The Other '68

STUDIES IN GERMAN HISTORY

Series Editors
NEIL GREGOR (SOUTHAMPTON)
BRIDGET HEAL (ST ANDREWS)

Editorial Board
SIMON MACLEAN (ST ANDREWS)
FRANK REXROTH (GÖTTINGEN)
ULINKA RUBLACK (CAMBRIDGE)
JOEL HARRINGTON (VANDERBILT)
YAIR MINTZKER (PRINCETON)
SVENJA GOLTERMANN (ZÜRICH)
MAIKEN UMBACH (NOTTINGHAM)
PAUL BETTS (OXFORD)

The Other '68

A Social History of West Germany's Revolt

CHRISTINA VON HODENBERG

Translated by
RACHEL WARD

OXFORD
UNIVERSITY PRESS

Great Clarendon Street, Oxford, OX2 6DP,
United Kingdom

Oxford University Press is a department of the University of Oxford.
It furthers the University's objective of excellence in research, scholarship,
and education by publishing worldwide. Oxford is a registered trade mark of
Oxford University Press in the UK and in certain other countries

© Verlag C.H.Beck oHG, München 2018; 2024 text
© Christina von Hodenberg; English translation © Rachel Ward 2024

The moral rights of the authors have been asserted

All rights reserved. No part of this publication may be reproduced, stored in
a retrieval system, or transmitted, in any form or by any means, without the
prior permission in writing of Oxford University Press, or as expressly permitted
by law, by licence or under terms agreed with the appropriate reprographics
rights organization. Enquiries concerning reproduction outside the scope of the
above should be sent to the Rights Department, Oxford University Press, at the
address above

You must not circulate this work in any other form
and you must impose this same condition on any acquirer

Published in the United States of America by Oxford University Press
198 Madison Avenue, New York, NY 10016, United States of America

British Library Cataloguing in Publication Data
Data available

Library of Congress Control Number: 2023916810

ISBN 978-0-19-289755-8

DOI: 10.1093/oso/9780192897558.001.0001

Printed and bound in the UK by
Clays Ltd, Elcograf S.p.A.

Links to third party websites are provided by Oxford in good faith and
for information only. Oxford disclaims any responsibility for the materials
contained in any third party website referenced in this work.

Contents

Preface to the English Edition	vii
1. Introduction: Voices from the Other Side	1
2. The Shah's Visit, in Bonn and Berlin	15
3. Of Wartime Children and Nazi Parents	39
4. Trust Nobody Over Sixty? The Role of the Elderly	69
5. The Female Sixty-Eight	92
6. Variations on Sexual Liberation	136
7. Epilogue: What is Left of Sixty-Eight?	168
On Sources	177
Endnotes	179
Bibliography	209
Glossary and Abbreviations	223
List of Credits	225
Index	227

Preface to the English Edition

This book is a translated, updated, and revised version of my title *Das andere Achtundsechzig*, which first appeared in print in German in February 2018. That year—the fiftieth anniversary of the '1968' protest movements—my arguments around the role of women, and the way the 'Sixty-Eighter generation' dealt with the Nazi past prompted lively and occasionally controversial discussion in Germany. For this edition, I have adapted the manuscript to academic audiences outside of Germany, setting the West German sixties within their wider European and global context, and the book now reflects on the scholarly debates during and after the fiftieth anniversary.

This translation has been made possible by a generous grant from the Alexander von Humboldt Foundation for which I am extremely grateful. My particular thanks go to Rachel Ward for her faithful but creative translation of the text, and to Jo Spillane, Cailen Swain, Sally Pelling-Deeves and Srividya Raamadhurai of Oxford University Press for their expert assistance in producing this edition.

This book rests largely on a wonderful sabbatical year at the University of Halle-Wittenberg, made possible by a Research Award 2014/15 from the Humboldt Foundation. It was then that I discovered the forgotten archives of the Bonn longitudinal study (Bolsa) and began my analysis. Katrin Moeller and Patrick Wagner of Halle helped in creating a new home for the Bolsa in the Historical Data Centre there, and the generous assistance of the Volkswagen Foundation enabled us to digitize the study. I would like to thank the psychologists Christoph Rott and Georg Rudinger, who had looked after the material until then. As well as making the study available for new historical research, they offered me active support in reconstructing its context and answering my questions. Former staff at the Bonn Department of Psychology, Ursula Lehr, Helga Merker, Insa Fooken, Norbert Erlemeier, and Ingrid Tismer-Puschner, were very open to conversations with me. I also owe thanks to Horst-Pierre Bothien of the Stadtmuseum Bonn, and Stefan Lewejohann of the Stadtmuseum in Cologne, who gave me access to the interviews conducted with students from the 1960s. My thanks to all their interviewees who allowed me to make secondary use of the material, and to Florence Hervé and Hannes Heer for their approachability. Boris Schafgans, director of the

viii PREFACE TO THE ENGLISH EDITION

eponymous photographic archive in Bonn, provided a great deal of background information on Bonn in the sixties, as did Thomas Becker, head of the university archive. In Halle, Felix Schneider and Franziska Kaschner assisted me in my research, as did Tabea Richardson and Alexandra Campana in London.

My thanks for the sabbatical that permitted me to write this book go to the School of History at Queen Mary University of London. Craig Griffiths, Fiammetta Balestracci, W. Daniel Wilson, and Paul Betts acted as both critical and creative early readers. Sebastian Ullrich of Beck Verlag was both considerate and understanding as editor. Cilla and Caroline Peddinghaus were generous hosts in Bonn. And my family—Dan, Martin, and Lucy, as well as my parents Barbara and Ferdinand—not only travelled to Halle with me from time to time, but also stood by me through all the highs and lows. There are very many reasons to be grateful.

I dedicate the book to my father, Ferdinand von Hodenberg (14 March 1938–19 February 2021), in loving memory.

1

Introduction: Voices from the Other Side

One day in February 2015, in Halle an der Saale, I started hearing voices. A young, male voice asked: 'In your opinion, how are young people today different from young people back in your day?' An older woman's voice answered emphatically: 'The youth of today...have a much larger horizon because they didn't have such a narrow upbringing as we did....So I think young people today are better off than we were because we weren't allowed to have our own opinions, our own will.' I heard footsteps, a window was opened, a bus drove noisily by. Then the elderly speaker began to talk about her youth. She had been born in 1897 and 'at any rate, very, very strictly brought up. My father's word was sacred....I wasn't allowed out of the house in the evening at any rate. I had to be at home by eight. You try telling that to a young person of 16, 17.' She sounded impassioned as she described the way her father had determined her hairstyle. 'In the old days, young girls weren't allowed to wear their hair any way they liked....I remember that I was never allowed to wear a ribbon in my hair, and I so badly wanted to.' She admitted having recently asked somebody's 18-year-old son (who had 'dreadful Beatles hair'): 'don't you think you'd look nice if you got your hair cut?' But when he'd answered 'I like it', all she'd said was: 'that's fine then'. And she never interfered with her 37-year-old son and his wife 'on principle', because that would be 'an intrusion into their personal affairs....After all, they were born into a different age...when I was young, it was a monarchy, now we have a democracy, to my mind, that's a massive difference.'

The young man on the recording agreed with the old lady. He said you could still tell that 'older folks' had grown up without free will. 'For example, discussing the student demonstrations with my father-in-law, where I take a middle view. I'm not in the SDS [the Socialist German Students' Union]. But I definitely see certain things that are worth demonstrating against.' Now the old woman talked in detail about a recent visit to her son in West Berlin: 'Then we witnessed the demonstration...well, there were so many police!' Strolling on the Ku'damm one evening, she'd seen 'smaller groups, debating' and in the afternoons, the demonstrators had been 'so polite' and had 'let [them] through in the car, everywhere'.

2 THE OTHER '68

I wasn't surprised that a housewife aged about 70 would disapprove of long hair on a man—that fitted my image of 1968—but I was amazed by how easily she accepted the student demonstrations and more liberal approaches to child-rearing. The door opened and my 10-year-old daughter stuck her head in. 'Who are you talking to, Mama?' I pressed a button on the reel-to-reel tape recorder, an ancient lump that weighed eight kilos. There was a click and the voices fell silent. I explained that the conversations had been recorded fifty years earlier. This was a Frau Friede, then aged 71, being interviewed in April 1968 by a 30-year-old psychology PhD student. But there were over 600 more tapes, so I had a lot still to do. With that, I promised to give my daughter more details over dinner. Frau Friede's voice returned, saying that you should beware of making distinctions between boys and girls. 'Because the girls have to win their battle with life, just as much as the boys', and are 'generally a bit more ambitious, actually.... And women are independent nowadays. I mean, most of them have a profession of their own, in the old days, women didn't work at all.' She had advised the young working woman who lodged with her that 'she shouldn't get married'. I changed tapes and the next voices I heard were those of two men talking animatedly about the student protests after the visit from the Shah of Iran in June 1967. They seemed largely to agree on their interpretation of events. The older voice said: 'But this violence, these demonstrations that you often see on the students' part, they cause—well, I'm not quite sure—they cause me quite a headache.' Similarly, the younger voice speculated that there was 'a certain danger in it. Some of them are pretty radical, you know, including some highly intelligent people.' The older man stressed 'that these radical groups are always considerably [intellectually] superior to the others... there is such a courage, such a doggedness in their discussions, and in their fanaticism, they don't deviate from what they have... they don't back down on anything. Like in the Nazi times: don't back down on anything.' Yes, the younger man agreed, 'so they do actually want to provoke...I see a fairly major danger there.' Again, I was flabbergasted. I'd expected old Herr Jäger, a tradesman born in 1905, to oppose the protests. But the man he was speaking to, who was only 27?

The voices I heard shook my preconceptions of Sixty-Eight. I began systematically collecting interviews. The old UHER Universal 5000 tape recorder kept running so hot that I was having to switch it off for longer intervening periods. Conversations with people who'd been at school or university at that time brought me fresh surprises. There was, for instance, a shy 20-year-old, who hated anything military and defended long hair, yet was mainly interested in earning money. Then there was the voice of Ulrich Rosenbaum, the

INTRODUCTION: VOICES FROM THE OTHER SIDE   3

chief editor of *akut*, Bonn's student newspaper in 1968. Asked about his parental home, he immediately reported 'that my parents had a Nazi past too'. But he went on:

> Well, that wasn't such a big deal for me, even though I've studied history. I just sort of accepted it, my parent's house was the way it was, and I didn't have a problem with that. I just saw to it that I went my own way. And the interesting thing is that basically my parents, when I joined the SPD [Social Democratic Party of Germany] in 1969, they suddenly switched to voting SPD too. So to that extent, we'd had an impact that way too.

This statement also seemed to contradict everything I thought I knew about the generational conflict of the late sixties. Why did the young student just casually accept that his parents had been Nazis? And why did his parents then follow him on his journey to the left?[1]

The voices I was hearing went beyond what I'd thought I knew for certain about 1968. Neither the young psychologist who criticized the left-wing activists, nor the student Ulrich Rosenbaum seemed to slot neatly into the 'generation of 1968' pigeonhole. And could Frau Friede and Herr Jäger be considered part of the establishment? As I delved deeper into the interviews, I gained a strengthening impression that our perception of 1968 is based heavily on visual sources, on potentially misleading pictures. The iconic images of the revolts are seared on the public memory: we see young white men, speaking into microphones, throwing stones, marching on the front row, in Paris, Milan, West Berlin, and Prague. This is how we imagine the sixties in Europe and across the world, dominated by iconic figures such as Mario Savio, Mark Rudd, Daniel Cohn-Bendit, and Rudi Dutschke. The German mass media reinforce these tropes; we see them on book covers, again and again: young men, their hair blowing in the wind, jogging arm in arm, waving flags and banners. Dutschke, the student leader, gesticulating wildly, standing on the podium in some overflowing lecture theatre. The members of a Berlin commune posing naked in their living room, their backs to the photographer. Is it a coincidence that all the household names of Sixty-Eight form a young, male, intellectual, metropolitan elite? Is it possible that the photos from those days, reproduced millions of times over in the media, merely lead us into fond misunderstandings? That they reveal only a vanishingly tiny fraction of the full extent of the revolts—namely those protagonists who won over the mass media?

This is the question that prompted this book. I wanted to believe my ears more readily than my eyes, and put greater trust in my tape recordings and

4   THE OTHER '68

files than in the visual icons of the revolt. My elderly reel-to-reel machine reawakened conversations between people of all social classes, recorded for posterity in the late sixties. Most of the interviewees had little formal education, and half were women. There were over 200 interviews with people over 60, compared to eighty-nine with those aged between their mid-30s and late-50s, plus both older and more recent conversations with twenty-seven former undergraduates and postgraduate students, male and female alike. My recorded voices thus captured the attitudes of three generations (the young, the old, and those in-between), who lived through the protest movements of the late sixties. And while the interviewees talked continually about politics and their views of other generations, they spoke at least as much about their families and personal circumstances.

Consequently, this book is a rather different portrayal of 1968, which takes in the whole of society. Working with a new set of sources, in which ordinary people's private, everyday experiences take centre stage, has enabled me to write a genuine social history of the late 1960s in West Germany, rather than just a history of a social movement. Many familiar events and protagonists in the protest movement come to the fore: the SDS and Kommune 1, Rudi Dutschke and Benno Ohnesorg, the Shah's visit, and the major demonstrations, West Berlin, and Frankfurt. But the characters generally labelled 'the 1968 generation' today—a small student elite numbering no more than a few thousand, in the heartlands of the protest movement[2]—will play key roles in only a few scenes of the drama unfolding here. They often appear as supporting actors or onlookers.

Because I aim to reveal not only the media-friendly confrontations between students and police, professors, and politicians, but also conversations within families, private relationships between generations and sexes, I will give a voice to people over 30, women, the middle and working classes, and those who lived outside the big cities. My aim is to de-centre the story of 1968 on the social, generational, and geographical levels. I hope to open up new perspectives by focusing on interactions between the centre and the periphery, and on the gendering of '1968'. After all, changing lifestyles at the heart of society, women's emancipation, and sexual liberation were just as important as the political theories espoused by the New Left and their striving for socialist revolution.

In many Western European countries, the mass media idea of 1968 has ossified. In both France and Germany, there is very little variation from the classical narrative, established over the last five decades, which continues to haunt feature articles, talk shows, bestsellers, and textbooks. Television and magazine reports from 1967 to 1969 made Rudi Dutschke, Kommune 1, and the SDS the stars of the show. Even then, the mass media paid 'disproportionate levels of attention' to the protests in West Berlin, at the Freie Universität, or in the first communes. Reporting in *BILD*, *Stern*, *Spiegel*, *Quick*, and the public service television channels followed the established North American pattern. Sit-ins, long-haired students, and brawling policemen flickered across TV screens and dominated photo features in magazines.[3] West German historiography followed in their wake, concentrating just as heavily on the cities of Berlin and Frankfurt, and on left-wing university students. Political scientists and historians relied on eyewitness testimony from contemporary activists to write a legend of 1968, where young male students were the standard-bearers for change. Dozens of similar accounts appeared in 2008 to mark the fortieth anniversary of the revolt; they centred, yet again, on barricades in Berlin and demonstrations in Frankfurt, confrontations in lecture theatres, and the battle of ideas on the left.[4] It was not until the fiftieth anniversary in 2018 that this narrative was first challenged, thanks to numerous contributions by younger historians.[5] Yet the tunnel vision frequently remains, and the intense focus on the SDS, students, and West Berlin still sometimes prevails, even in thoughtful writing that sees 1968 in West Germany as more of a cultural revolution or media spectacle than a political rebellion.[6]

It is by no means new for German historical research to pay such disproportionate attention to students and academics. The historian's lens is focused on the *Bildungsbürgertum*, a social class defined by university education and considered a cultural elite. This mindset encourages an overly detailed investigation of small constituent parts, while the whole object remains out of focus, and its contours blur beyond recognition. German historians' deep identification with middle-class intellectuals has frequently led to an overreliance on sources written by a male, educated elite, thus skewing the way events are interpreted. The classic, easily accessible sources mainly reflect debates between articulate, educated voices, almost all of which belong to middle-class men. Highly educated men monopolize our perspective on the past through ministerial files, *Spiegel* articles, parliamentary debates, party manifestos, literary fiction, and autobiographies. Perceptions of '1914' show how easy this makes it to miss the significance of turning points for society as a whole. For decades, the German narrative around the First World War was shaped by a focus on the academic male youth, and gushing newspaper articles on his enthusiasm for war. It was only in the 1990s that historians drew on fresh sources, which tapped the very different reactions of the rural population and working classes to the outbreak of war, and discovered that the

6 THE OTHER '68

much-vaunted 'August madness' and 'Spirit of 1914' among the volunteers had been misleading. The war had met with far greater levels of scepticism, temporizing, and worry than previously thought.[7]

I have therefore also used new sources to discover the other 1968, beyond the fixation on the *Bildungsbürgertum*, to privilege other voices—those with lower levels of education, women, and the elderly. My other stratagems include giving equal weight to the private and political spheres, and considering a small town as a counterexample to the way that Berlin and Frankfurt nag for our attention. To date, it has been rare for historical research to focus squarely on the provinces. The few existing regional studies have generally treated small towns as deficient sideshows, offering a faint reflection of events in West Berlin and Frankfurt.[8]

Yet 1968 played out across almost the whole of West Germany. There were hotly contested student parliament elections in all the provincial universities, a multitude of active student associations, vigils for Benno Ohnesorg, and demonstrations relating to university politics.[9] I take Bonn as my example, firstly because the voices on my recordings are from there (more on this later). Secondly, its status as the capital of the Federal Republic of Germany (FRG), the West German part of a divided nation, was intentionally provisional. The 'federal village' on the Rhine was thus home to an unusual combination of a small-town outlook and global politics, and saw worlds collide on a daily basis. The *General-Anzeiger für Bonn und Umgegend* (General Advertiser for Bonn and the Surrounding Area) dedicated as many column inches to nineti-eth birthdays, golden weddings, and cockerels crowing at night as to glittering state visits from controversial dictators, and enormous protest marches by the extra-parliamentary opposition. Bonn could not compete with the cultural elites, media concentration, or transport connections of West Berlin, Frankfurt, or Hamburg. Yet the non-stop stream of state visits and demonstrations, unusually rich cultural programme, and the presence of numerous politicians, lobbyists, and foreign ambassadors brought high politics into everyday life. A quarter of its 280,000 residents were federal employees, diplomats, and journalists; a further 25,000 were students. National political scandals, such as that surrounding Federal President Heinrich Lübke's record during the Nazi era, were expressed in confrontations between police and students at the University of Bonn that were scarcely less radical than anything happening in West Berlin. It was hard for anyone living in or around Bonn to avoid politics—women students, blue-collar workers, housewives, and OAPs alike.[10]

Moving out to the periphery is one way to escape the *bildungsbürgerlich* perspective. Another is to deliberately reject the 'political generations' interpretation of events. A good deal of writing on German history takes the view that unrest in the sixties represented an intellectual battle between two political generations: the 'Sixty-Eighters' challenging their predecessors, the 'Forty-Fivers'. The generation of 1945 were born in the twenties and early thirties, and labelled the 'Sceptical Generation' by Helmut Schelsky in 1957. Today, they are often called the *Flakhelfergeneration* (anti-aircraft auxiliary generation), or the 'Hitler Youth Generation'. This cohort, who were aged between around 35 and 50 in 1968, only experienced Nazi Germany as children and teenagers, and were thus sufficiently unencumbered that, as young adults, they rose rapidly to leading positions in politics, the media, and universities. The end of the war in 1945 became the turning point in lives which many subsequently dedicated to the Westernization and internal democratization of the Federal Republic.[11] This group included figures such as Helmut Kohl, Rudolf Augstein, Ralf Dahrendorf, Jürgen Habermas, Joachim Fest, and Hans-Ulrich Wehler. Some historians laud the Forty-Fivers, not the students of 1968, as the pioneers of a long-term liberalization of West Germany. This makes history itself into a duel between the political generations.[12]

Yet seeing 1968 as a conflict between two political generations means focusing, yet again, only on male intellectuals. The very concept of a political generation was first propounded in 1928 by Karl Mannheim and is therefore ultra-*bildungsbürgerlich*. In Mannheim's thinking, men were socialized politically at the Front or in youth organizations, and educated elites battled to see one creative political will prevail over others. Thus, even today, seeing oneself as a member of a political generation is a typically masculine thing to do. Many women's experiences and aims in life simply do not fit into this model. We find it hard to think of female political generations.[13] Yet German historical scholarship clings to the concept, and is therefore particularly prone to seeing the clashes of the late 1960s primarily through the lens of diverging world views held by younger and older academics.[14] Newer studies on topics ranging from the views of the New Left, to international relations, to university reform, to wider intellectual debates are still ultimately mainly concerned with the role of intellectuals.[15] Consequently, even now, we know considerably more about students, professors, and conscientious objectors who did community, not military, service in the late sixties than we do about the working classes, housewives, white-collar workers, or the retired.[16]

So, this is why I was unable to fit the voice of Frau Friede, and other female or non-middle-class speakers, into the familiar pattern of 1968. The people in my recordings were speaking another language. Even when asked directly, they were reluctant to talk about ideologies, political aims, and disputes. To

8 THE OTHER '68

them, it was more a matter of everyday frictions, personal relationships, money, and emotions. They saw themselves less as part of a political generation than as a link in the sequence of generations within a family: grandparents, parents, and children.

The idea of familial generations also figures frequently in current discussions of 1968 in Western Europe. It is usually argued that the student protesters in West Germany were the children of Nazified parents. In his *History of Europe since 1945*, Tony Judt claims: 'If there ever was a generation whose rebellion really was grounded in the rejection of everything their parents represented...it was "Hitler's children", the West German radicals of the Sixties'.[17] There is further speculation that the young rebels had accused their parents of being involved and staying silent. The consequence was said to have been deep private family quarrels between old and young. The protests were often seen as a collective psychological response to the parent–child conflict. Thomas A. Kohut, for example, diagnoses the children born between 1940 and 1950 with 'feelings of inadequacy, resentment and an unacknowledged but intense identification with their parents'. The parents' attempts at distancing themselves from the Nazi past created tension and laid

> the psychological groundwork for their [the Sixty-Eighters'] rebellion in the late 1960s against their parents...What distinguished the generational conflict from that in other Western countries was primarily the confrontation over the National Socialist past in the family and in society.[18]

There was also a frequent masculine overtone to this idea, with the popular trope of father–son rivalry being invoked to explain the 1968 protests. Writers allude to young men being aware of 'the sins of the fathers', generational conflict over 'the fathers' guilt', and the young attacking the 'silent patriarchs' who represented the 'generation of Nazi functionaries'.[19] In the first place, there is scant evidence for such bold theses (a few individual cases aside), and secondly, they mix familial and political generations inadmissibly. For these reasons, this book will not start by seeing 1968 as a generational conflict, but will attempt to investigate the disputes of that era without preconceptions. Where people were arguing, what were they arguing about? How often did disagreements relate to the Nazi past? And who fell out with whom—children with parents, or possibly grandparents? Did tensions flare up between sons, fathers, and grandfathers—or could they have been more common among daughters, mothers, and grandmothers, whose gender roles were then diverging far more dramatically than those of the men?

My attempt to consider 1968 from a social history perspective and, in the process, to expand the grounds under investigation, fits with related trends in historical research into the sixties in Western Europe. Research on several highly industrialized Western countries has recently begun to open up in precisely this direction (several decades after successfully integrating more global and transnational perspectives[20]). Kristin Ross has written workers' strikes and colonial militants back into the picture of May 1968 in France, arguing that an exclusive focus on student milieus and lifestyle changes wrongly depoliticizes the historical narrative. Other historians of France have also questioned the media-driven narrative put forward by former leftist student activists such as Daniel Cohn-Bendit, and begun to look at non-elites, beyond Paris and beyond hegemonic narratives of generational conflict.[21] Gerd-Rainer Horn has taken a regional approach and focused on working-class radicalization in Italy, France, and Spain to emphasize a Mediterranean pattern of class conflict underlying 1968 in Southern Europe.[22] A British-led oral history team, working on a collective biography of nearly 500 European Sixty-Eighter activists between 2007 and 2011, were careful to 'decentre' their story away from Paris, Milan, and West Berlin, and to include women among their subjects, along with rural and conservative activists.[23] Despite growing awareness of the ways this history has been distorted, it is still rare to find book-length studies on activists or groups who do not conform to the dominant storyline. Anna von der Goltz' study of conservative reformers in West Germany is a recent exception.[24]

The gendered aspect of 1968 is similarly under-researched, yet it is a fiercely contested field. As Rebecca Clifford, Robert Gildea, and Anette Warring wrote in 2013:

> Given the centrality of issues of gender and sexuality to the period, there has been surprisingly little work by historians that focusses on 1968 and gender, yet even studies that pass these issues over tend to recognize that challenges to received gender roles—linked to the emergence of second-wave feminism—were among the most significant legacies of 1968.[25]

Though a few important studies on feminist activism have appeared in print since then, the 'historiographic silencing' of women's voices in the narratives of the sixties has mostly continued.[26] As before, most books on 1968 discuss gender or the women's movement in one brief paragraph, or as one chapter among many, without linking these aspects to the overarching narrative.[27] It is only recently that the fields of the history of feminisms, and of the sixties in Western Europe have begun to intersect more fruitfully.[28]

10 THE OTHER '68

When it comes to discussing Western Europe in 1968, the relationship between long-term cultural change and the core phase of the protests in the late 1960s is also key. I will concentrate on the short period of social unrest in 1966 to 1969 so as to gain a closer understanding of the role of Sixty-Eight in societal change and ask how the intervention of collective, media-friendly protests related to longer-term processes bringing about social change. Historical scholarship has developed a range of similar variations on the theme of long-term cultural change across Europe, all of which proliferate in the shadow of 1968. In France, for example, there is talk of '*Les Années 68*' (the 1968 years), which run from around 1962 through to 1981. In Italy, new practices of self-expression have been characterized as gradually prevailing 'cultures of 1968'. Arthur Marwick's wide-ranging study of changing lifestyles and counter-cultures in Britain, France, Italy, and the United States dates the period of 'cultural revolution' to 1958–1974.[29] Similarly, events in West Germany are typically embedded in the 'long sixties', generally reckoned to extend from the late fifties to the 1973/74 oil crisis.[30] Lastly, European social sciences have paid increasing attention to the concept, deriving from political science and sociology, of a slow move towards a change in values that transformed 'materialists' into 'post-materialists' and culminated between around 1965 and 1980.[31]

In practice, however, historians differ in their assessment of the relationship between the 'political' events of the critical years of protest (1966 to 1969) and the 'cultural' changes of the long sixties. Some authors criticize an emphasis on the long-term lifestyle revolution as a way of whitewashing and depoliticizing class conflict and socialist insurrection. Others focus their studies primarily on the broad and deep societal impact of changing lifestyles because they see everyday life and popular tastes becoming more liberal, individualistic, and/or internationalist as a lived democratization and politicization.[32] The 'political' short Sixty-Eight is sometimes even seen as a flop compared to the resounding success of the 'cultural' long sixties. There is particular disagreement over the extent to which changes in gender roles and sexual morals can be directly linked with 1968 in Western Europe. Which events can be defined as 'political', and which elements find their way into the overall narrative of 1968? And to what extent was the Federal Republic, with its Nazi past and perpetual socialist 'Others' in the East (the German Democratic Republic, GDR), unique and different to every other Western European state? I will return to these questions later.[33]

But first, let us go back to that winter day, when my daughter pulled me back into the real world and away from the land of those recorded voices.

INTRODUCTION: VOICES FROM THE OTHER SIDE   11

Over dinner, she demanded the details I'd promised of the 600-plus boxed tapes in my study. I tried to explain. The conversations had been part of a major academic project begun in 1965, known as the 'Bonner Längsschnittstudie des Alterns' (Bonn Longitudinal Study of Ageing) or Bolsa for short. A total of 222 elderly people regularly travelled to Bonn from the Rhineland, Ruhr, and Rhine-Main areas, to be interviewed at the University of Bonn's Psychological Institute. They were lower-level employees and shopkeepers, skilled crafts-men, tradesmen, and housewives. A rapidly growing group of academics in Bonn, around Professor Hans Thomae and his assistant professor Ursula Lehr, were researching the way the human personality changed with age. Research into ageing was still a very new field in West Germany. The Bonn psychologists were Germany's first gerontologists, and would go on to hold significant professorial chairs across the country, and to play a leading role in government policy on the elderly from the 1980s onwards.[34] They had pro-cured millions of marks in funding from the Volkswagen Foundation, which enabled them to reinterview the participants every few years for two decades. And this is how a shop assistant from Weiden, a cleaning lady from Mannheim, and a hairdresser from Frankfurt came to spend hours talking about their life stories and every aspect of their everyday lives, as did a chem-ical worker from Kelsterbach, a miner from Oberhausen, and a policeman from Wuppertal.

Now my 13-year-old son piped up. Who'd picked those people, and how, he asked. Having just learnt about the basics of statistics at school, he was sure that it hadn't been a representative sample. I tried to argue that psychologists in those days had seen themselves as serious scientists. They had recruited a broadly representative sample, with equal numbers of men and women, while the educated elite made up only 3 per cent of participants. They had also relied on the very latest technology available to them: recording the conversa-tions on reel-to-reel tape and evaluating the results on the machines in the university's nascent computer centre. Thousands of hours of interviews had been encoded, people's various emotional states and degrees of personal intimacy had been converted into figures, ready for number crunching.[35] But as this merely made both children roll their eyes, having recently honed that skill to perfection, I tried appealing to their creativity. Perhaps they could help me with a visualization issue? I couldn't possibly label each of my recorded voices a 'participant in the Bonn Longitudinal Study of Ageing' every time. I urgently needed an abbreviation before I was driven to despair. My daughter wasn't falling for such a laughable ruse, and rolled her eyes again; but she suggested 'Bolsaners' or 'Bolsers' all the same. My son made a

12   THE OTHER '68

case for 'Bolsacs' before we settled on 'Bolsianers'. The term 'Bolsianers', which I use throughout this book, therefore derives from our conversation that evening in February 2015. The 222 study volunteers became my key witnesses for the role of the older generations (those born up to 1908) in the late sixties.

By coincidence, a second, smaller group of researchers around Professor Hans Thomae were investigating generational conflict. Between May 1967 and August 1968, a team led by doctoral student Helga Merker questioned women and men 'in mid-adulthood' about their opinions on 'the youth of today' and changing parenting norms. A total of 180 people from the Cologne-Bonn area, all born between 1909 and 1934, spoke about their own youth and compared it with young people's lives in the sixties. Again, they selected predominantly middle- and working-class people who had left school at the age of 14. Many of the interviewees got to talking in detail about student protests, mini-skirts, and beat music, as well as about their own time in the Hitler Youth and as *Flakhelfer*, Reich Labour Service Girls, and soldiers' wives. Eighty-nine of the 180 interviews have survived in the form of typed verbatim transcripts and been analysed here.[36]

I have no desire to neglect young people's voices in favour of older generations or those in-between, so I augment these sources with conversations with young students. Here, I have benefitted from oral history initiatives begun by two local museums, in which numerous former students were interviewed for exhibitions to mark the fortieth and fiftieth anniversaries of 1968. The Stadtmuseum Bonn's archives contain twenty-two interviews featuring Bonn students who were politically active in 1967 and 1968. These were conducted in 2005 and 2006 by Horst-Pierre Bothien of the museum; he was particularly interested in 'the students' work to raise awareness of the university's Nazi period' and paid less attention to other aspects such as their approach to sexuality or women's emancipation. Horst-Pierre Bothien said of his role as interviewer:

> I had nothing to do with the 68ers, more with the moderate left of the 70s.... I should not deny that in retrospect I had a certain sympathy for the undogmatic and non-violent 'lefties'. All the same, I consciously spoke to 'right-wing' students too, and wanted to see them included in the work.[37]

As thirteen of the sixteen interviewees who allowed me to re-use their material in Bonn were men, and the Bonn project did not take the local women's groups of the 1960s, or the issues they were tackling, into account, there was a gender imbalance for the younger generation. To counter this, I arranged my own conversations with women who had then been either undergraduates in Bonn or PhD students on the Bolsa team. I also called on print and film interviews carried out with women at the time.[38] For this English edition, I was additionally able to access recent video interviews with five women who were former students of the nearby University of Cologne.[39] These had been conducted by students from the Department of History at the University of Cologne for an exhibition at the Kölnisches Stadtmuseum, with the intention of giving a voice to 'different political camps', 'from as many perspectives as possible', and referred back to public discussion in 2018 about the female experience of 1968. Therefore, the project leadership had been aiming for 'gender parity' among the participants. The Cologne team had at first, however, found it 'rather difficult' to recruit female interviewees because 'mainly men' had responded to the press appeals.[40]

Oral history sources always present historians with similar methodological challenges—whatever the participants' genders. Conversations of this kind present a filtered version of past experiences. The subjects read meaning into their own life stories with hindsight, while also reacting to the interviewer's specific expectations and circumstances at the time the conversation takes place. I have taken this into account, and also considered who was conducting the interviews, and how their questions were asked.[41] Wherever possible, I have compared this kind of account with other sources, such as contemporary press reports, university archive files, and transcripts made by the Bolsa lead investigators.

Although the book thus draws on a range of interview material, I have not given it all equal weight, preferring to let the voices of the young, middle-aged and elderly, bystanders and activists be heard. The Bolsa recordings, files, and statistical data are much wider ranging and much more representative than the other resources I have referred to here. The larger and more broadly representative Bolsa sample, and its link between qualitative interviews and statistical data queries, gave particularly robust results. Bolsa is an example of 'social science data', a comparatively new kind of historical source. This term refers to surviving materials (both qualitative and quantitative) collected by contemporary social science research. They increased in number and complexity over the twentieth century as social science became more 'scientific'. Before historians can use social science data, however, the material must be historicized, archived, and processed for re-evaluation. In this case, I was involved in creating an archive for the Bolsa materials, interviewing surviving team members, developing a metadata system, and repairing and updating the quantitative database.[42] My analysis of the Bolsa interviews goes beyond

14 THE OTHER '68

citing qualitative examples and employs statistical methods wherever possible; this includes re-classifying some of the 5,553 variables.[43]

In this way, this book taps into three levels of intergenerational encounter in West Germany in and around 1968. Young psychologists at the Bonn Psychological Institute met with middle-aged and older volunteers. Young people, parents, and grandparents discussed their altercations with members of the generation above them on the streets, at work, and within the family. And last but not least, a public confrontation played out at universities and on the streets in Bonn and West Berlin alike, between rebellious students and the 'establishment'. These three levels are often intertwined and overlapping, and cannot be understood in isolation from each other. We need to bring together the private and political, the centre and the periphery, the intelligentsia and the broader population, generations and genders, if we are to get to the bottom of the meaning of 1968 for German history. I benefit, or at least I hope I do, from not writing from my personal experience. I was a toddler at the time of the revolt; my parents' university days were long behind them, and the events had little impact on them. This is another reason why I am not interested in either romanticizing or demonizing the events of 1968, or denying them their political significance. The aim of this book is to abandon the network of myths woven by the people who were there, and to use fresh sources and new perspectives to gain qualitatively different knowledge of the scope and impacts of 1968 on society.

2

The Shah's Visit, in Bonn and Berlin

Monday, 29 May 1967, was a warm, muggy spring day. Götz and Hedwig Langbein, aged 72 and 68, were sitting on a bench in the Hofgarten, a park in front of the main University building in central Bonn, enjoying the midday sun. The Langbeins had an appointment in the nearby Department of Psychology at 2 p.m. but first, they were resting after the journey from Frankfurt. Frau Langbein was minding her own business, enjoying the green, sunlit trees. Herr Langbein, a retired bank clerk, liked to read the newspapers. He had bought the local paper, the *General-Anzeiger für Bonn und Umgegend*, at the station and this Monday, it was full of the glittering state visit made by the Shah of Persia that weekend. 'Glorious Sunshine for the State Visit of the Year—Peacock Throne Royal Couple Kept Protocol and Police in Suspense—Children Presented Posies of Lily-of-the-Valley—Empress Farah Wore the Crown Jewels—Imperial Gifts: Two Carpets', Langbein read. 'Thousands upon thousands of people' had lined the streets of Bonn 'to see surely the world's most popular imperial couple, ... Shah Reza Pahlavi and his fairytale-princess wife Farah Diba'. But he also read that there had been a few slightly jarring notes amid the celebrations: 'Whistles disturbed the wreath-laying ceremony—the Shah ignored chanted slogans—demonstrator with dislocated arm—opponents of the Shah hidden behind masks made of newspaper'.[1]

Five days before what would become the pivotal event of Sixty-Eight from the student perspective—the serious clashes between demonstrators and police at an anti-Shah demonstration in West Berlin, in which the student Benno Ohnesorg was killed—the Shah, dressed in his white gala uniform, had been chauffeured from Bonn to Schloss Augustusburg, Brühl, where he was received by Federal President Heinrich Lübke. The state visitor had also laid a wreath at the 'Memorial to the Victims of Wars and Tyranny' in the Hofgarten. Frau Langbein observed that the bronze memorial was still being guarded by several policemen.[2] Despite her arthritic joints, she strolled over to the southern side of the park to have a look at the Shah's wreath. At last, it was almost two o'clock. The Langbeins, who had dressed up for the occasion, now tweaked their outfits into place before setting off for the Institute. The plumpish Frau Langbein had a gold brooch on the lapel of her black blazer.

16 THE OTHER '68

White-haired Herr Langbein was wearing a pinstriped suit, white shirt, and dark tie. The couple knew what to expect. They didn't travel often, but this was their third trip to Bonn. They would be greeted by a swarm of young psychology graduates. Now they were wondering which investigator they might be assigned for this week of interviews and psychological tests that lay ahead of them.

A total of nine elderly ladies and gentlemen would gather in the reception area at the Department of Psychology—this week, they had come from Frankfurt, Heidelberg, Kelsterbach, Darmstadt, and Friesenheim, and were between 64 and 76 years of age. Meanwhile, outside the building, a very different kind of encounter between young and old was taking place. Three Persian students approached the memorial. They were carrying a green wreath with a white bow and the inscription 'For the victims of the Shah regime: Confederation of Iranian Students', which they intended to lay beside the Shah's wreath. A hundred or so Bonn students, predominantly young men wearing suits and ties, followed this vanguard. But the police called in reinforcements. Almost immediately, 200 police officers blocked the way to the monument and forced the three to set their wreath down at the feet of a chain of riot police. The officer-in-charge informed the demonstrators that their action represented an 'insult to the Shah' and was thus 'unlawful'. Because the students refused to leave the area in front of the memorial, the police kettled them there for hours, along with various uninvolved bystanders. When two other students, Helmut Böttiger and René Herrmann, turned up 'with a wreath of thorns and barbed wire', dedicated 'To the Victims of the Shah's Tyranny', they were also enclosed within the cordon. In the end, sixty-one young people were arrested as many people looked on, and taken to the nearby police headquarters for questioning. The detainees numbered fifty-eight German students, including three members of the Bonn *Allgemeiner Studentenausschuss* (AStA, General Students' Committee) and the editor-in-chief of *akut*, the Bonn student newspaper, and the three Iranians. They were not allowed to leave until the late afternoon, by which time their fellow students had gathered outside the police station, chanting slogans calling for their release.[3]

Bonn police's panicky reaction to the demonstrators would trigger heated debate. While the Shah shook hands with the police chief to thank him for the outstanding security escorts that he had provided, thirteen students pressed charges against the incident commander and described the kettling as an 'arbitrary measure'. The AStA protested 'in the strongest terms against the grotesque (200 police versus fifty bystanders), incomprehensible and, given the questionable legal situation, unjustifiable behaviour of the police'. Surely 'even in the "exceptional circumstances" of a state visit, every citizen's fundamental political rights must still be respected in every regard'? And why had the film been ripped from the camera belonging to the student newspaper photographer, seeing that 'the police were in the habit of photographing the students at every other event'?[4] After all, the state visitor and his entourage hadn't even been in the Hofgarten that afternoon. The royal couple had then just set off from the quay below the Beethovenhalle for 'an imperial day trip' on a Rhine steamer, cheered by thousands of 'decidedly pro-monarchist' onlookers. As a result, there was a student march in Bonn, protesting against police violence, the day before the death of Benno Ohnesorg and long before the Berlin demonstrations. There were around 1,200 demonstrators waving placards with slogans such as 'Bonn has Guests—the Police Make Arrests', or 'Are We Living in a Police City?' (Figure 2.1).[5]

The second type of intergenerational encounter that took place close to Bonn's Hofgarten that week was somewhat different: semi-private meetings between young PhD students and the Department of Psychology's 'senior guests' (Figure 2.2). They were due to spend a week in face-to-face individual conversations, while the tape machine recorded their words for posterity. The academics working on the Volkswagen-funded longitudinal study wanted to find out more about the way the ageing process influenced the psychological, social, and physical health of the elderly. The chief investigators, Hans Thomae and Ursula Lehr, hoped that the results would contribute to the public debate on how West German society should treat its growing cohort of pensioners.[6]

Figure 2.1 Bonn students demonstrating against the police action on 1 June 1967

Figure 2.2 In the Psychology Department's waiting room, from left: Maria Renner (seen from behind), Karl-Georg Tismer, Heribert Simons, Reinhard Schmitz-Scherzer, volunteer, Ingrid Tismer-Puschner, volunteers

First of all, however, they sat together for a coffee and a chat about the plan for the week. Eight young psychologists had welcomed the senior citizens warmly and paid each of them a generous allowance. The atmosphere was formal, but friendly. The Bolsianers had 'dressed up smartly, and came in wearing jackets and suchlike', Norbert Erlemeier remembered. At the age of 31, Erlemeier was one of the oldest interviewers on the study. He had only recently completed his degree, having first worked as a metalworker at a colliery in Essen and studied for his *Abitur* (school leaving exams) at evening classes. As always, he was wearing a suit and tie while on duty, and trying 'not to sit around quite as casually'. He was talking to Maria Wellhöfer, a widowed accountant whom he would be interviewing in the week ahead, and had already met the previous year. Norbert Erlemeier assured Frau Wellhöfer that she should see the time in Bonn as 'a little holiday' and 'a very pleasant week'. Admittedly, the schedule was tightly packed—as well as three one-to-one conversations over several hours, there would be a medical examination, an intelligence test, a reaction time test, questionnaires on their attitudes, handwriting analyses, and several projective tests designed to tap into their fantasy worlds. This time, the investigators would also bombard their volunteers with a barrage of questions on the 'youth of today'. But as a reward for all these

THE SHAH'S VISIT, IN BONN AND BERLIN   19

exertions, they would all go on an excursion into the Ahr valley on the Thursday afternoon. They'd be able to have a bit of a walk, come back and drink Portuguese red, maybe even take to the dance floor; in short, he hoped that it would be a 'little social highlight'.[7]

The participants were in an upbeat mood. The Langbeins were volubly greeting the Tödtmanns, who were related to them by marriage. Both couples were happy to see Frau Wellhöfer again, having got to know her last time around. Götz and Hedwig Langbein had been allocated to their usual interviewers: Karl-Georg Tismer and Maria Renner. Their conversation turned to travel. Frau Wellhöfer told them all about her trip to Passau and Austria. She had visited 'this little pilgrimage chapel' on the mountainside, where even the priest had served in the inn.

> And behind the altar—because you can walk all the way round it there—they've hung up the crutches that people didn't need any more, and the special shoes that were meant to sort out where one was shorter than the other, their legs, you know. And all kinds of thank-yous in pictures.

Herr Langbein was proud to report that he had travelled to Florence in the spring, and that it had given him 'a lot of mental stimulation'. He emphasized that it had been 'very interesting but very strenuous'. The 73-year-old Herr Tödtmann replied, somewhat snippily, that he didn't like travelling, especially not abroad. He'd only gone along on the holiday to Wildbad to please his wife, because she had hip trouble. Besides, he was still working (as a salesman) and they couldn't do without him. Sitting beside him was his interviewer, the 29-year-old doctoral student Reinhard Schmitz-Scherzer, who smiled thinly and kept his thoughts to himself. In his eyes, Herr Tödtmann had 'sought refuge in work' as a way of running away from his problems, and was now self-aggrandizing the 'status quo'. The young psychology graduate Karl-Georg Tismer also held back as Herr Langbein now argued that you couldn't just concern yourself with 'banalities' in your old age, and let the television 'wash over you'. His trip to Italy, for example, had been productive; he had learnt about the Etruscans and the Tarquinians, and Byzantine history. While he would never have said so, Tismer considered Herr Langbein a prissy pedant who actually aspired to peace and banality, but thought he 'needed to project…a particular image' for the Bonn department.[8]

The conversation fell silent as Professor Hans Thomae pushed open the door and hurried into the white-painted common room with its modern furnishings. The 51-year-old lead investigator greeted each guest with a friendly

20   THE OTHER '68

smile and a handshake, and asked how they all were. Despite his dark suit, white shirt, and tie, the psychology professor still had a youthful air. His staff seemed to look up to him. Thomae also briefly addressed his study team: he asked them all to gather in the 'Bear' after work as he had something important to tell them. After that, he made his apologies to the group on the grounds that he had a lecture on developmental psychology to prepare for the next day. But he wished them all every success with their 'explorations' (the name given by the Bolsa team to the individual interviews) and said that he was looking forward to seeing everyone again for the excursion on Thursday.

After the door had closed, psychologist Maria Renner ran through the timetable for the week with all participants, and answered a few more questions on the sights to see, and the nearby steamship pier. With that, they adjourned until the next day. Chatting excitedly, the Langbeins and the seven other guests strolled back to Hotel Löhndorf, which was a few minutes' walk away, at Stockenstraße 6. They were looking forward to the days ahead, although some of the upcoming examinations, such as the intelligence test and reaction test, would be strenuous. The Bolsianers enjoyed coming to Bonn a great deal, and a poem by retired engineer Albert Schubert gives us an idea of why. Herr Schubert was a short, plump man with dark glasses, a bald head, and a moustache, who wore a flat cap and liked to entertain the others 'loudly and boisterously' with jokes and anecdotes. After his visit in the summer of 1967, he dedicated this verse to Professor Thomae and his colleagues:

> When your youth is in the past,
> you'll find that old age creeps up fast....
> You wave goodbye to all the strife
> And hope to lead a quiet life
> You're thinking—this could be quite nice
> —but you're the problem, in a trice!
> Before you pass away, you'll be,
> Studied at university!...
> The dreams of youth are swept away!
> What's in the future? Who can say!
> But the big VW boss
> Holds his finger up aloft—
> And hands out funding, to explore
> ways to beat what we deplore!
> He sought for help, he found a don,

a professor—now in Bonn!
He calls the elderly, to find
out everything that's on their mind.
The doctors and psychologists,
are full of questions, tests and lists.
Those questions can be quite profound
so they research in fruitful ground.
...But first of all, they take great care
to get the dosh all clear and square.
Our board and lodging is all free
and there's spending money too you see.
We learn who every guest here is
and they're assigned to their own whizz.
...In the conference room, your thoughts
will be disclosed—whatever sorts.
Images and cards reveal
and filter out the way you feel....
All of this and more beside—
while the tape machine whirrs on nearby.
You sometimes get to go next door:
A room with neat machines galore....
Blinking green, white, red lights shine.
You need to get them into line.
The beat picks up, the tempo's high—
and that gets tiring by and by.
...And so there is for every case
a gadget standing on its base.
No worries here that someone will
pull your leg: no, time stands still.
As a departmental guest
you'll discover all the rest.
The shrinks have questions which they stick to,
some straightforward, others trick you.
Five days of talking here and then
our time in Bonn comes to an end.
But there is still our farewell treat
when our bus heads down the street.
Frau Doktor brings her son along
on our outing—and now: so long![9]

22 THE OTHER '68

The study participants definitely found the knowledge that they were acting in the service of science uplifting. They enjoyed the personal esteem that the departmental team conveyed to them all. Whatever your concerns, you'd be listened to here, and considered important. However tiring the programme of tests might be, the fact that 'Herr Professor' and 'Frau Doktor' (and sometimes also their children) took part in the Thursday outings in person made up for that. And, last but not least, they appreciated the ample daily allowance, a comfortable hotel, and the break from everyday pensioner life offered by a trip to Bonn and a glimpse into the university world. Most of them returned home from one of these weeks 'in very high spirits'. The manager of an old people's home, which sent several residents to take part in Bolsa, wrote: 'They were all in high spirits. Still talking enthusiastically about it today. The whole atmosphere, the kindliness they'd been offered, everything, especially the interesting questions, had inspired this enthusiasm.'[10]

Old people, who often no longer expected anyone to be interested in them, found open ears on the Bonn research team, and an apparently highly interested audience. Given this motivation, the long-term drop-out rate remained low.[11] Herr Schubert addressed PhD student Schmitz-Scherzer as his 'dear father confessor', who was certain to use the recordings for an 'analytical x-ray examination of his victim'. All the same, he, Schubert, had been 'pleased...to conduct profound conversations'. Herr and Frau Liebig from Mannheim waxed lyrical about Bonn as 'the shining star' that brightened up their old age, and about how much they liked going to the 'the metropolis of intrigue', i.e. the seat of government. Herr Liebig, a tradesman on a meagre pension, had developed a close bond with Mr Tismer, calling him 'my strict and thorough psychologist and grinder'. He wrote a humorous Christmas letter in 1968:

> Dear honoured Herr Prof. Thomae, dear, revered Frau Dr. Lehr, the staff & all the pretty stafflings, the nice, kind people we had dealings with 1½ years ago, and that we hope to see again in the summer, hale and hearty, and assiduous for the study, provided that you haven't perished in the protests... Please excuse this long, but heartfelt salutation from a representative of the moderate kind of extra-parliamentary opposition, in short a little man on the street, who only gets to have his say in one place, & is even affectionately invited to do so. That one place is the Uni Bonn, Psy. Dept.[12]

People who were otherwise rarely asked their opinions had the opportunity to speak here.

Thomae's team were aware of the importance of Bolsa to the self-esteem of many of their volunteers. At the same time, they were careful to maintain a professional distance and to convert the long hours of patient listening into statistically relevant results. All the interviewers had studied under Hans Thomae or Ursula Lehr, and been trained in the 'explorative approach'. This meant gaining the trust of the interviewee and promoting free-flowing speech, while still working through the central points on a pre-defined list (Figure 2.3). Georg Rudinger, then a PhD student aged 25, described 'this balancing act':

> An exploration was like, or this is what I was taught, at any rate, it wasn't like some kind of empathy business, where you cried along with the people. It was about working through a set catalogue of questions, it was already kind of semi-standardized.... We did get chatting too, but all the same, I wanted an answer to every question.

An investigator was only allowed to express limited emotions—Rudinger called this 'I robot'—so as not to intensify particular elements of what they were told.[13] The Bolsa team had been trained to 'ask open questions' and to avoid leading ones. Neutral formulations such as 'And what else can you think of?' were ideal. Classic reactions to the volunteers' words, such as 'hmm' and 'uh-huh', crop up frequently on the tape recordings.[14]

Thomae's stated goal was to model his research after North American studies, giving it such an open and comprehensive structure that the material

Figure 2.3 Norbert Erlemeier interviews a volunteer; the tape machine can be seen on the table

produced would still be of value to 'the gerontologists of 2020 to 2050'. Although psychology in the 1960s and 1970s had little time for 'soft' case histories, focusing instead on 'hard' statistical analysis, the Bonn team continued to stress the value of the biographical approach. For this reason, they preserved not only the 2,529 encoded variables, but also the study's raw materials—tape recordings and investigators' notes.[15] They aspired to square the circle. The large numbers and representative selection of interviewees, and their strictly statistical methodology, were intended to assure that the results would be objective and generalizable, even when they were discussing highly individual experiences and actions. Both the categories under which the findings were encoded and the guidance for the various rounds of Bolsa interviews intrinsically reflected Thomae's philosophy.

Hans Thomae was primarily concerned with elucidating the way in which the personality was formed, and developed throughout a lifetime. He understood human behaviour as informed by what he called *Daseinsthemen* (existence themes) and *Daseinstechniken* (existence techniques). *Daseinsthemen* were long-term, reinforced key themes within an individual's biography, while *Daseinstechniken* were typical response patterns for coping with stressful situations (these included, for example, 'seeking help' and 'aggression').[16] Bolsa was intended to prove that ageing processes varied in each individual, and were not so much determined by biology as shaped by historic and social conditions. Thomae saw a driving force behind the lifelong process of personality development in how old people dealt with everyday challenges.[17] Both he and his student Ursula Lehr turned against the then-dominant 'deficit hypothesis', whereby ageing essentially meant continual degradation and loss. They also argued against the idea of 'disengagement': old age as a life phase during which a person increasingly withdrew from social attachments and obligations. With the aid of the Bolsa study, the Bonn team developed their own theory, which held that successful ageing presupposed a high degree of social activity and interpersonal skills.[18]

The guidelines varied for each round of Bolsa interviews, and contained something for each of the investigators involved, all of whom were working on doctoral theses based partly on biographic profiles and partly on complex arithmetic calculations. Each of them was interested in a very different aspect: Karl-Georg Tismer was studying formative 'existence themes'; Maria Renner was investigating social roles lived out in everyday life; Georg Rudinger was evaluating the intelligence tests; Manfred Schreiner was looking at expectations for the future; and Reinhard Schmitz-Scherzer was exploring leisure activities. Norbert Erlemeier and Ingrid Puschner were concerned with the

THE SHAH'S VISIT, IN BONN AND BERLIN   25

informative value of new psychological methods such as the Rorschach test or a new 'wish list' technique.[19] Professor Thomae had great aspirations for his PhD students. He wanted to establish gerontology, which then had a strong tradition only in North America, as a field of study in West German universities. Here, he was acting in concert with the Volkswagen Foundation, the funders of the longitudinal study.[20] The Bolsa researchers would indeed become the trailblazers for the new discipline of psychological and social gerontology in West Germany. In the seventies and eighties, they filled new professorships all over the country. Even so, there was a dry spell of about a decade during which the freshly qualified, Bonn-trained gerontologists came up against universities that had not yet set up chairs of research into ageing. As Ingrid Puschner, one of the researchers, put it: 'We were…a group of gerontologists that nobody needed.'[21]

But back to 29 May 1967. The Bolsa investigators were still working on their doctoral (or, in Ursula Lehr's case, post-doctoral) theses, and confident that they would soon establish gerontology as a pioneering subject. Once they'd said goodbye to the study participants, they strolled together to the 'Bear', Bonn's oldest pub, just around the corner on Acherstraße. The team often met up there at lunchtime, and, more occasionally, in the evening. Tonight, however, almost everyone was there, keen to hear what Thomae had to tell them. As everyone in the department knew, Hans Thomae had, some time previously, been offered a chair at the University of Heidelberg. What they did not know was what he would decide. The question of whether or not West Germany's star gerontologist would stay in Bonn, would have a direct impact not only on the personal futures of the young psychology graduates, but also on the future of the longitudinal study, which had been running for just two years. Everybody was hoping that Thomae would turn Heidelberg down. Many of his team had a deep respect, admiration even, for their boss. Norbert Erlemeier, for example, found him 'a very, very impressive person' and spoke warmly about the way the professor gave his researchers 'great opportunities' and allowed them 'considerable [academic] freedom'. Georg Rudinger was highly appreciative of the fact that Thomae was 'not just a pencil pusher', but also interviewed volunteers himself, and took part in the day trips and team conferences. Ingrid Puschner was impressed that even the youngest team members were involved in designing the guidelines and evaluating the data: 'We were able to play a part.'[22] Under Thomae's professorship, there was more cooperation than conflict between young and old. Neither was Thomae ever accused by students or colleagues of being tainted by a Nazi past, as other senior academics were. In Bonn, he was considered on the liberal side, friendly to students, and one of the most ardent mediators between US and German research.[23]

When Thomae entered the inn *Im Bären*, he was greeted and bombarded with questions. Spontaneous applause rang out when he confirmed that he had turned the position down and would be staying in Bonn. The landlord pulled a round of beers. The mood was relaxed. Two Bolsa researchers, Ingrid Puschner and Karl-Georg Tismer, were flirting intensely with one another. Tismer was 32 and had relocated from the GDR. As a result of a spinal cord injury, he used a wheelchair for the rest of his life. He studied under Thomae and attained the position of assistant professor. Ingrid Puschner was a few years younger: a blonde woman of Sudeten-German extraction, who had also come to Bonn from the GDR. She had studied with Ursula Lehr ('For me it was really like a sigh of relief. My goodness, there's a woman and she gets to be a lecturer!') and had joined Bolsa straight after her final examinations. It was an open secret that there was a spark between Mr Tismer and Ms Puschner. At the other corner of the table, there were people with their heads together, arranging something special. The team wanted to drum up students and colleagues to stage a torchlit procession to sing songs of praise outside Thomae's house in nearby Roisdorf, as thanks for his loyalty to Bonn.[24]

Around another couple of corners, the Langbeins had settled into the Hotel Löhndorf for the week. Frau Langbein had approved the Persian rug and immaculate net curtains in their room. Herr Langbein particularly appreciated the hotel's brand-new lift but wished there were a television in the lounge.[25] The next morning, they met Frau Wellhöfer and the Tödtmanns there for breakfast.

A member of the hotel staff was serving coffee while the eight o'clock news played on the radio, which stood in the corner of the room beneath a rubber tree (Figure 2.4). Only the clatter of coffee cups interrupted the announcer's voice: the Shah was continuing his tour of Germany. Rush-hour traffic in the Ruhr area had ground to a halt that day because many motorways had been closed for the state visitor. Reza Pahlavi was to visit a steel mill in Duisburg, where they had a golden helmet ready for him. After that, he would travel via Rothenburg to Munich and Berlin, where the police had already been put on alert. Anti-Shah protests were expected everywhere. Events were dramatic elsewhere too. Israelis and Egyptians had exchanged fire in the Gaza Strip. Chancellor Kiesinger had flown from Bonn to Rome, where the European Community was continuing to discuss the United Kingdom's accession request. Meanwhile in Bonn, there were arguments over the proportionality of the previous day's police operation in the Hofgarten. Students had initiated

Figure 2.4 The Hotel Löhndorf breakfast room, c. 1960, with a view of the University building

legal proceedings against the incident commander and were now calling for a demonstration against 'police brutality'.[26]

When the weather forecast and music followed the news, Frau Langbein turned down the volume and whispered to the other Bolsa guests: wasn't it a shame that this protest march on Thursday would be happening at the same time as their trip to the Ahr valley? She'd have loved to have experienced the spectacle at close quarters and have 'direct contact' with students. Because otherwise, you only got to see 'what we read in the newspaper, what we see on the television and so on'. The breakfast party did not get drawn into discussing this topic, however. Frau Wellhöfer was very worried about 'this crisis over there in Egypt and Israel' and engaged Herr Langbein in a lively conversation about the events that would lead, not long afterwards, to the Six Days' War. As the mother of three sons, she was worried: 'I hope the business gets settled well. It'd be awful if we get involved in another war, that's not out of the question, you know.... Although they weren't in the army, but if push comes to shove, they'll just call them up.' Herr Langbein also admitted that 'the stupid Egyptians' were making him particularly annoyed and so he would definitely need to buy a newspaper before the start of the day's testing programme.[27]

As a result, they set off together for the Psychology Department a little earlier than planned.

There, the young gerontologists invited each of their senior guests into a small, modern conference room. To start with, the ladies and gentlemen were allowed to report back on what they had been doing for the last year, and the microphones on the desks were soon forgotten. Frau Tödtmann reminisced about her class reunion fifty years after leaving school, and a meeting for the Silesian *Heimatgemeinden* (ethnic Germans from Silesia who had been expelled from their villages after the Second World War) in Nuremberg. Herr Langbein talked about his niece's engagement party, and Herr Blech related his deep disappointment in his daughter, who didn't want him to move into her newly built house with her. This was followed by a medical examination, after which a machine was used to test their handwriting pressure. Finally, everyone's fine motor reaction speeds were measured using a rapidly rotating metal plate. Over the next few days, the Bolsianers underwent a whole raft of further experiments. They answered hundreds of questions on childrearing norms, their own retirement, and television use. They were sounded out about their past and the youth of today. By then, the mood was often a little more relaxed, and the interviewees made no bones about their opinions.[28]

While the reel-to-reel tapes whirred in the Bonn psychology rooms, the week's domestic and foreign political events were heating up. On the Wednesday, President Heinrich Lübke was leaving the Freie Universität in Berlin when he was booed and whistled at by 200 students, who were collecting for the Vietcong. On the Thursday, Munich saw the largest demonstration against the Shah to that point. Around 500 protesters demanded freedom in Iran and accused the state visitor of multiple murders. At the same time, 1,200 people gathered in Bonn for the city's 'biggest student rally in years'. Every student organization, whatever its political leanings, supported the protest against the police actions on the Monday, as did sixteen professors. The demonstrators declared themselves 'against the police state' and demanded the resignation of Valentin Portz, Bonn's chief of police. The latter hotly refuted 'insults and affronts of this kind' and described the wreath-laying as 'vulgarity' and 'affray': 'I cannot understand how the students can misbehave so badly, when a foreign head of state is honouring our dead, the victims of a regime of violence.'[29]

In retrospect, these events seem only a pale prelude to Friday, 2 June 1967. Having now landed in West Berlin, the Shah was greeted outside Schöneberg Town Hall that afternoon by around 400 students, throwing smoke bombs, eggs, and flour. The Berlin SDS handed out hectographed 'Wanted' posters featuring Reza Pahlavi. That evening there was a two-hour street battle outside the Deutsche Oper, where the Iranian imperial couple were watching Mozart's *The Magic Flute*. Amid the violent scuffles between the police, Shah loyalists, and demonstrators, detective constable (and Stasi agent) Karl-Heinz Kurras shot the 26-year-old Benno Ohnesorg, a German studies student, in the head. By the time Ohnesorg died in hospital that same evening, the final tally from the clashes stood at one dead, forty-four injured, and widespread shock at the brutal behaviour of the police. All the same, the mayor of West Berlin, Heinrich Albertz, immediately defended the forces of law and order, imposed an indefinite ban on demonstrations, and announced that the walled-in city could 'no longer allow itself to be terrorized by a minority'. The Senate promised summary courts for rioters and stressed that Kurras had acted 'in self-defence'. The *BILD* newspaper's front page called the students 'hooligans' and compared them to the Nazis: 'We don't hold with SA methods. Germans don't want a brown SA, or a red one either. They don't want gangs of thugs, they want peace.'[30]

The violent death of a fellow student and the partisanship of politicians and the press created a major stir among students across the country. 'We're recording an incredible level of political activity, unlike anything we've seen before', marvelled the chair of the *Verband Deutscher Studentenschaften* (VDS/Association of German Student Unions). In the seven days from when Ohnesorg was shot until his funeral, around 100,000 West German students gathered for silent marches, vigils, and rallies in his name.[31] In West Berlin a kilometre-long cortege of students accompanied Benno Ohnesorg's coffin to the border with the Eastern zone, where it was transferred into a convoy of cars to be driven to his home city of Hannover. On the day of the funeral, which was restricted to close family only, 6,500 students marched through Hannover city centre. They carried black banners and wore black armbands, handed out leaflets, and assembled in the evening for a 'Congress on University and Democracy'. This featured lively debates, not least between Rudi Dutschke and Jürgen Habermas, on the need for 'organized counter-violence'.[32] Practically every university town in the Federal Republic was swept up on the wave. Local protests had previously flared up in an unsystematic way, but this now grew into a political movement.[33] Moreover, the student movement spokesmen—still famous today—now emerged in the mass media.

The television cameras, *Spiegel* magazine, and the Springer press were all equally fixated on Rudi Dutschke, the SDS, and West Berlin. On the day of Ohnesorg's funeral, Dutschke—who had previously featured only once in the

30   THE OTHER '68

Springer press (in 1966), when he was called 'the spiritual leader of the Berlin Provos'[34]—was discovered by *Die Welt* to be 'the rabble-rouser and Marxist-Maoist sloganeer at the Freie Universität'. The SDS was identified as a hotbed of progressive thinkers 'who might not organize the unrest but certainly give it an ideological direction'.[35] Besides Dutschke, Springer's newspapers concentrated on Reimut Reiche of the Frankfurt SDS; 'the Student Lawyer', Horst Mahler; and commune member Fritz Teufel of West Berlin.[36] *Der Spiegel* also focused exclusively on Berlin. Three days after 2 June, it published an eleven-page cover story on student protests at the Freie Universität. It put Dutschke ('highly gifted', according to his professors), the Berlin SDS headquarters on the Kurfürstendamm ('the beds are still unmade at noon'), and the 'muddle-heads' of the 'Horror Commune' right in the foreground. The AStA chairmen, Knut Nevermann and Hartmut Häußermann, were quoted in passing. West German provincial cities did not even merit a mention. The student protests were characterized as specific to West Berlin, feeding on the city's precarious position in the Cold War, the American influence on the Freie Universität, and immigration from many young West German men fleeing military service.[37]

Television news was equally Berlin-centric. Reports on the West German student movement from June 1967 onwards focused almost entirely on West Berlin and Rudi Dutschke, at least partly on technical grounds. Numerous camera teams had been live in Berlin for the Shah's visit, and almost every subsequent news bulletin and political magazine show relied on the clips filmed at that time. In television terms, it was only logical to single out a few protagonists, 'who were already known to the viewers and editors'. Consequently, a total of three in-depth television profiles of Dutschke were broadcast from late summer 1967 onwards. Horst Mahler, described by the television magazine show *Monitor* as 'a prominent representative of the demonstrators since the Shah's visit', was also frequently interviewed. Mahler had appeared at the press conference after Benno Ohnesorg's death as legal adviser to the AStA at the Freie Universität.[38] Similarly, Kommune 1 featured on the television, although it appeared on screen more rarely than in the glossy magazines, which were obsessed with naked bodies and free love.[39]

Yet despite the portrayal on television, in *Der Spiegel*, and in the Springer press, things were brewing far from Berlin, outside the SDS, and away from the flagship communes. The shot at Ohnesorg had massively changed the political climate in university cities across the Federal Republic, as could also be seen in Bonn. A week before 2 June, students and professors had taken part in a panel discussion on the question of whether or not Bonn University was really an 'oasis of peace in political matters', as art historian Professor Heinrich Lützeler had maintained. At the heart of the argument was whether Bonn's AStA was allowed to operate on a general political level: whether, for example, they were permitted to discuss foreign policy in lecture theatres, compose resolutions on Vietnam, or invite speakers from the GDR. Left-leaning students were in favour of these things, while the university management and conservative students were opposed. The AStA at that time was politically centre-right and had been in office since May 1967, chaired by classics student Rudolf Pörtner; it tried in vain to arbitrate between the fronts. It faced a challenge from a kind of extra-parliamentary opposition (APO) within the university. Left-wing and liberal students, who rejected the conciliatory course, had withdrawn from the student parliament and established a 'Student Union'. This faction, which consisted of about a third of the members of the student parliament, included the SDS, and candidates from the *Sozialdemokratischer Hochschulbund* (SHB), who were close to the Social Democratic Party; the *Liberaler Studentenbund Deutschlands* (LSD), who were linked to the Free Democratic Party (FDP); the left-liberal, anti-clerical *Humanistische Studentenunion* (HSU); and a few independent left-wing representatives.[40]

The events of 2 June considerably intensified the politicization of the Bonn student scene. It was certainly no longer possible to speak of an oasis of peace. As Pörtner, the AStA chairman, recalled it, the 'Red June of '67' so polarized the camps that they ended up with the 'bizarre situation' of having two competing memorials for Ohnesorg. The guest speaker at the heart of the Student Union memorial, billed as a 'teach-in', was physics professor Siegfried Penselin, who stood up for the students' political mandate. The other event was a semi-official memorial put on by the AStA and the Senate; the speaker was political scientist Karl Dietrich Bracher. He railed against 'police terror' and Springer's 'smear campaigns', and even gave a clear warning against the 'tradition of the German authoritarian state' and a new '1933'.[41] Bracher thus expressed much greater criticism of the government than Penselin. Nonetheless, the Student Union described the AStA event as a mere matter of duty that had helped to conceal societal problems. The Student Union, in which the SDS quickly gained the upper hand, focused on organizing events with a broader impact, even outside the university. The very next Monday, they got a demonstration in the Hofgarten off the ground, in which about 1,000 students took part. This was followed by a solemn vigil by the Beethoven Monument on Münsterplatz. They laid a book of condolence on a table for passers-by to sign, which was continually flanked by two students bearing

32 THE OTHER '68

torches. For days, small groups of Bonn residents and students would gather there to discuss things.[42]

The student body's political voice seemed suddenly louder than ever before. Within a few days, the people of Bonn had witnessed not only the demonstration against the police actions, the protest marches, and acts of mourning after the death of Ohnesorg, but also a large AStA rally in response to the Six Days' War. This third Arab–Israeli war had broken out only three days after the riots in West Berlin. While Israeli pilots launched surprise attacks on Egyptian airfields, and Israeli troops conquered the Sinai Peninsula, the student government in Bonn had brought itself to 'take a stand' on this question too, and to arrange a 'large demonstration...on Münsterplatz...for peace in the Middle East'. Rudolf Pörtner had been able to attract Günter Grass to speak at the event, as a result of which the rally, attended by 2,000 students and residents, 'unintentionally...developed into a pro-Israeli demonstration'. In his speech, Grass did however also clearly criticize the actions of the Bonn police during the Shah's visit.[43]

The new visibility of the students' campaigns astonished the Bonn residents, and divided opinion. On the letters page of the local newspaper, the *General-Anzeiger*, feelings were running high. 'What's up with the students anyway?' asked Frau A. W. She was afraid that 'riots' like this would 'discredit' the German nation abroad. Other correspondents described the student protests against the Shah as 'senseless and pointless' (Th. Gansen), 'primitive' and 'immature' (H. F.), 'ungrateful' (Willy O.), and 'loudmouthed' (Franz Merck). The 'student howling' (M. Schallus) was probably the consequence of 'excessive freedom, of the sort that, in this country, we sadly mistake for democracy' (H. Schl.). Elisabeth Vogel, aged 83, felt sorry for the 'poor police'. In W. E.'s opinion, the students would be better off not 'kicking up a rumpus', but 'doing something on the barbed wire in East Berlin for the sake of those who had been killed or abducted'. Meanwhile, W. M. of Bad Godesberg raged: 'These students, no matter whether they're yahoos or not, ought to be sent for two years in the Reich Labour Service again, so that they could put their surplus energy at the disposal of the *Volksgemeinschaft* [national community].'

These voices were certainly in the majority, with eighteen letters criticizing the students, but they were by no means representative. Fifteen people from Bonn wrote to support the young people's political engagement (W. B.) and defend 'the right to opposition' (Dr. E.). It was not uncommon for the police to be blamed for the escalation. They had violated the constitution (Rosemarie Kappis), used 'all available means...to silence dissenting opinions' (Klaus Runge), and assumed the role of 'an instrument of destruction for enemies of the state' (according to professor of law Helmut Ridder).[44] Like him, many liberal professors publicly declared their allyship with the students by signing messages of solidarity or speaking at demonstrations.[45] It is worth noting that the local press largely sided with the demonstrators. While the Bonn *General-Anzeiger* issued a clear condemnation of the protests in West Berlin ('terror on the streets in the guise of the democratic right to demonstrate'), it defended the Bonn students against accusations of 'professional protestership' and did not shy away from criticizing the police. 'Pensionopolis'—as Bonn was known on account of its population of 15,000 retired people—was thus divided.[46] In the two weeks between the Shah landing at Cologne-Bonn airport and Benno Ohnesorg's funeral, the local political camps had been seriously stirred up. The scale of debates and demonstrations at the university, on the streets, and in the local press had seldom been seen before.

The political convulsions of the fortnight had only a tangential impact on proceedings in the university's Department of Psychology. While the Persian royals strolled through Munich, and Bonn's professors and students held their panel debate on AStA's political mandate, the Bolsianers were answering a multi-page questionnaire on the youth of today. While Bonn's students were demonstrating against the police, the Langbeins, the Tödtmanns, and Frau Wellhöfer were heading out to the Ahr valley in a minibus. The expedition enabled the psychologists to observe the participants' behaviour, although their guinea pigs were evidently unaware of this (Figure 2.5). Most of the volunteers had travelled very little, and experienced the trip mainly as tourists, all expressing 'their enjoyment of the excursion very animatedly'. Psychology graduate Maria Renner meticulously noted the way one of the ladies on the bus 'went into fresh raptures with every bend in the road', loudly 'struck up several songs', and told jokes. A second lady kept alternating between 'outbursts of wonder at the landscape' and accounts of her past travels elsewhere. In the café after their walk, a spirited conversation developed on the question of whether or not the actor Hans Moser had been Jewish. This animated discussion was only interrupted by the waiter, who served up assorted postcards on a silver tray; these had been bought by Herr Schubert—the engineer with a penchant for verse—for the women present. Thereupon, a third lady played somewhat conspicuous court to Herr Schubert, with 'remarks that were sometimes less than distanced'. When he offered her a cigar, she even let herself be photographed with it 'in a theatrical pose'. On the homeward journey, Albert Schubert insisted on sitting right at the front of the bus, testing the investigator on 'geological formations' and 'Latin grammar', and continually 'skilfully' weaving 'his erudition' into the

Figure 2.5 A study participant reads a poem during the day excursion. From left: Ursula Lehr, Hans Thomae, volunteer, Norbert Erlemeier, volunteers, driver

conversation. Maria Renner, who was in charge of the trip, characterized him in writing as a 'ready-on-my-command type' including some 'rather impolite outbursts'. All the same, the mood was euphoric, almost tipsy—even if one old woman had expressly insisted that she was able to 'get the party going even without wine'.[47]

The Ahr valley trip was the undisputed highlight of the week for the Bolsa participants. Nevertheless, they had to report in again on the Friday morning to undergo a last series of tests. In one of these, their concentration and resilience were measured by means of buttons, pedals, and levers to be pressed or pulled in response to flashing coloured lights and buzzers. They were also questioned on their ideas about the future before saying goodbye.[48] As soon as they had left, Thomae's team met for what was known as the 'Friday round table' in the department's windowless, soundproofed Room 9. Here, the researchers jointly ran through each of their 'senior guests' to obtain a statistically grounded personality profile. They all shared the individual observations they had made over the week and on the excursion. The views compiled in this way were then 'aggregated into an overall impression': they quantified how excitable, active, controlled, conforming, and confident the behaviour of each Bolsianer had been. There was a lot of laughter—the Friday round table was less 'a seat of dry, earnest academia' than 'a space for collegial sociability and relaxation'.[49] They frequently listened to sections of the week's tape recordings so that their colleagues could hear pivotal passages in the conversation.

Influenced by the local student protests, the young researchers also spent that Friday discussing the old people's attitudes towards the clash of the generations. Maria Renner dug out the tape of her volunteer Hedwig Langbein. Frau Langbein had tried to make distinctions:

> When the Berlin students are constantly running riot, well that's not exactly nice, is it—and badgering all the professors like that, so they all quit...But most young people are all right really, aren't they? They study, they apply themselves, they're hard working...They aren't all drop-outs and beatniks and whatnot, whatever they're all called.[50]

Maria Wellhöfer had also seen a difference between respectable young people and the others: 'Well now, you can't measure them all by the same yardstick now, can you? There are still some...young people who take life seriously. But most of them just don't want to fit in with the general public.'[51] Many of the voices preserved on the tape showed deep unease. A 76-year-old master metalworker exclaimed: 'The youth have no respect for age...students reckon the professors ought to arrange things to suit *them*...where will that lead us?' Housewife Marie Tödtmann was outraged by the young people she'd seen walking in the city:

> These mini-skirts and drop-outs..., it's scandalous...Unwashed and hair down to their shoulders, colourful jackets. And sometimes they've got Jesus written on them, and that. It's just awful. Draped all over each other—that would never have been possible in the past. It makes you feel really queasy to see that.

The voice of Götz Langbein could also be heard, indignant that 'the youth of today have so much less respect for age than in the past...Young lovers, kissing, slobbering over each other—if you say anything, the most you'll get is a gruff answer.'[52]

The Friday round table was briefly paused following a cautious knock on the door. It was Helga Merker, a brand-new psychology graduate, inviting her friend Maria Renner for a coffee in the refreshment room. Merker wanted Renner's advice, having just had a conversation with Professor Thomae. He had suggested that she write her PhD on the attitudes of the Bolsa participants towards youth, as she had just sailed through her oral examination with him. The excited Helga Merker told her friend that she'd even been late for the exam because of the war in Israel. 'There were these big American bombers flying over...I almost went nuts over them, I was stressed about the exam, and then the stress about the war too!'[53] Maria Renner congratulated her on her pass and asked about the planned doctoral thesis. Helga Merker said that she was to compare the Bolsianers' statements with a 'middle-aged' sample of 33- to 58-year-olds, with the aim of finding out whether the intensity of prejudice against young people increased with the age of the interviewees, and how widespread stereotypes were in the various age groups.

Maria Renner laughed and assured her she'd find plenty of material on the tapes. They were always talking about drop-outs, students, and girls in miniskirts! The budding PhD student was looking forward to her task. From then until the middle of the next year, six young women students would be delivering her with fresh conversations with 120 middle-aged adults on the subject of young people. She would then transcribe and categorize these interviews and subject them to statistical analysis with the aid of the university computer centre.[54] The friends' conversation broke off, however, when their colleague Erlemeier popped in to remind them of the torchlit procession that had been arranged in honour of Hans Thomae. Despite the slight drizzle, they set off together for the Bonn suburb of Roisdorf, where the Thomae and Lehr families shared a large, old villa.

Almost 200 undergraduates and postgraduate students gathered in Roisdorf towards 9 p.m., with fifty private cars, dozens of torches, and bunches of flowers. Once they reached the villa's garden, the crowd struck up the Latin drinking song 'Gaudeamus igitur', which celebrates youth and academic culture. They handed the professor a scroll, thanking him for having turned down the job offer from elsewhere (Figures 2.6 and 2.7). Hans Thomae was surprised and visibly touched. Helga Merker found the subsequent celebrations 'wonderful', even 'romantically beautiful'; they went on until midnight, and not even the rain could detract from them. It helped that Mrs Thomae had been pre-warned, and bought up 'almost the entire supply of bottled beer' to be had from the landlords of Roisdorf.[55] Thus, two different student rallies were held in Bonn that evening: a tribute to a professor, which could have played out very similarly in centuries past, and a vigil held by the Student Union on Münsterplatz, which brought the new forms of symbolic provocation into the public eye.

There were many facets to Sixty-Eight in Bonn, and many types of intergenerational encounter. Elderly residents came face-to-face with demonstrating students, Professor Thomae with his up-and-coming psychologists, retired

Figure 2.6 Hans Thomae receives the scroll from the torch-bearers

Figure 2.7 Torchlit procession, singing in Roisdorf on 7 June 1967

study participants with their young interviewers, passers-by with young hippies and pairs of lovers. Ohnesorg's death on 2 June was the moment that polarized and galvanized the student movement. The Shah's visit, and the following week, changed the situation in Bonn and across the country. The University's political rigidity broke open, existing rifts in the student body were deepened, a multitude of direct, symbolic actions mobilized thousands of students. Non-students took sides and split into camps. Many saw an existential threat to democracy in West Germany, either from the police or from the demonstrators.

Yet the mass media focused not on Bonn, but Berlin, and television images of, and press reports from West Berlin dominated perceptions of the movement. The media's working conditions and genres prescribed the way they painted the icons of Sixty-Eight. The public view of the protests was narrowed to a few places and people: Cold War West Berlin, the Frankfurt of the Frankfurt School, Kommune 1, the SDS office on the Kurfürstendamm, Rudi Dutschke, and Horst Mahler. The SDS, with its targeted strategy of provocative and subversive campaigns, gained considerably more publicity than other student associations, which stuck to traditional resolutions and well-mannered events with visiting speakers.[56]

Consequently, the fact that Sixty-Eight also took place elsewhere was lost from view. Student politics was polarized and intensified in the West German provinces too; rallies of all kinds, against police violence, and Ohnesorg's shooting, were organized; a little later, grassroots initiatives such as alternative nurseries and women's groups were formed. From June 1967 onwards, regional student leaders also began to emerge. In Bonn, SDS activist Hannes Heer's spectacular performances made him the best-known local student hero. Yet his reputation was limited to the Cologne-Bonn area, and the national media came late to reporting on him, and then only sporadically.[57] It was not until the 1990s that he gained nationwide attention, in his capacity as the head of the 'Wehrmacht Exhibition' on the violent crimes committed by German soldiers during the Second World War.

3

Of Wartime Children and Nazi Parents

September 1968, in a forester's lodge on the river Sieg. Fifty-six-year-old Paul
Heer is writing to his 27-year-old son Hannes, who is studying history, Latin,
and German studies in Bonn. The Russian invasion of Prague had shown Paul
'once and for all what you want, you and your comrades. Dutschke, Langhans
and whatever they're all called.' Hannes wanted to

> smash up everything we rebuilt after the war; to deliver the rest of Germany
> up to the Communists too. I no longer consider you our son. I have spoken
> to the notary in Wissen, to ask him to disinherit you. I forbid you ever to
> enter our house again. I have done this out of consideration for Mother, who
> has been very hard hit by the awful things that are written about you in the
> newspaper. But in your blind fanaticism, that will not interest you anyway.
> Your Father.

The son, born in 1941, did not even answer, and first explained himself two
decades later:

> The disinheritance made me laugh because a forester has nothing to
> leave anyway, and I kind of took the banishment from the family in my
> stride. We were busy with more important things at that time, with world
> revolution...Your letter only proved our theories correct. You were on
> the other side. Son of a smallholder who rose to become a civil servant,
> Nazi Party member and soldier, a CDU voter after the war. For me that
> was a logical trajectory.[1]

In 1966, Hannes Heer had founded the Bonn SDS with a group of friends,
having been a member of the university's student parliament since 1965. In
1967 and 1968, he was the city's best-known student activist—'Bonn's answer
to Rudi Dutschke'.[2] After his travels to the GDR and Auschwitz, which made a
deep impression on him, he had developed an interest in Marxist politics and
theory. 'Dear Father', he responded, 'you never asked me why I joined the
SDS....I had visited Auschwitz in 1965. On my return, I discovered that the

same people' who had enabled the murder of the Jews were now 'representatives of our democracy'. The young Hannes Heer was worried by the Emergency Acts, a hotly contested law pending approval by the ruling Grand Coalition, which put in place far-reaching emergency government powers that would take effect in the event of an internal or external attack on West German democracy. Heer also abhorred the acts of brutality committed by the Americans in the Vietnam War, and—above all—the Nazi past of West German politicians. Allegations against Hans Globke, Adenauer's Head of the Chancellery; Theodor Oberländer, Minister for Refugees and Expellees; Chancellor Kurt Georg Kiesinger; and Federal President Heinrich Lübke roused him to action.[3] Together with fellow student Glen Pate, Heer steered the Bonn SDS onto an orthodox Marxist course, which came closer to the GDR line, and later that of the German Communist Party (DKP), than the SDS in West Berlin. The spectacular protests at the University of Bonn, led by Heer, made the national headlines in February 1968 and thus led to the rift with his father.

On 6 February 1968, Hannes Heer had led a group of fifteen to twenty students into the office of the Rector, ecclesiastical historian Professor Wilhelm Schneemelcher. He had asked the receptionist if he could wait for the absent Rector to return, and been given access. Heer wanted to force a conversation with him about Heinrich Lübke, having already written to Schneemelcher twice in vain. The Bonn SDS were demanding that the university withdraw the title of honorary senator that it had bestowed on the West German president in 1966. The SDS had declared the week beginning 29 January a 'Lübke Week' and had displayed incriminating documents in the main university building, in the canteen, and on Münsterplatz in Bonn.[4] Lübke had been facing public criticism for months because a campaign instigated by the GDR in relation to his Nazi past had been picked up by the West German mass media. *Stern* magazine and other publications were increasingly treating the documents, presented by the East and only partially faked, as genuine. The Federal President was vilified as a 'concentration camp architect'—in reference to blueprints for prisoner barracks that he had signed during the Second World War. In fact, Lübke had been a construction supervisor responsible for building prisoner barracks in armament factories, and had used forced labour squads on the work. Now he tried to hush his involvement up.[5] The president did not respond until March 1968, when he gave a belated, less than convincing, and inaccurate television address, in which he spoke of libel, and insisted that he could not remember ever having planned buildings for concentration camps.[6]

But back to Schneemelcher's office. Once the students had been ushered out, a surprising new entry was discovered in the university's book of honour: appended to Lübke's signature were the words 'concentration camp architect'. The university management were outraged. The Rector considered the golden book 'defiled'. The following day, he accused the students of 'naked terror' and 'serious assault'. He spoke of 'affrays that necessitated police intervention' and of 'insults and lies'.[7] What had happened? During a meeting with representatives of the student parliament and the AStA, to which the SDS contingent had not been invited, SDS members had staged a sit-in, led by Hannes Heer and Glen Pate. To gain access, they blocked the corridor to the Rector's office, broke windowpanes, and threatened to break down the door. The Rector called the police, who cleared the passageway by non-violent means at first, but then by force, and subsequently sealed the building off for several hours. The demonstrators chanted slogans such as 'Nazi out! Thugs!' and sang both 'We shall overcome' and the GDR anthem 'Risen from the Ruins'. That same night, furious students painted slogans such as 'Schneemelcher—Friend of Nazis'; 'Schneemelcher test runs the Emergency Acts'; 'This is a Police School'; and 'Uni Closed to Students, the Police Study Here' on the walls of the main building.[8]

The confrontation between the SDS and the Rector polarized the camps at the University of Bonn (Figure 3.1). Conservative students, represented by Jürgen Rosorius, spokesman for the Association of Christian Democratic Students (RCDS), demanded that SDS representatives Heer and Pate be expelled.[9] The Student Union, as the mouthpiece of the left-wing students, demanded the resignation of 'Police Rector' Schneemelcher and spoke of brutal 'purges' and an act of 'provocation against the students of Bonn'.[10] The centre-right AStA under Rudolf Pörtner tried to mediate by condemning violence on the part of both the students and the police. He warned 'that the SDS and its supporters in Bonn have now also succeeded in using targeted actions to provoke the university leadership into wrongdoing, and that as a result it now has the illusion of right on its side'.[11] This escalation can only be explained by taking the influence of the East German state into account as an additional factor.

During its 'anti-fascist' Lübke week, the Bonn SDS had clearly declared its solidarity with the GDR campaign against the FRG President. The evening before the sit-in, the SDS had extended an invitation to a public lecture by Friedrich Karl Kaul. Kaul was not just anybody. He was the top lawyer within the Socialist Unity Party (SED), Professor at the Humboldt University in East Berlin, and, as a communist and Jew, had been persecuted under Hitler's

Figure 3.1 After the raid on the Rector's office in February 1968, the police take down the particulars of thirty-six students. Centre: Hannes Heer

regime. He was especially known for his involvement in the West German trials of perpetrators of Nazi atrocities, in which he appeared as joint plaintiff on behalf of victims living in the GDR, and frequently contributed evidence from East German archives. He had published several volumes featuring incriminating documents relating to the Nazi past of West German dignitaries and been heavily involved in the Lübke case. In the SDS view, Kaul was thus a champion of 'unmasking well-to-do Nazis'.[12] Bonn was just another stop on Kaul's tour of West German universities, and he had already spoken in Tübingen, Marburg, and Münster.[13] But the Bonn lecture was crashed by anti-communist students, most of whom were members of traditional student fraternities, or the RCDS. Some, such as Busso von der Dollen, were refugees from the GDR themselves; they had researched 'former National Socialists in the services of Pankow' in advance, and circulated a leaflet on ex-Nazis on the SED Central Committee and within the Volkskammer, the GDR parliament.[14] Dollen and his fellow campaigners did not let Kaul get a word in, and demanded instead 'immediate discussion on Nazis in important positions in the GDR'. They also unrolled two banners, accusing Kaul of inactivity when it came to 'Freedom for political prisoners in the GDR' and 'Murder at the Wall'. The visitor from East Berlin flounced out of the hall, whereupon Hannes Heer, the co-organizer, denounced the conservative invaders as

'The Rector's *Schutztruppe*' (Protection Force), a colonial-era term implying authoritarian militarism. An SDS leaflet later described them as 'organized fascists'.[15] The row about the West German president's Nazi past was inextricably linked with the anti-totalitarian fundamental consensus of the West German state (both anti-communist and anti-fascist). And it was by no means over after the Kaul evening and the sit-in.

The Rector rang the bell for the next round by announcing severe disciplinary measures against the students involved in the sit-in. Hannes Heer and Glen Pate were identified as ringleaders and threatened with expulsion. The case was passed to the university's disciplinary arbiter, Professor of Criminal Law Hellmuth von Weber. But the SDS went on the counterattack by appointing Friedrich Karl Kaul for the defence, and putting out a leaflet about von Weber's actions during the Third Reich, with documents that had been hastily procured from Jena.[16] Again, backing from the GDR proved very valuable to the SDS.[17]

It turned out that von Weber was seriously tainted. In 1933, he had written an expert opinion on the Reichstag fire on behalf of the Nazi regime, which recommended the summary trial of the arsonist.[18] He had served in other prominent positions too, such as deputy *Gaufachschaftsleiter* (regional head) of the National Socialist German Jurists' League.[19] Now he, of all people, was to decide on whether or not Heer and other SDS members should be thrown out of the university. Hundreds of students demonstrated—successfully— against this. The university Senate established a commission to investigate the allegations against von Weber and put the disciplinary proceedings on ice for the time being. The SDS were ultimately victorious. The expulsion was rescinded and Hellmuth von Weber resigned.[20] Although the Senate commission did not name and shame him as a Nazi, he was publicly rounded on by many students and assistant professors, as well as nine professors (the total later came to twenty-six full professors). His critics argued that his position was no longer tenable and was damaging the 'university's reputation'.[21]

This was a completely new look for the University of Bonn. Since 1964, the weekly newspaper *Die Zeit* had criticized the tainted past of its Rector Hugo Moser on several occasions and, over the years, the university management had generally responded by stonewalling. Then, in 1965, there had been vociferous protests against Siegfried Ruff, Professor of Medicine, who was heavily implicated for his involvement in barbaric experiments into the effects of low pressure on the human body carried out on prisoners at the Dachau concentration camp. Once again, the university response was hesitant. It even exerted legal pressure on the assistant professor within the Department of

Psychology who first made the accusations against Ruff. In the end, Ruff resigned his adjunct professorship in May 1966, before a Senate commission could investigate the case.[22] Dealing with the past was yet to be prompted by the students: in this instance, the impetus came from the media and junior academic staff, although some students were politicized by the scandals around Moser and Ruff. Of the twenty-two activists interviewed by the Bonn Stadtmuseum, two stated that the debates about the professors' involvement with the Nazis had played a part in their own developing political awareness.[23]

Disproportionate policing at demonstrations was, however, cited far more frequently. Four of the twenty-two referred, unprompted, to the police actions during the Shah's visit in May 1967 as a formative political experience.[24] Another five described similar eye-openers at other protests.[25] Eckehart Ehrenberg, an independent, right-leaning AStA member, was 'inwardly appalled' at the police behaviour during the blockade of the Rector's office in February 1968. 'I found this police action indefensible,...unnecessary and unwise, because it escalated the situation....That played a considerable role in shifting me further to the left.'[26] Similarly Ulrich Rosenbaum, a member of the student parliament with links to the SPD, experienced the same actions as a shocking breach of taboo.[27] The police truncheon became the catalyst for the student movement. Social Democrat student Guntram von Schenck recalled: 'We benefitted the most, as they did at other universities too, from police actions. We could count on fresh intake after every police operation.'[28] By contrast, few students seemed particularly offended at this point by the fact that almost all their professors had gained their academic qualifications under the Nazi regime.

The conflict around Lübke, which led to the sit-in, police actions in the Rector's office, and the von Weber scandal, followed the anti-Shah demonstrations of May 1967 as a second step towards the political mobilization of Bonn's students. Hannes Heer was becoming an ever-clearer leader of the radical students, especially after his fellow campaigner Glen Pate returned to the USA in April 1968.[29] The *Kölner Stadtanzeiger* called Heer the 'most eloquent SDS man', whose 'fighting speeches via megaphone' were 'particularly uncomfortable' for 'the University management and police'.[30] The press reports on the camp-architect campaign, and his (threatened) expulsion from the university were the ones that worried Hannes Heer's mother and prompted his father to disown him. The headlines seemed to speak for themselves: 'Charged With Sedition', 'Sit-In Ends in Rioting', 'Radicals Plan to Storm the Rectory', 'SDS Chief Frogmarched Away'.[31] The ensuing letter of

OF WARTIME CHILDREN AND NAZI PARENTS 45

excommunication cited above was followed by decades of silence on both sides. Hannes believed that he had found his father out as an 'old Nazi':

> As a student in Bonn, I chanced to come across a newspaper cutting in some old papers. It was a report from 1939 on his speech as champion marksman and Party member in Wissen an der Sieg, where I was born, in which he thanked the Führer for our beautiful Germany. There were simple explanations for why he had joined the Party. But he never said a word about it, and he didn't speak about his war years either.

His father never discussed the world war, his imprisonment, or how close he had been to the regime.[32] Nor did he enquire about his son's political opinions. Just as Hannes Heer's image of his father was based on a yellowing newspaper article, Paul Heer's view of his son was composed of press reports about riots at the universities.[33] This was a 'communication at second-hand' via the media. The 1988 docudrama *Mein 68. Ein verspäteter Brief an meinen Vater* (My '68. A Belated Letter to my Father) was an attempt by the son to break through this silence. It was broadcast on WDR, the regional third television channel, but still not followed by a personal reconciliation.[34]

'We would never have been able to have a conversation', Hannes recalled. And he extrapolated this view to take in his entire generation and their confrontation with their parents:

> At first we were facing your wall of silence. Then we felt the force of your hatred.... You called us 'anarchists', 'hellraisers', screamed 'gas [them]', 'put [them] up against the wall', 'labour service'.... Did you shout so loudly because we reminded you of that blood-soaked, lost part of your lives?[35]

Hannes saw yesterday's murderers in the elderly citizens on the streets expressing loud anger at the demonstrators, considering that they 'had lived through a time when action was taken, had joined in with the action themselves...letting streams of real blood flow all across Europe'.[36] In his view, members of the Nazi Party (NSDAP), and adherents of the Führer, such as his father, were 'not fellow-travellers, but perpetrators'.[37] He understood 'Auschwitz' as that generation's Achilles' heel. At a demonstration staged by groups of Germans displaced from the East in 1966, he had a hostile encounter with the police, who confiscated his placards opposing the expellees' goals. He would later write:

46 THE OTHER '68

Perhaps the police commissioner and his accomplices, who sought in 1966 to enforce the law against a placard, had travelled in 1941 to the Eastern front via Auschwitz, after Józefów and Łomazy, after Białystok and Riga... to all those little Auschwitzes that they had staged with their police battalions. Where else would all that rage come from.[38]

His actual parents, the father who had cast him out, were conflated with parents in the abstract: the police, the columnists, the disciplinarians, politicians, and professors of the late sixties.

Heer would wrestle with these abstract fathers, and their Nazi taint, all his life. He remained politically active at the university until 1974. He was in the Bonn AStA until 1970, a member of the 'Revolutionary Cells' and communist K-Gruppen splinter groups until 1974. He and fellow SDS campaigners briefly managed to take over the VDS, the umbrella group for German student associations, in 1969, and to steer it along revolutionary lines.[39] After the *Radikalenerlass*, a decree banning the employment of teachers or civil servants considered to be radicals, the teaching profession was closed to him, and he became an author, curator, and filmmaker. He headed up the Reemtsma Institute's first, controversial Wehrmacht Exhibition, which clearly and visually laid a share of the blame for mass Nazi atrocities at the feet of ordinary soldiers, and many conservatives thus considered him 'the greatest denigrator of our fathers' generation'. He and his own father never managed a heart-to-heart. In his mid-60s, Heer wondered self-critically, whether he had been just as blinded by ideology in his youth as his father had been before him. 'We were fanatics—we were your sons', he reasoned. 'By getting rid of our fathers, our families, their morals and religion, "all that same old shit", and declaring it "fascist", "bourgeois" and "reactionary"', he and his comrades had withdrawn from conversation with their parents. He and the others had shied away from the task of fighting 'the fascist, bourgeois and reactionary structures within ourselves'.[40]

To what extent was the generational conflict arising from the burden of parents' Nazi past, which Heer invoked so insistently, truly the core of Sixty-Eight in West Germany? The conventional historical opinion has been that young people's moral outrage 'at older generations, at their fathers, even their grandfathers' was specific to West Germany and at the heart of the revolt there: 'These conflicts even reached into individual families.' Fury at their parents, who were silent about their own complicity, was said to have driven radical young people to rebel against 'everything their parents represented—everything: national pride, Nazism, money, the West, peace, stability, law and democracy'.[41] 1940s children were said to be alienated by their silent parents, giving rise to a generation born 'out of the spirit of opposition to National Socialism'. The actions of these rootless 'children of repression' were seen as a perpetual 'moral protest against their fathers' guilt', because 'nowhere else was the generation that fathered the "68ers" as politically compromised and morally weak' as in the Federal Republic.[42] The parents' cold behaviour and glossing over their Nazi past helped escalate the conflict: 'The radicalism exhibited then was the result of real psychological damage caused by the intergenerational transfer of the psychological legacy of Nazism'.[43]

Historical scholarship frequently reads this much-vaunted father–son antagonism directly into family relationships. The discord 'between the (Nazi) parents and their children' had produced 'a generation of emotionally freezing children', according to Götz Aly. A 'lack of *Nestwärme*' (the warmth of the nest, i.e. parental affection) had been 'the central problem for the 15- to 25-year-olds of 1968'. Aly asserts that there were 'countless' incidents of clashes 'within families, over dinner'.[44] Interpretations of this kind are often based partly on Sixty-Eighters' autobiographies, and partly on literary sources. After all, a student rebel cutting ties with his guilty father—whether the latter had been a direct perpetrator or a fellow traveller—is a classic theme in such memoirs: the Sixty-Eighters were 'choosing to be orphans'.[45] From the early seventies onwards, the mental torment caused by these rifts found expression in the new West German genre of *Väterliteratur*: novels by predominantly young, male authors in which they denounced not only the silence and guilt of their Nazi fathers, but also their own trauma at losing their fathers.[46] Despite its popularity, other authors have occasionally criticized this interpretation. Ulrike Jureit warns that the generation of 1968 had only staged this genealogical divide. In her view, the parents' emotional rigidity and the shock of Auschwitz were often not the reality, but retrospective constructs, which enabled the younger men to put a heroic gloss on their own generation.[47] So is there any truth to the prevailing idea of father–son conflict arising from the Nazi past?

First of all, we need to clarify the birth cohorts of the different generations alive around the year 1968. Most families at that time spanned three generations living together: children, parents, and grandparents. The overwhelming majority of Sixty-Eighters were born between 1938 and 1948, while every former Bonn student interviewed in 2005 and 2006 by Horst-Pierre Bothien was born between 1940 and 1948, with the median birth year being 1944.[48] The files kept by the West Berlin SDS were out of date, so it had a larger proportion of older members on its books, but even so, over two thirds were from the 1939–1945 cohort.[49] This confirms the hypothesis, posited by historians such as Norbert Frei, Heinz Bude, Albrecht von Lucke, and Ulrich Herbert, that the student rebels were born from the late 1930s to 1950.[50] Thus, the Sixty-Eighters were aged between 20 and 30 in 1968.

Meanwhile, their parents were mostly between 40 and 60 years old, and belonged to the cohort born between around 1908 and 1928. They therefore approximate to the 'middle generation' questioned by Bonn PhD student Helga Merker in 1967 and 1968.[51] This means that they were mostly rather younger than the generation the majority of historians have considered to be the key supporters of Nazism: those born between about 1900 and 1910. Various terms have been coined for this latter cohort—*Kriegsjugendgeneration* (the generation who were teenagers during the First World War), *Generation der Sachlichkeit* (generation of objectivity), *Generation des Unbedingten* (uncompromising generation), or the *Jahrhundertgeneration* (the generation that spanned the twentieth century). But there is consensus that many of this age group were radicalized by defeat in the First World War and the political turmoil of the Weimar era, and that from the 1930s onwards, they constituted the relatively young adherents of the regime, endorsed the Nazi ideology, and took active part in its mass crimes.[52] These people, whom historians consider the most strongly Nazified age group, were between 58 and 68 in 1968, and were thus more likely to be the grandparents than the parents of teenage Sixty-Eighters. If we take the male volunteers in the Bolsa study as an example, we find that only 7 per cent of fathers born between 1897 and 1906 had an oldest child born in 1938 or later (median 1929, n = 32), while the youngest child of only 39 per cent was born after 1937 (median 1935, n = 28). We can see then that the Sixty-Eighters' parents do not fit the cliché of the perpetrator generation, merely on grounds of age.[53]

So what was the young students' experience of their parents? Serious conflict with a tainted father, such as that which dominated Hannes Heer's life, was rare. Of the twenty-two activists in Bonn from 1966 to 1968 who told their stories to museum curator Horst-Pierre Bothien, only two—Hannes Heer and Heidrun Lotz—mentioned open discord with Nazi parents. Twelve other interviewees did, however, describe at least one parent as having been an apolitical fellow traveller or a small-scale Nazi, without this having caused confrontations. By contrast, four of those questioned came from socialist, communist, or pacifist homes. Another four sited their families as close to the conservative resistance.[54]

At first glance, the strong showing (8:14) for the offspring of the resistance to Hitler—which was in historical fact relatively limited—may seem surprising. But on looking more closely, we can see that the four instances of conservative 'resistance' were by no means unambiguous. Rather, the interviewees often accepted and generalized vague stories told by their parents (more on this later). The four accounts of left-wing, anti-Nazi parents are more credible. They point towards a trend that has been confirmed by more recent research into the student movement in Italy and West Germany. Students who got involved in politics from early in their university career, and took up prominent positions, were more likely than average to come from radical or social democratic families, and to have been immersed in protest from childhood. After interviewing many SDS and APO members, historian Anna von der Goltz wrote in 2013 about frequent conversations that attested to positive family influences: 'Indeed, many activists came down on the same side politically as their parents and jointly attended demonstrations with older family members.'[55] The Italian student movement was also dominated by the children of communists, socialists, and anti-fascists, by a ratio of ten to three.[56]

It is therefore hardly surprising that, even in a setting such as small-town, Roman Catholic Bonn, perhaps as many as a fifth of the student protagonists came from left-wing backgrounds. It was easier to take the step into politics if, like Bonn SDS member Christoph Strawe, you had developed 'a particular critical stance' as a teenager because your family were critics of the arms race and supporters of the *Kampf dem Atomtod* (Fight Nuclear Death) movement. Strawe was already a committed Marxist when he arrived at the university.[57] Being able to depend on solidarity from your parents may also have had a liberating effect. Judith Olek, née Ramm, handed out anti-Shah leaflets on 28 May 1967 and was subsequently arrested and harassed by the police. Her father, a lifelong Social Democrat, who had been briefly interned in Bergen-Belsen by the Nazis, turned up at the Bonn police headquarters and 'kicked up a massive stink, after which I was allowed to go home'. He also helped her arrange an examination by an independent doctor, who attested to the bruises, sprains, and contusions she had suffered and, later, to press charges.[58] Judith Olek noted with amazement 'this doggedness', this 'outright hatred for the Nazis' that other students felt, such as a friend of hers, whose father had served as a judge during the National Socialist regime. 'They were ashamed...We had no need to be ashamed. We could deal with it better...[because] our parents had not been involved with that.'[59]

Eighteen of the interviewees' mothers and fathers had been conservative, apolitical, or National Socialist, and this group was both more numerous and more typical. As many as sixteen of them had not argued with their parents

50 THE OTHER '68

about their roles in the Third Reich, preferring to maintain family harmony. Moreover, they often engaged in retrospectively justifying their parents. There is a wide gulf here between our modern expectation of antagonism between the Sixty-Eighters and their parents, and the reality within families. When he interviewed the former activists from Bonn for the Stadtmuseum, Horst-Pierre Bothien consistently asked targeted questions about their parents' Nazi pasts[60] but gained slim pickings; indeed, many clearly rejected his assumptions. Rudolf Pörtner, chairman of the Bonn AStA during the summer of 1967, claimed 'that that really was no big deal in people's family homes':

> As I recall, addressing [their] parents' Nazi pasts played no role at all. I don't remember that in 1967 and 1968... OK, Hannes Heer's father had been a particularly staunch Nazi... [but apart from that] no... We talked about it now and then, but not awfully intensely. Although my father, it must definitely have been awkward with him because he was working as a journalist then, you know, on a Nazi newspaper, and so he must have written articles in those days that you wouldn't like to read nowadays. But on the other hand, he always maintained that he'd been against it. And, I don't know if that's all true and how it really was. I used to believe him, but I really don't know for sure. All the same, it didn't play any kind of decisive role for us at home.[61]

Eckehart Ehrenberg, then the social officer for the AStA, whose father had been killed in the war, had a very similar reaction. Coming to terms with National Socialism had been 'no motivation' for him:

> No, definitely not, that was disgusting and it didn't surprise me but... biographically I had nothing to do with it. I didn't consider my father a criminal. At the end of the day, I don't know what he did in the war, but there was no knowledge that he was a particular criminal, and nor was anyone else in the family. And that's a difference. Now let's say that if Heer had an uncle or a father who'd been a Camp doctor... well then, that's a whole different dimension.[62]

In answer to Bothien's questions, Ulrich Rosenbaum, the editor-in-chief of Bonn's student newspaper *akut* in 1968, conceded that

> my parents also had a Nazi past. My mother had taken part in the '36 Olympics and of course as a young girl, she was keen as mustard. But to me

OF WARTIME CHILDREN AND NAZI PARENTS   51

that was neither here nor there. It's not like it was for Hannes Heer, where
there was what you might call the incorrigible father who still didn't grasp
that we'd ended up in a democracy standing there in the background as
some kind of menacing figure.

It was only after both his parents had died that Rosenbaum investigated more
closely in surviving documents and archives. He wrote in 2017:

> Because I had a sheltered childhood, I always consciously deferred that until
> after they had passed away. So I now know that my mother was a leading
> BDM [*Bund Deutscher Mädel*, League of German Girls] official in the
> General Government [in Nazi-occupied Poland], and that my father was
> until April 1945 the senior editor at the SS publishing house *Nordland
> Verlag*, responsible for the production of morale-boosting literature, and
> that he taught at the SS training facility at Bernau (now a World Heritage
> site).[63]

Another *akut* editor, Hans Günter Jürgensmeier, certainly chafed against his
teacher father's authoritarian style, but did not link this with his past:

> I was firmly convinced that the [Third Reich] had been an utterly terrible
> business, but I hadn't concerned myself any further with how far my parents
> had been tangled up in it. My mother wasn't, at any rate, she came from the
> Catholic Rhineland, and they were resisters, Catholic resistance... My father,
> I wouldn't like to say that he was active in any way. Of course they were all
> organized, National Socialist Teachers League, German Labour Front and so
> on, but otherwise he sat tight. It was always Catholic, from what I heard in
> those days.[64]

Jürgen Aretz, who as a liberal-conservative student co-founded the Bonn
'Aktion 68' group, also classified his parents as Catholics who had been linked
to the Weimar Centre Party and had rejected the NSDAP. Aretz railed against
'sweeping judgements from a moral pedestal' made by 'students who were not
the least bit interested in facts':

> For some it was a confrontation with their own parental home, with their
> fathers' generation. I... can't really join in that conversation because I didn't
> have that problem at home. But I know Hannes Heer did, for example.... The
> thing that I found morally infuriating was that many of my generation of

52   THE OTHER '68

students practically identified themselves with the victims of National Socialism and used that to derive the moral legitimation to judge or condemn the actions and behaviour of their fathers', or our fathers', generation. I have a completely different mindset to that.[65]

These examples show that people did not ask more searching questions while their parents were alive—not even when the research would have been relatively straightforward, as in the case of the journalist father.[66] They accepted the way their fathers or mothers portrayed themselves, provided they could be reassured that they had not been 'particular' criminals. Here, the former students were adopting a widespread pattern of thought from that time, which set the fellow travellers, who had got tragically entangled but had no personal guilt, apart from the 'real criminals'.[67] Anyone who had not been a concentration camp guard, or who had no discernible blood on their hands could be presumed innocent. It is also striking that many interviewees spontaneously compared their own families with that of Hannes Heer, assuming—inaccurately—that Paul Heer must have been one of the main perpetrators, or a real hardliner.[68] Clearly, they were reacting to the many media voices that consistently broadcast the Heer family conflict, beginning with the 1988 TV film, and continuing with the controversial Wehrmacht Exhibition that toured Germany from 1995 to 2004.[69] In this way, the rift between the Heers, father and son, was transferred onto an entire generation of students.

Bernhelm Booß, who was the head of the independent left-leaning AStA in 1967 and thus a colleague of Heer's, addressed this retrospective invention of a generational conflict in depth in his interview:

My father was a lawyer too and, incidentally, a Nazi, and, well, I had a...a very close and affectionate relationship with him....Which is why I never asked him, for example, how far he was involved with the deportation of the Jews to Auschwitz. I can work out for myself that he was relatively central to it...He wasn't part of the Warsaw Reichsbahn [railway] division, which was responsible for Auschwitz, he was rather further to the east, but I am fully convinced that he would have known a great deal about it. But I never spoke to him about it because I personally [saw] him as a...person of integrity, you know. I never had this generational conflict. Personally, I don't believe it when it's presented like these 68ers were shaped by this generational conflict. That's a point of disagreement between me and Hannes Heer, for example, because he really plays up this generational conflict stuff...Apart from my own life experience, I don't think it's really true of others either.

Even for Hannes Heer...I visited Hannes Heer at his parents' home, saw him with his father. It's all just post-rationalization...I want to tell you how it really was from my point of view. People in my age group had to come to terms with the fact that parents, who you personally highly respected, and where you had ultimately no doubts about their integrity, even if they did some things differently, that through some kind of system failure, they'd gone in the wrong direction. What I mean is that this kind of analysis forced us to thinking in kind of systemic terms. What turns deeply thoughtful and likeable people—they weren't stupid, our parents, and they weren't unpleasant—what turns intelligent and likeable people into monsters? That was a question that you just couldn't ask your own parents, it was something that you could only ask the literature, so to speak...And Marxism was saying, offering, we know a system failure...the private ownership of the principal means of production.[70]

Booß was caught in a dilemma that was familiar to many people at that time. He figured out that his father probably bore a share of the blame—as a Party member, lawyer in the Transport Ministry, and a soldier in the war in the east. But he loved his father. So he refrained from asking questions. Instead of discussing the past in person, the students sought refuge in abstract concepts. You could determine a theoretical 'system failure': it wasn't Papa's fault; it was down to capitalism.

Other students made use of similar strategies, consciously or subconsciously reframing events in the abstract so as to avoid tricky confrontations with their parents. One possibility was to separate the 'fug of the Adenauer era' in general from their parents in particular, as Ulrich Rosenbaum did. You could distinguish between 'right-wing conservatives' on the one hand and Nazis on the other, and assign your parents to the first camp, as Wolfgang Breyer did. You could insist that your father had been subordinate to others and therefore had no scope to take his own decisions, like conservative-leaning Eberhard Crueger, whose father had been a career officer in the army. Or you could draw on stories of resistance from your extended family, and wash your own parents clean in their wake, as in the case of Wilfried von Bredow. In 1967, this scion of a conservative Junker family was a political science student and member of the Bonn Students' Union. A distant relative, Admiral von Bredow, murdered by Nazis during the Night of the Long Knives in 1934, was used as proof that the entire family group was a 'great distance' away from Nazism.[71] Individual fragments of apparent or actual resistance were cited as evidence. So Maria Zabel, who was involved in the Bonn RCDS,

54   THE OTHER '68

could say that her parents 'weren't members of the Party, not during the Nazi time either. On the contrary: my father saved a lot of these people from being punished afterwards.' Hans Günter Jürgensmeier's 'mother always told the story of how my Grandpa sent the Nazi Adjutants, who wanted to present my Grandma with the *Mutterkreuz* [Mothers' Cross], packing off his farm'. Similarly, his mother saying that the Jews in Endenich had been 'very fine people' and 'thank God they got out in time', enabled Jürgensmeier to conclude that 'she had nothing at all to do with it'.[72]

Evidently, the families involved never had a genuine conversation about this. None of the activists cited above had spoken to their parents about National Socialism to any deeper extent than semi-informative anecdotes and stories of their own suffering during the war. This is not surprising. During the 1950s and 1960s, detailed knowledge about the Nazi crimes was still relatively limited. This made it difficult for either the young or the old to have a fully informed discussion. Moreover, the Sixty-Eighters were active participants in developing what we can call the family memory of National Socialism. As the children of their parents, they were emotionally and normatively locked into jointly constructing (selective and frequently retold) stories about the past, without breaking with the family consensus. As we know from sociological research into the way stories of the Nazi era are handed down within multigenerational families, the family memory privileges accounts which portray the parents not as perpetrators, but as victims or good Germans. The ideal stories contain enough gaps and ambiguities to allow subsequent generations to fill the blanks from their own imaginations, often making use of ready-made scripts found in the media. This means that the younger generations are not just a passive audience, but actively involved in reinterpreting what they have been told. In one study, which ran from 1997 to 2000 involving forty three-generation families, the children and grandchildren even systematically closed their minds to stories from that time in which their fathers or grandfathers clearly outed themselves as perpetrators. The younger people could not and would not accept crimes committed by their own parents because such stories were simply unimaginable if brought up within the private family sphere. Tellingly, the study team talked about the 'so-called 68er generation' having a 'problem with the Nazi past and their carefully cultivated myth of the silent wartime generation':

> In marked contrast to the generally accepted assumption that the first-hand witnesses had a tendency to 'hush up' the past, the former soldiers and '*Trümmerfrauen*' [the women who cleared up the rubble] generally assented

spontaneously; it was far more likely to be their sons and daughters who refused to participate—often on the grounds that their parents would not want to discuss this subject.[73]

I have absolutely no intention of accusing the Sixty-Eighters of dishonesty. It is rather that they were born into a situation that made critical discussion within the family practically impossible. They were emotionally attached to their parents and materially dependent on them, particularly as students. Seeing the people you sat 'at the breakfast table' with as Nazis 'was not at all easy to bear... with yourself'. This is how Hans Günter Jürgensmeier put it, referring to a classmate who happened to be Hans Globke's son.[74] In the few cases where the Nazi past played a role in Sixty-Eighters' arguments with their parents, this had serious personal consequences, as we see with Hannes Heer and Heidrun Lotz.[75]

In 1968, Lotz (Figure 3.2) was a 25-year-old psychology student, a member of the SDS, and the student representative on the faculty council.[76] As a

Figure 3.2 Heidrun Lotz at a demonstration on 16 April 1968

teenager, she had fallen out with her father, because her parents had forbidden her older sister to marry an unemployed man. In addition to this, Heidrun, influenced by a pastor's wife who lived next door, had taken part in the Easter peace marches, and then come back home to a buffet party for officers with an 'Easter march symbol emblazoned across my arse': 'I was meant to marry an officer, that was out of the question.'

According to Heidrun, her father Georg Lotz, a professional army officer born in 1906, had been an 'SA *Obersturmbannführer*' (Senior Assault Unit Leader in the Nazi Storm Troopers). 'He also said that he was a Nazi and remained a Nazi.' His daughter never found out any more detail about his denazification status, his initial difficulties in re-entering the Bundeswehr as an officer, or even any possible conviction for Nazi crimes. As a result of their disagreements, she left home at the age of 17 without any financial support from her parents, and had to catch up on her *Abitur* while also working and saving. Although she resumed contact with her parents after completing her exams, and lived just around the corner from the family home, it was impossible to have an open conversation with her father until 'much, much later', when he was elderly. This reconciliation led Heidrun to re-evaluate her father, seeing him no longer as a Nazi but as a damaged and oppressed fellow traveller:

> Although he had actually reflected on that period and...had a very critical position on it, probably did so, even at the time....My father always had difficulties actually, clearly, he was being watched too....He had a hard time with me as a daughter, but all the same he stuck by me pretty well...And my father was also a traumatized person, if you like, this is where the loop closes again. And it wasn't until I understood that that I could find my way back to him.[77]

The striking thing about this account is that the father's guilt was still obscured by only superficial knowledge, even after decades. The conflict was originally sparked by his attempts to influence his daughters' choice of partners, with the Nazi past as an additional factor. Meanwhile, the quarrel not only forced Heidrun into years of poverty, but also led to a longing for emotional reconciliation, which could ultimately only be achieved at the price of denying her father's (presumed) guilt as a perpetrator.

The rift between Hannes Heer and his father was similarly dramatic. Here too, the father was comparatively old, having been born in 1912. Here too, there was a late reconciliation, but only after hurt on both sides and periods of no contact, which also damaged Hannes' relationship with his mother and left 'bitter wounds'. Above all, the son wanted to learn more about the 'family secret' of his father's NSDAP membership; he wanted to 'understand' his motivations. Hannes did not suspect his father of war crimes, or long-term far-right tendencies, especially as Paul Heer 'never used anti-Semitic slogans or aggressive Nazi language after his return from imprisonment'. During the war, the father had been deployed on the Channel coast in Flanders, a relatively 'quiet section of the Front'—'it seemed to me to be a harmless case'. 'He was not *the* Nazi perpetrator, like others that I got to know during my studies.' As a result, the son found it even harder to understand why his father refused to speak about having joined the Party in the early thirties. Two years after the 'banishment', they reached a formal peace agreement, at the insistence of his mother and an uncle. Hannes moved back into his room in the forester's lodge. But the 'remaining alienation' deepened in 1971 when, as the son put it, 'in a fit, after he'd laid hands on another newspaper report about me, he burnt my red flag in the furnace along with other revolutionary memorabilia', and they no longer spoke to each other. No reconciliation was possible until the end of the father's life, after he had been diagnosed with dementia. His father repeatedly asking 'have you got a steady job?' triggered Hannes' 'sudden understanding' that 'underlying this whole fight, his resistance to talking about the past...there was always a father's worry' about his son's wellbeing, given that his political activities had prevented him from becoming a teacher. His father, Hannes now realized, had had years of putting up with 'remonstrances' from his fellow foresters, who had constantly 'shamed' him with press reports about his lefty son.[78]

From an external perspective we can see that father and son traced the split back to different causes. While Hannes Heer blamed his father's refusal to speak about his NSDAP membership, Paul Heer took particular exception to his son's role as a communist agitator.[79] The same pattern can be seen in the families of other Bonn students who were interviewed. The GDR and communism were a red rag to a bull, and more likely than National Socialism to be the cause of political friction with parents. Dieter Gutschick, for example, remembered the way

Kiesinger...spoke about the 'Party of Recognition' [of the GDR as a separate state]...So I had this placard that said 'I'm in the Recognition Party' or something. And I went home with it, and there was serious trouble. [My father] said I couldn't be seen with that in our building, they're all civil servants, you know. You just can't imagine it, these days, how narrow [minded] everything was back then.[80]

58   THE OTHER '68

As the offspring of a middle-class family, the leap to Marxism was simply 'impossible'.[81] Tension with parents was generally not the cause but the consequence of involvement with left-wing politics.

The kind of radical breach with their fathers that Heidrun Lotz and Hannes Heer experienced was a difficult, uncomfortable, and rare choice. Peeking into the family histories of the Bonn activists as we have done here shows that arguments, fractured relationships, and emotional coldness were the exception. Hushing up, giving the benefit of the doubt, and selectivity in both telling and listening were far more common. Most students evaded the enormous challenge of exposing their own parents as either perpetrators or fellow travellers, taking refuge in an abstract understanding of Nazism, or in adopting apologetic family myths. People often had little concrete knowledge of the history of the Third Reich, as was only to be expected at that time, and research in libraries or archives was practically unheard of. In this respect, the Sixty-Eighters of all political hues were comparable. Nevertheless, the few students who experienced discord with their parents were all on the radical left. At the same time, left-wing rebels were particularly likely to come from socialist homes. A team of historians who interviewed many SDS and APO supporters between 2007 and 2011 found: 'However firmly the notion of generational conflict may be established in popular memory, many activists—in Germany and elsewhere—did not experience such a political conflict within their own families.'[82]

In every case, it was easier for the Sixty-Eighters to go after abstract father figures—professors, politicians, and the police—as Nazis than their own personal fathers. When Beate Klarsfeld slapped the incumbent chancellor, Kurt Georg Kiesinger, in the face in November 1968, her action was intended to redden 'the repulsive face of the ten million Nazis' with shame. On a journey east in April 1965, Rudi Dutschke noted in his diary: 'Too many memories of our fathers' involvement in the conquest of Poland.' At a meeting of the West Berlin SDS shortly after Ohnesorg's death, Gudrun Ensslin is said to have shouted: 'They'll kill us all…that's the Auschwitz generation we're dealing with—you can't debate with people who did Auschwitz.' It was an abstract accusation because Ensslin, like Ulrike Meinhof, came from a loving and comparatively untainted family home. Nor did the members of the K1 commune in Berlin break with their own parents. Dieter Kunzelmann reminisced fondly of a family 'in which I experienced love, solidarity, and tolerance'. Fritz Teufel was able to rely on his mother's support in court, and Rainer Langhans thought his father was great. 'The bourgeois-fascist family hell, that was…always other people.'[83]

OF WARTIME CHILDREN AND NAZI PARENTS 59

There is evidence from the social sciences for the overwhelmingly peaceful coexistence between young adults and their parents in the sixties and seventies. In comparison to earlier decades, parent–child relationships at that time were excellent. Sociological studies show a particularly high level of agreement on values between young and old—between 75 and 95 per cent—from the 1950s to the 1980s. Mutual financial, everyday, and emotional support, and close contact between parents and their adult children were the norm. Clearly, we like to overestimate the frequency of intergenerational conflict because media attention is always focused on spectacular exceptions.[84] 'Up to the mid-seventies', West German adults adopted 'an ever-friendlier stance towards their offspring'. While in 1950, only 24 per cent had a 'favourable' impression of the young generation, that figure had reached 44 per cent by 1960, and risen as high as 62 per cent in 1975. Because the young and old were making the same consumer decisions, 'adults increasingly [appreciated] teenagers as pioneers in the jungle of the consumer society'.[85]

A survey of young people carried out in 1965 is illuminating when it comes to the relationships between the cohorts of Sixty-Eighters and their parents. The Institut Emnid was researching the attitudes of over two thousand 15- to 25-year-olds towards their parents. Most were apprentices, still at school, or already working; only 2 per cent were at university. The findings were clear: the generations lived together, spent a lot of time together and, mostly, liked each other. Eighty-nine per cent of the teenagers were living at home. For 71 per cent of them, their parents were their closest confidants (in 1953 this was true of only 58 per cent), followed at a considerable distance by friends at only 21 per cent. Seventy-three per cent of the young people were perfectly satisfied with their levels of parental sympathy and interference; only 6 per cent felt patronized. The few conflicts were mostly around what time they had to be home after leisure activities. It was 'very rare' to argue, and then mostly about fashions or money. There was no trace of Götz Aly's generation of 'emotionally freezing children'. Only 4 per cent complained about uninterested or loveless parents. The pollsters even stressed that the majority of the youngsters were spending their free time in an intensely family-focused way:

Among the wider working population...the growth in leisure time ensures shared consumerism within families, shared leisure activities and holidays. The shared television, which now stands in two thirds of households, and the family car, which can be found in every second household, necessitate... new ways of doing things together.

60 THE OTHER '68

The parents often thought 'similarly to their children', liked the same music, went camping with them, and strove for a style based on partnership, even for an 'adolescent-laddish tone'.[86] The long-term trend was towards defusing family relationships. Studies of the sixties and seventies attest unanimously that children and parents alike loved consumerism and domesticity. The older age group frequently wanted to be modern, tolerant, youthful parents. The younger people expressed trust in and understanding for their parents, even if there were areas where they thought differently.[87]

When the representatives of the protest movement in the late sixties criticized the guilt of the older generation, they were generally speaking only about notional father figures—such as Heinrich Lübke, Kurt Georg Kiesinger, and Hellmuth von Weber. Yet even here, the Sixty-Eighters' attacks were highly selective, as we can see from the example of the University of Bonn. Nobody questioned the past entanglement of professors they were close to, or considered open to reform. But it was different for deans or rectors who responded to confrontation with rebels with authoritarianism, or by calling the police. In these cases, even those with no, or very little involvement, were vilified as Nazis. In February 1968, theologian Wilhelm Schneemelcher, the Rector of Bonn, was misrepresented as a 'friend of Nazis' despite having been forced out of his academic career on political grounds in 1939 and being unable to qualify as a professor until after the war. The dean, art historian Heinrich Lützeler, was derided as 'brown-spattered', yet he had been persecuted under the Third Reich both for his small stature and for his political views, and was ultimately banned from teaching in 1940.[88]

The rebels took a similarly imprecise approach to the histories of other professors they had personal dealings with. Hannes Heer, for example, began his doctorate with the renowned yet tainted Germanist Benno von Wiese. The latter had made rapid professional progress during the Third Reich, had been a Party member since 1933, *Blockwart* (block warden) since 1937, and, since 1936, an editor within one of Alfred Rosenberg's literary departments, which aimed to develop and purify the Nazi ideology.[89] Likewise, as Bolsa investigator Georg Rudinger remembered, nobody asked about the Nazi past of Hans Thomae, who held the chair at the Department of Psychology and headed up the study into ageing: 'sixty-eighter or not, nobody ever looked into Thomae's biography'.[90] In the sixties and seventies, students and junior academics considered Thomae a liberal, even a 'liberal with progressive views'[91] although he never took a public political stance. He did not, for example, sign the declarations in which the Bonn professors criticized President Lübke and university judge Hellmuth von Weber for their past actions. Yet in the summer of 1968, he became the preferred candidate for the post of Dean of Philosophy among students who hoped that professors like him, 'inconvenient because [they were] democratic', would be elected. The student leaders, Hannes Heer and Heidrun Lotz, organized sit-ins and stormed the dean's office to force the election of a liberal candidate by the Senate. During the election itself, the windowpanes were smashed, and the assembled professors panicked and fled through the window to get away from the students. Paradoxically, the outcome of these radical actions was that Thomae initially lost, was then elected in his absence, and immediately resigned the office. He was able to weasel out of a position he found irksome by arguing that the student representatives had been denied a role in the decision. Looking back, he admitted that the 'far-left groups' storming the meeting room had definitively relieved him of the 'worry that I might have to be dean'.[92]

As here, Hans Thomae consistently manoeuvred between the fronts without ever being asked about his past. On the one hand, he allowed the seriously implicated, anti-Semitic psychologist Friedrich Sander to give seminars in Bonn until the mid-sixties, even though Sander had been drummed out of every honorary post in the field, nationwide, back in 1960. On the other hand, Thomae helped his student Heidrun Lotz out of a fix when she was threatened with being thrown off her psychology degree course after the raid on the dean's office. Lotz said that she had had 'a very good discussion with Thomae', who then stood up for her within the department and forestalled proceedings.[93] Under Thomae's leadership, the Department of Psychology was, from 1970 onwards, the only one within the University of Bonn where there was de facto parity in decision-making between students, non-professorial teaching staff, and professors. Each of these groups represented a third of the vote in a 'departmental council', which took all key decisions. The increasing radicalization of the communist students on the council crossed Thomae's pain threshold in November 1974, however, whereupon the body was dissolved.[94]

There is no doubt that Hans Thomae was more tolerant of the student revolts than many of his colleagues in those days. But his past life might not have stood up to scrutiny had anyone looked. Thomae was born in 1915 and from 1938 onwards, he studied at undergraduate and doctorate level with the philosopher and Nazi Erich Rothacker. In 1937, Thomae had joined the Party, probably at the first opportunity open to him (new members were barred from joining between May 1933 and April 1937). From 1941 to 1943, he was part of the *NS-Dozentenbund* (National Socialist German Lecturers League), which enforced the National Socialist spirit at the universities. The post-1945 denazification tribunal classified him as a fellow traveller.[95] Although Thomae

62   THE OTHER '68

never served as a soldier on the grounds of gastric bleeding, he certainly served the regime ideologically. With hindsight, he stressed that he had 'first read about Auschwitz in 1946' and had 'not added an asterisk to the names of Jewish authors' in his theses and dissertations, yet his writings speak for themselves.[96] In 1939, Thomae published *Ruf des Lebens* (The Call of Life), an anthology of 'Thoughts of Great Germans of the Past'. These quotations were intended as reflective reading for people looking for affirmation in wartime. Thomae began by emphasizing the 'historical necessity' of National Socialism and the 'victorious way our world view permeates our entire national and personal lives'. His stated 'educational' goal for his work was to urge young people to 'independent contemplation [of] and hard work' at the core ideals of Nazism. Thomae showcased maxims such as: 'Life is Struggle'; 'war, hardship and suffering are the great educators of humanity'; and 'race lifts a man above himself'. The state was declared the crown of nationhood, the antidemocratic principle of Führer and followers justified on the basis of biologically determined inequality, and religion was repurposed to serve Germanness. 'Keeping one's own character pure, rejection of the foreign is the highest existential imperative for race and *Volk*', wrote Thomae. He feted Treitschke's anti-Semitism in the 1870s as a welcome 'beacon', against which the 'press, which even then was heavily judaized, had declaimed with howls'. Hans Thomae frequently cited such great minds as Houston Stewart Chamberlain, Nietzsche, Fichte, and Friedrich Ludwig Jahn, known as the 'father of gymnastics', who fitted most neatly into the *völkisch* model. Enlightenment philosophers such as Kant or Lessing were left out, as were Jews like Heinrich Heine, Marx, or Freud. This was more than just lip service—it was an outpouring of Nazi ideology.[97] Thomae's later publications were at least ambiguous. A pamphlet from 1941, intended for soldiers' kit bags, introduced the troops to the basics of Immanuel Kant's ideas, and focused several times on human dignity, the categorical imperative, and the experience of internal resistance. His habilitation treatise from 1944 forwent *völkisch* verbiage.[98] Presumably, Thomae's opinions had changed between 1939 and 1944, by which time the war was as good as lost; this was then clearly followed by a further, post-war conversion to liberal democracy.

Hans Thomae's 1939 book was nowhere to be found in the Bonn university library catalogue, and the fact of his Party membership was unknown. It would have cost rebellious students a degree of effort to prove that he was tainted—but they did not even try. As Thomae was one of the professors who were open to discussion, who could imagine liberal reform of the university, the Sixty-Eighters turned two blind eyes. In this way, the past of these abstract father figures was exploited as a weapon in their political struggle.

It was only in retrospect, in the seventies and eighties, that the Sixty-Eighters began to upgrade their differences with their (abstract or actual) parents and present them as a pivotal moment in their lives. Being 'different from my parents' and rebelling against their authoritarian mores, borrowed from National Socialism, was now part of the generational narrative.[99] Many voices told stories of a father–son conflict sparked by complicity in Nazi guilt, which were built on a century-old literary trope and spread by the mass media. Just as once Schiller's Don Carlos rebelled against his tyrannical progenitor, so the rebels of Sixty-Eight rose up against Nazi fathers in autobiographical accounts that became increasingly stylized with the passing of time.

There were a few such 'late oedipal scenario[s]' in the early days. Bernward Vesper's autobiographical novel *Die Reise* (The Journey) settled a score against his father, Will Vesper, a well-known Nazi author. The families of Hannes Heer and former SDS chair KD Wolff were also frequently mentioned in the media.[100] The emotional coldness of the parents' tainted generation was a feature of numerous bestsellers at that time, based on speculative collective psychological diagnoses. Alexander and Margarete Mitscherlich's 'inability to grieve' was the first of these ideas to do the rounds. The older generation were said to be so traumatized by the loss of their idol Hitler that they were emotionally stunted and only capable of manic defence responses.[101] Next to be exploited were the theories of Wilhelm Reich, in which fascism and crimes of violence were derived from the suppression of sexual urges in bourgeois families. Many theorists from the Sixty-Eighter generation, especially Klaus Theweleit, invoked a link between inhibitions at home and the Nazi guilt of their fathers.[102] Reimut Reiche, sexologist and former SDS chair, maintained that there was a 'collective intergenerational trauma among the student movement's generation' that could be traced back 'to the silence of our parents and especially to the way in which we were tied into, were meant to be tied into, their major post-war programme of denial of their involvement, whatever its source, in the collective German National Socialist crime'. People his age had reacted to this trauma with an unconscious 'sexualization' of the problem weighing them down: instead of tackling the guilt within their own families, they were said to have tried to free themselves from sexual repression and its gamete, the authoritarian nuclear family.[103]

At the same time, the first and second waves of *Väterliteratur* were rolling in.[104] Parental silence became a demonic power poisoning the Sixty-Eighters'

64 THE OTHER '68

lives. The 'unsettling pressure of a family secret' dating from the Nazi era was the driving force behind many novels, a trope begun in the 1970s and 1980s but continuing into the new millennium. The children and grandchildren encountered the generation of perpetrators, yet longed for healing and reconciliation. The literature typically featured emotionally cold fathers who maintained both authoritarian parenting styles and an icy silence.[105] These popular themes are recycled in the twenty-first century 'war children' genre, aimed at a readership who were children during the Second World War. This group happens to be of a similar age to the Sixty-Eighters: the 'war children' are generally taken to have been born between 1930 and 1945, while the Sixty-Eighters were mainly born between 1938 and 1948. Sabine Bode's bestseller, now selling in its thirtieth reprint, argues that the experience of war clinically traumatized large swathes of this age group, particularly as their overburdened Nazi parents had been unable to love them. Seeing that their parents had taken refuge behind a wall of silence, the children had supressed their own trauma as victims of war, and thus been permanently emotionally damaged.[106] This pop-psychological interpretation, based solely on a few memories from that time, perpetuates the myth of loveless, mute parents and the helpless, suffering Sixty-Eighter children, just with a slightly different emphasis. In the more recent war children discourse, everyone is ultimately a victim of their wartime trauma, including the Nazi parents. Furthermore, far more attention is paid to mothers and daughters than in the classic conflict narratives of the Sixty-Eighters.[107] Neither *Väterliteratur* nor the war children genre mentions daughters and sons being actively involved in hushing National Socialism up, however.

The popular success of this approach has led to ever more historians bringing out books in which guilt, trauma, and a family refusal to talk about the past play the starring role in the discord between political generations. One of those surfing this wave is Thomas Kohut, whose 'psychoanalytically informed' 2012 *Experiential History of the Twentieth Century* takes the form of 'composite life stories' based on transcripts of interviews with sixty-two *Bildungsbürger* born between 1900 and 1926. Kohut reads a classic dispute between Sixty-Eighters and their uncommunicative Nazi parents into his oral history sources, without either considering their relative ages, or challenging the narrative put forward by his interviewees.[108] We can see a similar situation in Karin Wetterau's 2017 book subtitled *Familienroman einer Revolte* (Family Saga of a Rebellion), written entirely from the Sixty-Eighters' perspective, and *Utopia or Auschwitz* by the journalist Hans Kundnani (2009).[109] A few individual cases taken from the narrow circles of the university-educated, middle-class New Left are extrapolated into a collective psychological argument about entire age groups within society as a whole. Moreover, autobiographical sources have often been evaluated selectively. Götz Aly, for instance, presents Christa Nickels, a member of the German parliament, as his chief witness for the allegedly 'central problem' of West German Sixty-Eighters: a lack of parental love. In a speech to the Bundestag in 1997, Nickels spoke of her father, born 1908, who—according to her mother—'cried out terribly in his sleep every night about fire and children' after the war. It was only in 1985 that she had

> noticed that in the only photo of my father that exists from that time, he is wearing a uniform, which is black and has death's heads on it. By that time, I'd already been elected to parliament for the Greens and I didn't dare ask my father; because I found it terribly difficult.

Götz Aly now takes it as a matter of course that this non-asking and non-speaking led to a withdrawal of affection, 'massive tensions' between generations within the family, and 'destructive energies' on the part of the younger people. He traces the excessive radicalism of the left, and even the 'disaster' of 1968, back to the 'consequential damage to family histories' caused by National Socialism and the Second World War.[110] In doing so, Aly supresses the fact that Nickels did not mention tension or coldness. On the contrary: she stressed that her father had loved his children and that she herself had 'of course very much loved' her father. Nickels herself had decided to keep quiet about the past so as not to hurt her father: 'I didn't have the heart to do that, I couldn't.' She expressed understanding for the dilemma that had made her father into a perpetrator: he had not had the strength to elude the pressure of the regime.[111]

Thus we can see that silence did not necessarily go hand in hand with either a lack of feeling, or the political radicalization of the children. Not every kind of silence is toxic—only the one-way, aggressive silence after a failed rapprochement. Not talking could be simply a matter of keeping the peace within a family, and could act as a distraction, as we can see from Cordt Schnibben's story, which made it to the cover of *Der Spiegel* magazine (Figure 3.3). Schnibben's father had been a convinced Nazi, an anti-Semite, and involved in a politically motivated murder, as the son only discovered after his death: 'I never enquired deeply enough...we settled up with our fathers' generation without speaking to our fathers...There was also a shying away from the truth...every encounter was a ritualized exchange of nothing.'[112]

Figure 3.3 Cordt Schnibben's father on the cover of *Der Spiegel* No. 16, 14 April 2014

This was typical of most families, where a deeper understanding of the precise role of parents or grandparents in the Third Reich was either never attempted or diverted into more harmless territory. The myth of emotionally cold parents and rebellious sons can be replaced by a picture where mutual, selective silence was a guarantee of harmony. This casts doubt on Jürgen

Habermas's assessment made in 1990: 'The 68ers were probably really the first generation in Germany who did not shy away from demanding face to face explanations, from their parents, from older people in general, within the family, in front of the television screen etc.' Two decades earlier, when the media had not yet started to build the intergenerational myth, Habermas had held a more realistic view of the situation. He wrote in November 1967 that:

> Protest among these young people from middle class family homes no longer seems to fit the usual pattern over the generations, of being primarily a protest against parental authority. This generation has probably grown up with more psychological understanding, a more liberal upbringing, and amid a more permissive mindset than any that went before them.

In those days, he also suspected, correctly, 'that the active members of left-wing student groups are more likely to have parents who share and encourage their critical mindset.[113]

The Sixty-Eighters eagerly adopted the generational narrative of themselves as trailblazers against their fathers' Nazi legacy because this retrospective story was the means by which they could constitute themselves as a political generation.[114]

A 1985 get-together of '*APO-Opas*' (Extra-parliamentary Opposition Grandpas), the ironic label middle-aged former SDS applied to themselves, shows how this worked. There was recurrent talk about the trauma of conflict with their fathers that had made them into anti-fascists. 'It was a rebellion against our Nazi parents', they said. The movement had been powered by 'existential outrage at fascism', rooted in 'impressions [of suppression] sedimented in biographies.[115] For those of the relevant age, joining the story-telling community of Sixty-Eighters was attractive as it upgraded the meaning of their own life story within the context of the Federal Republic as a whole. Looking back, you could laud yourself as part of a movement that had democratized West German society and, in the face of parental resistance, cleaned up the brown mess the Nazis had left behind. An older generation of die-hards made a suitably gloomy background, against which the young anti-Nazis could stand out all the more brightly. This narrative had legs, and consequently spread rapidly from the late seventies onwards, assisted by the mass media. The Sixty-Eighters became a 'generation drip-fed by the newspaper features pages.[116] Yet this involved accepting many distorted perspectives: a few thousand activists were turned into hundreds of thousands. The socialist left, which was in the minority, dominated memories in the media.

68 THE OTHER '68

Advocates of communist revolution were recast as champions of liberalization. Men, not women, were portrayed as the heroes of the piece. And of course, the intergenerational conflict and the Nazi past were stylized as the true driving force of the movement.

Yet the situation was different and, as always, more complicated. The majority of the young people who took to the streets in around 1968 wanted greater democracy. They took on authoritarian hierarchies at universities, and authoritarian structures in politics, when facing police batons to protest against the Emergency Acts or the weakness of parliamentary opposition during the Grand Coalition. But they were not primarily motivated by the Nazi past, let alone the wish to expose perpetrators. The impending descent into a new form of fascism was a politically expedient argument, yet even the more radical activists did not fully believe it. 'It wasn't that we were, that I was afraid of some kind of Nazi era being just at the door. That isn't how it was', recalled Bernhelm Booß, the chair of Bonn's left-wing AStA in 1967.[117] There was a central, generalized concern about consolidating democracy, but limited specific knowledge of National Socialism and continuities with the Nazi past in West German society and politics. By taking refuge in theory, the spokesmen for the student movement could avoid the need to consider exactly who had a tainted history. Searching for 'system failures' (Booß), which found expression in the theories on fascism and state-monopoly capitalism propounded by their leading thinkers, enabled an ongoing denial of concrete guilt, whether within or outside their own families. Even more problematically, the socioeconomic and sociopsychological explanations for Nazism popular in the New Left allowed the victims' faces to fade out, and resulted in an underestimate of continuing anti-Semitism. Influenced by the Six Days' War of 1967, certain leading figures among the rebellion staged a switchover of the victims, portraying the persecuted students as Jews and Israeli Jews as Nazis.[118] The young people's ignorance of the history of the Holocaust led to this insensitive behaviour, yet they deployed the Nazi past as a flexible political weapon against 'abstract fathers' at the universities and in politics. This often involved attacking authoritarian conservatives as Nazis while sparing tainted liberals. But they practically never confronted their own parents, or indeed any older people they knew personally, with demands to engage with their own involvement.[119] Thus we can largely rule out both father–son conflict, and anti-fascism based on a family past, as engines of Sixty-Eight.

4

Trust Nobody Over Sixty? The Role of the Elderly

A little cluster of older and elderly people had gathered at the entrance to the Hotel Löhndorf on Stockenstraße. They were watching in fascination as the seemingly endless procession of protesters passed before their eyes, on its way to the Hofgarten. Now and then, the demonstrators sat down on the asphalt with their banners and placards, before moving on again a little later. That must be what they meant by 'sit-ins', commented an old gentleman. The woman watching on beside him was worried by 'this army of red flags—is this meant to be an argument for freedom?' An elderly lady was astonished to see how many of the demonstrators were older than she had been expecting. And indeed, a good number of the marchers were mature adults: trade unionists and socialists, professors and academics, 400 Protestant clergy, and even former concentration camp inmates.

It was the morning of 11 May 1968, and 50,000 demonstrators of all ages had travelled to Bonn in motorcades, special trains, and flotillas of ships to protest against the Emergency Acts. These laws, which were intended to allow a state of emergency to be declared in West Germany (thus permitting government by decree in cases of disaster), were shortly to be adopted by the Bundestag. As demonstrations were not permitted around the parliament building, the protesters were marching to the Hofgarten, where keynote speakers—the authors Heinrich Böll and Erich Fried, numerous professors, and a smattering of FDP politicians—warned of the danger that the Emergency Acts could pose to democracy in West Germany.

Marchers converged on the Hofgarten from various starting points in a demonstration that formed the high point and culmination of the political revolution that some radicals were then hoping for. The march remained peaceful and without incident (Figure 4.1). This was in stark contrast to events happening at the same time in France, where thousands of Parisian students had been fighting running battles with the police for five days. The students had set up barricades in the Quartier Latin, which they defended by throwing cobblestones and Molotov cocktails.

Figure 4.1 Bonn demonstration against the Emergency Acts on 11 May 1968

The three major trade unions had declared solidarity with the student rebels and called for a general strike: President de Gaulle's government wobbled. By contrast, the Federal Republic remained quiet. Before the march, the Bonn *General-Anzeiger* prophesied that it would be the 'hottest Saturday since the war', but later played things down. There had been a run on the hotdog stalls, but nothing else had happened. There were no violent clashes between police and demonstrators this time—unlike over the Shah's visit a year earlier, or the unrest a month back, at Easter, after the assassination attempt on Rudi Dutschke. Bonn's middle classes breathed a sigh of relief.[1]

By contrast, the left-wing students watched disappointedly as the energy fizzled out of the anti-Emergency Acts camp after the march. The Bundestag debated the emergency constitution during the second and third readings from 15 May onwards, finally passing the Acts on 30 May. Meanwhile, students in every university city held plenary meetings, went on lecture strikes, occupied lecture theatres, and even mounted isolated hunger strikes in increasingly desperate, yet vain attempts to mobilize the general population against the bill. The calls for strike action went unheard. Students with leaflets were chased away from factory gates in the Ruhr district, by the very workers they were trying to convince to protest. Friedhelm Meier, then a 34-year-old steelworker in Dortmund, considered the students trying to get into a debate with him pretentious, and found their language incomprehensible: 'Most people didn't even take the leaflets... Well, they didn't get read... The stuff they wrote in them was hard to understand... the proletarians, first we had to clarify the term: what's a proletarian. We felt insulted.' In rejecting the students' endeavours, the factory workers were following the German Trade Union Confederation, which spoke out against the general strike and thus snubbed the student-led extra-parliamentary opposition.[2] In Bonn too, the last days before the Emergency Acts were passed were characterized by feverish activity. A two-day embargo on lectures, on 29 and 30 May (Figure 4.2), was supported by many professors and lecturers. Teaching staff in the Department of Psychology united in solidarity with the students, postponed their seminars and recommended that instead of studying, they should 'follow the parliamentary debate, which would be broadcast into the university, very closely'.[3]

Figure 4.2 Student strike in opposition to the Emergency Acts outside the Bonn Department of Psychology on 30 May 1968

72 THE OTHER '68

The fact that there were many university professors and mid-career academics, trade unionists, clergy, and victims of Nazism on the march against the Emergency Acts shows that the extra-parliamentary opposition in around 1968 did not consist solely of students and young people. Middle-aged and elderly people were also involved, but their exact role is barely known. Both current media discussions and academic research focus almost exclusively on the young. There are numerous publications dedicated to students and young bohemians, but the attitudes of older generations have attracted little interest, those of professors and politicians aside. Ulrich Herbert's most recent overview of German history subdivides the young protagonists of the 1960s according to gender, degree of political radicalization, levels of education, university, political stance, and musical subculture. By contrast, older people are dealt with in a few broad-brush sentences. They represent conservatism, the Nazi past, authoritarianism, the primacy of (post-war) reconstruction, frugality, sexual taboos, militarism, and alignment with the state, while no detailed evidence is provided for these blanket characterizations.[4] Admittedly, West German society in the sixties was younger than today: almost a third of the population was under 20 years old, compared to a fifth in 2011.[5] We should also acknowledge young people's prominent role in the cultural avant-garde. Even so, a major blind spot remains. Those aged over 60, and the middle generation of 35- to 59-year-olds, were more than just a negative backdrop to display the young rebels to greater advantage. How did their parents' and grandparents' generations react to the unrest, and to what extent did they actually correspond to the bogeyman of an anti-reform, antidemocratic, Nazi-supporting establishment?

Contemporary opinion polls on the student unrest at Easter, and the Emergency Acts demonstrations in April and May 1968 all reflect a clear age divide. The older the interviewees, the more likely they were to see the student protests as 'a nuisance' rather than 'expressing a serious political opinion'.[6] Nonetheless, we should take a closer look. The differences between age groups were often only gradual. In the immediate aftermath of the violent riots at Easter 1968, West Berliners were asked for their opinion. Sixty-seven per cent of over-50s considered the protests by the students unjustified, but the same was true of 63 per cent of 30- to 50-year-olds, and 46 per cent of those aged 16 to 30. This was because of the demonstrators' use of violence, which 95 per cent of the older age group, 94 per cent of the middle-aged group, and 86 per cent of the younger generation opposed. Police use of batons had been 'appropriate', or even 'too soft', according to 87 per cent of the elderly, 83 per cent of the older group, and as many as 67 per cent of young people.[7] In spring 1968, a large majority across all age groups were thus afraid of violent riots. All the same, the police, whose advertising posters at that time bore the slogan 'Your Friend and Helper', suffered a loss in popularity. They were now more associated with batons than with being the friendly forces of law and order. In Bonn, when asked 'What do you first think of when you hear the word "police"?', 20 per cent of the younger and middling age groups, and 12 per cent of older survey respondents spontaneously referred to water cannons, truncheons, and kicks.[8]

The unease caused by the Emergency Acts was not limited to young people. In mid-1968, almost a third of West Germans were opposed to such laws. The figure was 29 per cent for those aged over 59, and 36 per cent for those aged under 30, so hardly a striking difference. Thirty-nine per cent of interviewees in both the older and younger age groups were *for* the emergency constitution proposed by the government, as were as many as 55 per cent of students.[9] In the run-up to the Bonn marches in May 1968, the local newspaper interviewed various stallholders and traders on the marketplace and found that reservations about the emergency powers were widespread among older people too. Forty-eight-year-old market trader Max Lüneburg criticized the laws as unnecessary and the government as power-hungry, but was not intending to join the march: 'there's no point'. A 41-year-old was similarly opposed to the changes to the law, but would 'keep away because it's pointless'. A 59-year-old radio and television salesman did not want to pass judgement on the planned emergency constitution but was opposed, on general principles, to taking part in demonstrations: 'I didn't do that under the Nazis and I'm not doing it now.'[10] The age groups showed less difference in their attitude towards the Emergency Acts than in their emotional stance towards politics. Where the young were keen to force political change, the elderly took a back seat and responded almost in panic, especially when faced with street violence or communist ideas. Consequently, their sympathy for student demonstrations decreased markedly the more the SDS dominated the debate, or the more the students resorted to violence (as at Easter 1968 in Berlin and May 1968 in Paris).

In the interview rooms at the Bonn Psychological Institute, many of the Bolsa participants, who were all aged over 60, expressed harsh criticism of the fractious students. Pensioner Till Schumann, for example, complained that the 'student ruckus' had been 'instigated by communists or nationalists'. There were just too many academics, and 'they're not thinking about studying any more, but about rioting', declared a 70-year-old skilled tradesman. A 77-year-old construction supervisor referred to 'the students where there are

74 THE OTHER '68

the riots' as 'an entirely ungrateful society—live off the state and don't even know what they want'. He emphasized how different his young days had been when, at the age of 13, he had already been doing sixty-hour weeks of hard work on the building sites.[11] Rejecting the protests was not just a knee-jerk reaction, however, but a reasoned position. Julius Heise and Friedrich Schmiedeknecht are two typical examples of this. Heise was 68 and retired; he was religious, had served in the First World War, and after 1945 he had sometimes been involved with the CDU at the local political level. As a young man, he had experienced the revolution of 1918/19 in Berlin, when he'd 'made himself scarce' faced with 'rabid sailors', and as an innocent bystander at the time of the Kapp Putsch in Merseburg in 1920, he had escaped three shots fired into the crowd. Heise could 'largely not understand' the 'students of today': 'when did that ever happen before, that they whistled and booed the professors?' While he was critical of the 'expense of the Shah's visit', and pointed out that the militarized youth of his day had 'preferred playing soldiers, and I condemn that too', he was opposed to the student revolt, largely out of fear of political instability. His main concern was for 'the currency to remain stable'. There was an urgent need to get public finances back in order, he explained, and another period of inflation would radicalize the entire population politically: 'losing money three times' in one lifetime really was 'a bit much'. However, 'democracy was not entirely ideal' as a way of imposing economic discipline, given its lengthy compromises and negotiations: there was a need for a 'bit of authority'. Young people did not understand that; he even felt 'that it didn't bother them if the state was in a bad way'.[12] Bricklayer Friedrich Schmiedeknecht was also concerned that a rebellion by the young people carried the risk of ungovernability, hyperinflation, and even a Soviet invasion. At the age of 60, he was still working on building sites in the Ruhrgebiet, as well as being active in the local Kolping Society, as staff representative, and treasurer of his trade union. He attended a Roman Catholic church and sang in the choir. He followed politics closely and was particularly worried about the Vietnam War, the Prague Spring, and the 'race riots in America'. 'The Russians'll march into the FRG at the first opportunity', he thought, and Vietnam could set 'the whole world in turmoil again'. The biggest turning points in his life had been the Second World War, which had 'thrown (him) back in everything', and being expelled from Czechoslovakia after the war ended. Thereafter, he had 'worked day and night' to get back on track. Fundamentally, he wanted 'peace and quiet' in the country, but was afraid of 'spiralling prices' and 'another endless struggle over wage and price increases'. 'I wouldn't want to go through all that again, to have to start again from the beginning a third time with acquiring everything that makes up a household.'[13]

These two pensioners were not alone with their fears of civil war, a Third World War, and hyperinflation. As an age group, the over-60s had been shaped by their experience of political turmoil and the catastrophic consequences of war, and were ready to pay a high price for economic and political stability. Opinion polls show that West Germans aged over 60 felt considerably more 'threatened by Russia' than the under-30s. They were more likely to be afraid of another war (41 per cent, compared to 33 per cent of young people).[14] The oldest generation was especially concerned about the Vietnam War. In around 1965/66, older West Germans were more likely than the young to think that the Americans should withdraw.[15]

When it came to their attitudes towards the students, the old people were worried by their shift towards political violence and new, actionistic forms of protest. Of course it was wrong 'for the people to be suffering like that' in Persia, and criticism of the Shah was justified, argued Herr Jäger, a CDU-voting master carpenter. But 'stones and clubs' were the wrong tools, let alone 'murder threats': 'the people don't want these demonstrations' and 'everyone had to submit' to the police as a force of order. He suggested 'podium discussions' as a more suitable form of action.[16] Albert Wiegner, who was a trade unionist and member of the SPD, saw things similarly. In politics you should 'stand your ground, hand out leaflets, put up posters at elections', as well as 'debating sometimes' and 'offering criticism', but 'not talk endlessly'. You should always recognize that democracy was the 'best system of government', 'even if it isn't always put into practice correctly'.[17] Similarly, a 75-year-old gardener asserted that the students were simply too impatient and their goals were too utopian:

> They're living in a delusion that they have to improve the world, but you can't achieve anything by jumping the gun...I hope the whole thing doesn't go wrong. There are a lot of disruptive elements among the students, that's how it started in 1933 too.[18]

Quite a few of the elderly tempered their criticism of the student protests by remarking that their age group had made major political mistakes themselves. Businessman Siegfried Dänhardt, for instance, argued that 'the student ringleaders want locking up, they're giving all the rest of the students a bad name'. But he also admitted that 'my youth and my generation didn't get it right, or the Nazis would never have come'. Two other pensioners agreed that they had

76 THE OTHER '68

grown up too 'trustful of authority' and 'nationalistic'.[19] 'Mere obedience isn't right', said a former land surveyor, who welcomed a critical-minded, reform-oriented youth, but not 'excesses' like the 'young people on the rampage' in Berlin, or either right-wing or left-wing extremists.[20] A minority of the retired labourers from a trade unionist background expressly supported the student protests and defended the demonstrators' just cause against individual troublemakers, who, they thought, were creating a false impression.[21]

Old and young differed in their attitude towards consumption as well as to politics. The elderly study participants were almost unanimous in criticizing what they saw as an excessive consumerism among their children and grand-children. 'My daughter needs more money for the household than my wife does', complained retired foreman Herr Erbss.[22] Similarly, Hermann Weider praised his wife for her frugality, but objected that his daughter and grand-daughter were 'too lavish' and had no control over their purchases.[23] For the Bolsianers, frugality was the ultimate virtue, along with modesty and self-sufficiency in everyday life. 'I'm very pleased with my wife, she counts every pfennig...she never just gets anything for herself alone...she saves up cou-pon books...You wouldn't believe how happy she is if she can get a towel a bit cheaper', explained a worker from Oberhausen.[24] A housewife born in 1895 praised her daughter for doing all her own sewing. She reported that she her-self cooked vegetables from her own garden and got meat from her sister, who still did her own butchery.[25] Herr Bohe spent several hours a day toiling in his vegetable garden, while Herr Suhle kept rabbits and chickens: 'They lay our eggs.'[26] A 70-year-old retired cobbler would get up at dawn in blackberry sea-son to pick berries: fifteen pounds per day, one-and-a-half hundredweight per season.[27] Old people in those days even viewed the use of tinned food with suspicion.[28]

The scarcity with which the elderly generation had grown up, and the mul-tiple economic slumps caused by wars, displacement, and currency devalu-ation had cemented a deep-rooted ethic of thrift. The Bolsianers practically never mentioned having made major purchases during their sessions in Bonn. It was more common for the pensioners to give their children or grandchildren money towards a car or an item of furniture, or to settle their offspring's debts (with varying degrees of willingness).[29] Lists of the old people's favourite leisure activities did not even feature items based on mass consumption, such as shopping or listening to records.[30] The only major con-sumer aim on which the oldest and middle generations could agree was to build their own home. Fathers and sons often did bricklaying together after work, and adult children would frequently club together with their elderly parents, putting their savings towards the construction.[31] The vast majority of the interviewees aged over 60 cited a house—generally self-built—as one of their lifetime goals.[32] The mantra 'work, save, provide for yourself, build a house' is a pretty accurate description of the financial ethic of the generation born between 1890 and 1910.

Despite their differing attitudes towards consumerism, relations between pensioners and their children in West Germany had 'substantially' improved since index-linked pensions were introduced in 1957. This reform, a manifesto pledge of Adenauer's, had significantly reduced poverty in old age at a stroke. In 1955, a retired blue-collar worker would have been entitled to only 38 per cent of the average labourer's wage, but from 1957 onwards, this was raised to a 'standard pension' of 60 per cent of the average pay. This figure was regularly updated as it was pegged to rising wages. The older generation's new material independence defused familial relationships between old and young. Index-linked pensions acted as a vent, releasing the pressure on intergenerational relationships. Financial security improved the status of the elderly and battles over the distribution of family resources became rarer. Material assets were now flowing in the other direction, generally from old to young. At the same time, the children's obligation to accommodate and care for frail parents was gradually reduced as the welfare state expanded.[33] Established forms of intergenerational mutual aid persisted, though, with assistance varying according to age and sex. The sons of elderly parents took on repairs, garden work, household renovations, or heaving heavy bags upstairs. Their daughters might wash curtains, clean stairways and windows, or do the shopping. By contrast, 'the actual domain in which parents could be of help' was 'the financial sphere', as the Bolsa research team noted: 'the possibility of helping their children to build a house or make major purchases, to enable them to travel, or to clothe their grandchildren', conferred 'a gratifying feeling of independence and strength' on the elderly.[34] Even badly off widows would save on heating and food to be able to give 'regular gifts of money' to their grandchildren 'at Christmas and birthdays, when they visited, for good [school] reports, as a contribution towards a purchase'. 'Given that the elderly often felt more capable in this regard than at any previous point in their lives', they enjoyed 'expressing their affection in this way'.[35]

Beyond the index-linked pensions, two other factors were central to maintaining good relations between grandparents, parents, and grandchildren: the tradition of 'intimacy at a distance' and the new post-war behaviour pattern of 'intimacy through silence'. 'Intimacy at a distance' was a century-old pattern of relationships, the dominance of which was continually reaffirmed by

West German social scientists from the fifties to the eighties.[36] Being intimate at a distance meant that both generations valued having their own home and independence, while still living close to each other and helping each other out in their everyday lives, both financially and emotionally. The increased prevalence of telephones and cars made it ever easier to reconcile physical distance with frequent communication and emotional closeness.

Thus, the Bolsa participants kept in close contact with the next generation, yet sought a distance 'that permitted independence while still guaranteeing an inner connectedness'.[37] Thirty-one per cent of these elderly people lived in the same building as at least one of their adult children, although most maintained separate households. In two thirds of cases, the children lived within a hundred-kilometre radius.[38] Two thirds of the elderly 'expressly' ruled out sharing a home with the younger generation because they wanted to be independent, not to be a burden, and not to be bothered with their children's everyday concerns.[39] All the same, they saw each other regularly. Two thirds of respondents met up with their children at least twice a week; a further 17 per cent saw each other once a week. As a rule, the Bolsianers were very emotionally attached to their children, even more than to their spouses. In only two of 222 cases had 'contact with their own child been wholly or largely broken off', this being 'accompanied by seriously unsatisfactory emotional engagement'.[40] Normally, breaches in communication had less to do with arguments than with unavailability (where the children had emigrated, lived in the eastern bloc, or were in prison), or divorce, after which a father had no longer seen his children.[41]

After 1945, 'intimacy at a distance' was joined by 'intimacy through silence': maintaining harmony by the shared hushing up of Nazism. There was a need to distance themselves from the recent past so as not to jeopardize emotional closeness and amicable family life. All three generations abided equally by the rules of this game. They were also reflected as strongly as ever in the Bonn longitudinal study interviews: the Bolsa conversational guidelines quite deliberately skipped over the Third Reich and the Second World War. The interviewers asked detailed questions about the participants' childhood, adolescence, and early adulthood. Then the script for the researchers continued: 'so, we'll now pass right over the whole period of the war, and the time before it. And we'll pick it up again in 1948. What was your experience of the currency reform?'[42] The volunteers were thus intentionally not asked about their past in the Nazi era. But the memories emerged all the same. War, violence, implication, crime, racism, and anti-Semitism were recorded on the tapes and in the investigators' notes, even though the Bonn psychologists did not evaluate them further at the time.

TRUST NOBODY OVER SIXTY? THE ROLE OF THE ELDERLY   79

The investigators in Thomae's department certainly didn't see the elderly ladies and gentlemen sitting opposite them as former Nazis. 'I can't remember us ever saying straight out of any of them "so-and-so was definitely a Nazi"', said researcher Ingrid Tismer-Puschner. She even felt 'almost a kind of sympathy...My goodness, what did you all get yourselves into there!' with many interviewees, who conveyed 'more of an excitement, all of the things we did and everything we experienced', about the Third Reich.[43] This is consistent with psychologists Norbert Erlemeier and Georg Rudinger, neither of whom could remember a single 'ex-Nazi' in the Bolsa cohort. Although Erlemeier reported that the men had 'always' confided in him about their 'war experiences', it was his view that they had been just as heavily influenced 'by the hardships of the post-war era, the economic miracle, and the boom that followed the war'. His approach had been to meet the interviewees 'without prejudices'.[44] PhD student Helga Merker, who analysed the interviews with adults from their mid-30s to late-50s, confirmed: 'you had sympathy with them, with my parents' generation, many of whom had believed in Hitler'. A friend and neighbour of Merker's family, who had been awarded the Golden Party Badge, had killed himself after the war. As a result of this experience, 'I saw that generation as victims: believers, betrayed, life over—this arc was something I could observe at close hand, you know'.[45] The young investigators' remarks resonate with considerable sympathy towards the old people. When they opened up in conversation, it created a personal relationship that mitigated against having a poor opinion of them. Here, in a situation of personal intimacy outside the family, the rule also held true: Nazis had always been other people.

The trainee psychologists had had plenty of practice in their cautious approach to the older generation at home. Norbert Erlemeier's father was born in 1898, and was thus the same age as the Bolsianers he asked to step up to the microphone at weekly intervals. Yet 'there was no way I could have spoken in such depth to my father as to the Bolsa participants...So, I never experienced my father as a Nazi, I really only knew him as a caring father.' According to his son, Erlemeier senior had 'admittedly [been] in the Party, but not an active Party member' and as a 'lower-level civil servant' he had been required to be 'a Party member, at least formally'. Given that his father had never been at the front, and had 'always been present' at home, the son had not considered it 'particularly urgent' to 'pump him' for information: 'I never made accusations against my father over his past.' Although his father sometimes made anti-Semitic remarks about rural money lenders—'you know, that cliché, *Geldjuden* [money-oriented Jews], they drove lots of farms

80   THE OTHER '68

to ruin'—the Nazi past was 'a taboo subject, as was frequently the case in families back then'. The only conflict arose when a female relative 'had to get married'.[46] Meanwhile, there were no arguments about National Socialism in his colleague Georg Rudinger's family either—his parents were a decade younger. If anything, disagreements were over money. 'For me, the Nazi problem with my father didn't exist, he was a soldier and was wounded during the war and...just used as cannon-fodder. I don't care whether he voted for the Nazis or not back then.'[47] It is not our place to judge the Bonn researchers' fathers, but it is apparent that their children had little appetite for unmasking and confrontation—an attitude that carried over into their professional lives.

Of course, it was only natural that many participants in the Bonn study had a tainted past. Half of them had been born between around 1900 and 1910, and were thus in the age group that held key positions in the Third Reich.[48] Even at the time of recruiting, which was largely done through contacts in firms, social security offices, and charitable associations, some of the men had been flagged up. A company nurse noted of one candidate: 'Retd. teacher, now 131er (aha).' '131ers' were officials who had lost their jobs before or after 1945—mostly due to denazification—and been given preferential treatment for reinstatement after 1951, under the recently amended Article 131 of the constitution.[49] Some encounters quickly showed the interviewers quite clearly that they were dealing with Nazis. Georg Rudinger, for example, wrote in his interview notes that a candidate had told the 'story of how he became a Nazi'. Files on two others state matter-of-factly: 'forced retirement...because of NS membership'.[50] Another interviewee, Martin Gärtner, wallowed in such detailed tales of heroism from the Second World War that it had cost his young listener 'a certain degree of effort' to stay patient and professional. Gärtner, born 1904, bewailed the 'distinguished position' he had held 'during the 3rd Reich', and liked to quote Hermann Göring.[51] A former skilled worker 'at the Anilin' (i.e. the BASF chemical plant) stated that there had been several occasions between 1942 and 1944 when he had spent some weeks at the Auschwitz camp, where he had 'seen and heard a few things'. The interviewer did not follow up on this and even gave him three points out of a possible nine for the response pattern (Daseinstechnik) of 'active resistance' on the grounds that he had not let himself be forced into joining the Party and had only seldom given the Hitler salute.[52] Wilhelm Odermann was another obvious Nazi, who admitted in the very first conversation that he had been 'involved' in the 'thousand-year Reich', as a result of which he'd been interned by the Americans until April 1946 and suspended from his teaching post for a full five years. The investigator responded tactfully: 'Well, yes, many Germans were involved, many idealists…the *Führer* was really just a criminal.' Odermann's reply was plain: 'a criminal, you couldn't say that. He was an Austrian, from the border lands, had no backbone, wasn't truly German.' Odermann made no secret of the fact that he disliked Israelis, Africans, foreigners in general, and communists, and that he was an FDP-supporter, but referred only nebulously to his role prior to 1945.[53]

The relative openness with which Gärtner and Odermann spoke about their proximity to the Nazis was rare, however. Normally, interviewees would only admit to having been a 'PG' (*Parteigenosse*, Party member) after some time, and in a lowered voice. Speaking about their own involvement in National Socialism was effectively taboo—despite the high number of ex-Nazis. A statistical analysis of all the Bolsa interviews shows that 22 per cent of the men stated unasked that they had been members of the Nazi Party. If we add in those who, of their own accord, cited other instances of a tainted past (such as involvement in war crimes), this figure rises to 27 per cent. This also fits with the fact that 17 per cent voluntarily mentioned the serious disadvantages they had suffered after 1945 as a result of the denazification process. A further 3 per cent admitted to slight disadvantages. Given that over half the interviewees wrapped themselves in a resolute silence, we can conclude that the percentage of men with murky pasts was likely to have been considerably higher. Only 18 per cent asserted that they had never been a 'PG'. Almost 12 per cent of the men told reasonably credible stories of opposition or persecution. Comparing the two age cohorts—those born in the 1890s and the younger group, born after 1900—does not produce any significant differences.[54]

So the Bonn 'explorations' certainly did touch on people's implication in Nazism. But this was bound up with difficulties. The volunteers often seemed to lack the vocabulary. The flow of their speech halted and the Bolsianers took refuge in abstract formulations when describing their careers during the Third Reich, or the damage denazification had done to their prospects and earnings. Paul Wiecierzki, a chemical worker born in 1899, for example, gave a somewhat opaque answer to the question of what the most important event in his life had been:

> What shall I say. It's hard to make a judgement as to that. After 1933, events happened so quickly. We sort of let ourselves drift. You couldn't overlook the future. Everybody had to see to it that he got through. The war came, the post-war time. I went through a lot.

82 THE OTHER '68

In answer to the investigator's next question, 'which event in your life was the greatest hindrance?', he once again stuck to insinuations: 'What I told you about. I was still young in those days. Things just went down the drain thanks to the political business.' At work, after the war, other people were preferred over him, the Party member: 'Who are the high-ups these days? Communists, the rest all got thrown out after '45.' The precise role Wiecierzki had played was not clear.[55] A retired railway worker expressed himself equally cryptically: 'Followed the crowd during the war. During the war, a lot of things went wrong... Totally set me back.'[56] A teacher, one of the few who had been classified as a major offender (Group 1) by the denazification court, put it like this: 'You slipped into the whole thing without knowing it... You attracted yourself a batch of enemies. Once the war was over, you got your nose rubbed in it.'[57] Words such as Nazi and denazification were missing from these semi-informative accounts, as were precise roles, ranks, and deeds. An unmarried former teacher, Paula Mühlberger, beat about the bush:

MÜHLBERGER: well and added to that, might be a particular issue.
INVESTIGATOR: Yes.
M: Yes. Um. The National—uh—Socialist period.
I: Yes.
M: I was in the Party in those days.
I: Yes.
M: Particularly the Women's League.
I: Yes.
M: And, uh, now, what was I about to say? Where had I got to? Yes, you see. So then I was keeping house for father, and doing this work, and that was already over by then, wasn't it. That was already over, you know. '47. It was already over then.... I'd been out of service for two years by then.
I: Two years afterwards.
M: Yes. After '45
I: After '45
M: Yes.
I: '45
M: Yes.
I: '45 after the end of the war.
M: I was out of service.
I: Oh right.
M: Out of service...
I: So how did you make your living then?

M: Yes, we rented out the house, I gave lessons, you know....Had a lot of friends, who we kept—colleagues too—who we, because we weren't the only ones in town who were, who, uh, were out of service.[58]

The social stigma of denazification, which could only be labelled with the codeword 'out of service', continued to have an effect for this study participant. It was similar for Hermann Demmer, a civil servant born in 1900. In the forties, he had rapidly risen to be head of a municipal authority—'that was quite something, I can tell you'. But then he whispered, barely audibly: 'And I was a PG too. I got back in in '52, and by then I said to myself, I've missed the bus.' His suspension represented an irreversible damper. He never became a head of department again. By the time he retired, he was a senior inspector: 'I got on with the job for those ten years, reached the highest level I could reach.'[59]

Nineteen of the ninety-six men reported difficulties with denazification. Almost all of them had been removed from office for several years and some, such as a judge and a police commander, were required to take early retirement. Admittedly, all of them were eventually reinstated, at least after May 1951 when Article 131 took effect.[60] Yet the lost years and demotion in rank resulted in a reduction of prestige and pension payments. Consequently, the denazification process, however patchy it was in application, had lasting effects.[61] As an example, electrician Christian Nitsche, who had worked his way up from the shop floor to the technical staff, remembered:

In 1947, all the PGs were fired from the company. The wife of an acquaintance of mine ticked him off, saying: 'You wouldn't have got fired if you were any good'—and the man was a hard worker! My wife didn't say that, she said: 'We'll just have to hold on through this together.' Then you got rehired, on the shop floor, but your previous years in the factory didn't count.[62]

Teacher Gustav Crauert, who was only allowed back into his school in 1954, was still complaining bitterly at the age of 68:

The experiences...made us feel like 'second-class Germans', to some extent. Being no longer fully recognized as a public servant, and so having to struggle for your existence, that eats away at you...You always strove to support the state...I was no wartime profiteer, no, we just made sacrifices! And then there are people who went at it more skilfully or who were better at smelling the way the wind was blowing than the likes of us, and now they've got

84   THE OTHER '68

themselves onto a good financial footing...If people then say: Yes, absolutely, you lot [Nazis] lost that, but you have to...lump it, then that hurts, it
hurts a lot![63]

A commercial clerk who had forfeited his senior position said of his professional reinstatement: 'All right, so it was primitive, but at least it was starting
again.'[64] Another suspended teacher spent five years struggling through with
eleven different jobs, all badly paid. They ranged from woodcutter to ware-
houseman and postcard painter.[65] A third teacher, who had been prominent
in the Party and the SS, worked as a street sweeper, cemetery warden, and in
the sugar beet factory. 'Those who had been at the bottom were then at the
top, and those from the top were at the bottom', he said of the end of the war.
He came to terms with his reduced pension, and with the social indignity of
denazification: 'It's all the same to me...I'm thick-skinned, you know...You
can tell me to sweep the floor here and it'll be done right away, won't it.' In the
immediate post-war period, he had not dared to stand up for his interests with
landlords and neighbours because 'as an NSDAP member' he had had 'few
rights', and he had not been keen on speaking publicly. The only thing was that
his wife had 'taken it rather to heart' that he had 'been sacked from office'.[66]

Many of those affected lost respect in the eyes of their relatives and
acquaintances due to years of being unable to provide for their families.
Hermann Demmer described the years after 1945, during which he had 'only
lived off his father-in-law' and not earnt a pfennig, as humiliating.[67]
Housewife Marie Voigt divorced a policeman in 1952 and complained that
back then, he 'went straight into the SA...He didn't earn much, but still
bought rounds for the others...After the turnaround, he was afraid and
hid away.' She should have married a 'more business-minded' man, she
grumbled.[68] Colleagues and schoolfriends were even more likely to show
these men the cold shoulder than their wives. Teacher Wilhelm Odermann
remarked of his reinstatement in 1951: 'Certain colleagues acted like they
hadn't seen me.'[69] The Göring fan cited above, Martin Gärtner, complained
that, after 1945, 'a lot of friends' had 'spoken badly about him', just because he
had been a Nazi and a member of the Waffen-SS. Affrontedly, he declared that
'a friend in need is a friend indeed...I want nothing to do with people like
that.' As a result, he had 'become reserved' and now only spoke to 'casual
acquaintances'.[70] The police commander forced into retirement also found the
'social isolation' in his small town 'painful'.[71]

Clearly, the denazification interlude mainly had long-term consequences
for those who had held public roles, such as headteachers, senior police

officers, or heads of government departments. The Bolsa participants with more senior positions or higher education levels were most likely to talk about denazification. The majority of the volunteers, however, were manual workers, tradespeople, skilled workers, low-ranking employees, farmers, and housewives, with only primary education.[72] They may well have been Nazis but they seldom spoke about their past during the interviews in Bonn. This was because it had been easier for them to slip through the many holes in the denazification net. Moreover, they were less accustomed to voluble reflections on their own past. The lower their education level, the less likely the interviewees were to have suffered any disadvantages through denazification. The Bolsa data set shows a highly significant correlation between the variables *Höchster Schulabschluss* (highest educational qualification) and *Entnazifizierungsnarrativ* (denazification narrative) with a chi-squared value of 0.002.[73]

Regardless of education level and social status, the ex-Nazis knew better than to make any extreme right-wing remarks, even among people of their own age. Only two of the 118 Bolsa men can be considered self-confessed die-hards. In both cases, their opinions caused offence. The Bonn psychologists described Martin Gärtner's 'lack of integration into the group' as follows:

> In some cases, he himself notices that he advocates highly prejudiced views on political questions, but he expresses them all the same by…initially specifying that his belief may appear to be borrowed from Nazi thinking, but that he would like to propound it here all the same.[74]

Wilhelm Odermann boasted that he had 'not been a fellow traveller, but had led the way'; the investigator wrote that he was 'still heavily influenced by prejudices—against Americans, Jews, [President] Nasser etc', but that he 'holds back more in the group'.[75] It was unusual for people with a tainted past to go on the offensive. They generally banked on a dual strategy: depoliticization and withdrawal into private life.

The incriminated turned away from politics and kept silent. Many, having once been bitten, were shy of ever getting involved with a political party again. Some were opposed to the political situation in West Germany, but knew that they formed a small minority. Hermann Demmer, the man who could only whisper 'PG', railed loudly against any kind of advancement on party-political grounds and swore unambiguously: 'to me, no party is the idol—none, neither on the left nor the right'. Although he participated in the elections and voted for 'my staunch party', he stated with resignation: 'You have no

86   THE OTHER '68

influence over things, and consequently no politics either. Don't agree with some measures, it's pointless to go against the flow.'[76] A 76-year-old qualified engineer commented that he didn't always vote because he didn't like the parties: 'You can't even influence things by voting... Troublemakers in Berlin have more influence than voters.' The ex-police commander maintained that he had lost all interest in politics as he had 'no influence on events, either in private or in general'. A steelworker gave it as his opinion that 'strictly speaking, you ought to vote, or you don't get to complain later. But you soon get tired of it'; he had simply been 'disappointed too often'.[77] Similarly, a former journalist stressed the duty to vote but 'fundamentally' didn't care about politics: 'If things get dicey, I'll notice it soon enough.'[78]

Even those who had—as far as anyone could tell—played no active role in National Socialism, tended to express themselves in terms of a passive civic duty. A civil servant remarked soberly that 'in the end, it had always turned out for the best that he had never been particularly politically active'. 'I'm in favour of not needing to worry', said a retired factory inspector; after all, we 'have an elected parliament'.[79] They were unenthusiastic converts to democracy. The Bolsa team concluded from the collected data: 'In most cases, their activity did not extend beyond a superficial desire for information, and exercising their right to vote.' Although the men were on average a little more interested in politics than the women, their overall interest could be described as 'barely moderate'. Even the most inveterate joiners, who were at the forefront of choirs, carnival associations, and rifle clubs, showed little involvement in community or political affairs.[80] There were, however, clear differences between the men who had, by their own account, been badly affected by denazification and those who did not mention any such disadvantages. Not a single one of the former group was involved in communal affairs or politics at any level beyond going to the polls, or having formal membership of an organization. By contrast, 7 per cent of the latter (considerably less educated) group could point to their regular participation in community or political groups.[81]

Retreat from politics and public life corresponded with increased involvement in the private sphere. Consequently, a grandfather's Nazi past often led not to conflict but, on the contrary, to greater intimacy between the generations of a family. Karl-Georg Tismer wrote of the teacher Gustav Crauert, for example:

> Herr C's life is particularly based on his children and grandchildren, and also on his wife... After his return from the Second World War,... as a

TRUST NOBODY OVER SIXTY? THE ROLE OF THE ELDERLY   87

former member of the NSDAP, [he] was suspended from the teaching profession. As a result, he faced social discrimination and a loss of external prestige, and also experienced economic difficulties, a situation that lasted until 1955, but which continued to play a constant role thereafter. Against this background over the last twenty years, he developed a fundamental attitude marked by resentments and prejudices...A stabilizing effect [is exerted by]...his identification with his children and grandchildren, i.e. the achievement of satisfaction and happiness through their successes.[82]

A payroll clerk who counted the two occasions when he joined a political party—the SPD in 1933, and the NSDAP in 1941—as his greatest mistakes, put it in a nutshell: 'That was the major flaw in '45. I had to start again from the beginning...then, in 1946, I was through with the lot of it and now I just live for my family.'[83]

But for all this close family life, we can assume that the three generations seldom or never discussed the parents' lives during the Third Reich. Vocabularies were limited and there was little appetite for open conversation. The Bolsa study does not record a single case where the old people talked about having discussed National Socialism within their families. Indeed, only one of the 118 men mentioned occasional political conversations with his children.[84] Likewise, there was only one instance of any of the 222 Bolsianers objecting to the political orientation of their sons or daughters. This was Wilhelm Odermann, the strident Nazi, whose arguments with his 39-year-old daughter had at least a political tinge. They shared a house, but kept separate households, and he said of her:

She's let a room to a Jordanian student, and I'm against that. Admittedly the man is intelligent and seems OK for now; and he runs the Jordanian Student Group in X. But in the end, he's a typical Levantine, and I just have no sympathy for those people.

Here then, are a father and daughter arguing over the father's racism, but we have no evidence of whether they ever spoke about the Nazi past. The man's relationship with his daughter had been strained since he had criticized her choice of partner. 'That man was no good', he complained. His son-in-law had drunk, cheated, and spent too much money. So their years of conflict had much more to do with finances and romantic partners.[85] This was a typical pattern. In the few Bolsa families where there was tension between elderly parents and their children, this revolved around who they married, at what

88 THE OTHER '68

age they married, and their choice of professions—and therefore the level of independence allowed to the younger generation, and the timing of their major life decisions. Political disagreement played little part.[86]

Discord could also be traced back to the gulf between the grandchildren's values and those of their grandparents' generation, but this rarely led to open conflict. While 40 per cent of the Bolsianers expressed some degree of criticism of their grandchildren's behaviour, they generally refrained from interfering, to avoid meddling in their grown-up children's business, and to keep the peace.[87] The grandparents and parents had different childrearing styles, as a survey from 1971 shows. At that time, 'anti-authoritarian parenting' was favoured by almost a third of those aged below 30, a fifth of those aged 30 to 44, a seventh of the 45- to 59-year-olds, and only a twelfth of interviewees aged over 60.[88]

Many of those in the middle age group—i.e. the Sixty-Eighters' parents' generation—considered the grandparents 'intolerant' and out of touch. Frau Seifert, aged 45, had three generations living together in her house; to her, 'the grandparents [being] very rigid' was a 'major obstacle.'[89] According to Herr Urban, who was the same age, the problem with the over-60s was that 'their earliest youth began in the Imperial Era' and that they had never overcome the 'strictly authoritarian, highly traditional expectations' of those days. He speculated in relation to the student unrest that 'for them, the upheaval now basically represents a repeat of 1918'.[90] Another 38-year-old thought that the elderly could no longer keep pace 'because they basically come from a completely different world', a world full of 'authoritarian practices'.[91]

At the height of the West German student protests between May 1967 and August 1968, six women students fanned out across the Cologne-Bonn area to question 120 adults born from 1909 to 1934 for Helga Merker's PhD thesis. These interviewees were unrelated to the Bolsa participants but found themselves sitting opposite the same microphones, answering the same questions: what did they think of the youth of today, and how had their own youth been different from young people's lives today? Naturally, these middle-aged adults frequently referred to the ongoing student unrest, but they also described in detail their own position as intermediaries between old and young. Most of them emphasized their sympathy for the turbulent young people, clearly differentiating themselves from the over-60s. A good many of them defined themselves surprisingly clearly as members of the generation we now label '*Flakhelfer*', 'sceptical', or 'Forty-Fivers'. This refers to those who were influenced by Nazism as teenagers, but who were still young enough at the end of the war to make a complete political about-turn to democracy and thus to forge a career in the post-war society.[92] Of the fifty surviving conversations with middle-aged men, sixteen (a third) could be classified as Forty-Fivers. They described their youthful indoctrination under the Nazi regime (either in the Hitler Youth or on the Front) in negative terms, actively distanced themselves from the authoritarianism of the older generation, and welcomed their children's desire for freedom, or their political engagement. The women were generally less likely to express political opinions, but here too, five of thirty-nine described themselves as Forty-Fivers. Middle-aged right-wingers, who defended Nazi-adjacent values and were strongly critical of the APO were considerably rarer, with four men and four women among the eighty-nine surviving answers.[93]

The Forty-Fivers were unanimous that they felt cheated of their youth by the Nazi regime, and that they had learnt to regret their childish enthusiasm for Hitler and the war. Consequently, they tended to defend the students' right to express their views, but to reject the protests at the point where they crossed into utopian thinking and acts of violence. They were far clearer than the elderly in condemning the legacy of the Third Reich. Herr Russ, aged 42, for example repudiated the 'phony boy-scout romanticism', '*Blut und Boden* literature', 'insularity', 'basic principles of racism', 'martial (role) models', 'leadership through orders', and 'slavish obedience' of the Nazi period. This was the background against which he disparaged the elderly because they 'construed every youthful exuberance as sedition' and 'rejected anything that's unlike the past'. Russ had every sympathy with the young people's ongoing protests as an expression of their yearning for individual freedom and a critique of police violence.[94] A Herr Kaym thought similarly: having grown up in the absence of freedom, the grandparents considered it 'abnormal' for youngsters just to want to 'express their own opinions'.

> I'm sure it is hard for the general public to understand that if an assassination attempt is made on Dutschke, then an hour later, massed students march on the Springer building to demonstrate...Well, I do have to criticize the form that that kind of action takes...[but] if they don't hurt anyone or attack anyone's private property, I have no problem accepting it, because I'm sure there are plenty of valid reasons, just the form. I'm sure the students aren't the only guilty party...in fact I admire how active they are.[95]

A PE teacher argued that older people should also engage more constructively with 'the general wave of protest' that was underway: 'So why are the young people rebelling against this democracy at the moment? Because it's just too

90   THE OTHER '68

rigid for them, too inflexible...Nothing happens if you stay that rigid.' She talked about a sit-in staged by the girls at her school the week before: 'I was in the middle of teaching the fifth form the Western roll technique...and my pupils sat down in the hall and said: nope, we're not doing this anymore! The high jump again!' Although she'd found this 'shocking for a moment', the situation had been resolved by discussion and compromise.[96] Around a third of the parents' generation showed this relative open-mindedness towards the youth protests, while most people in their mid-30s to mid-50s sat on the fence or reacted with little interest, and a small minority expressed harsh rejection.

The in-between generation saw the old as overly authoritarian and inflexible, and the young as overly impatient and radical. In many ways, they took a transitional position between the Sixty-Eighters and their grandparents, who had been shaped by the Wilhelmine and Nazi eras. This helps to explain why, soon after the protests of the late sixties, reform-minded alliances grew up between middle-aged and young adults in many fields, leading to the accelerated dismantlement of hierarchies and traditional authorities.[97] Most of the older generation, the over-60s, were unwilling to make these kinds of compromises. They clung to the pre-war ethic of thrift and, however much they might have objected to the Vietnam War or the Emergency Acts, their fear of political instability led the vast majority of them to reject the rebellions with their violent or unfamiliar forms of protest and utopian aims. Many of those aged 60 plus also had a tainted political past, although a vanishingly small number of them were still professed National Socialists. Although the postwar denazification process had been limited to a few years, its effects were still being felt in the loss of social prestige, blocked career progression, and reduced pensions. Even in the grandparental generation, die-hards were socially ostracized. Former Nazis typically reacted to this situation with resignation and by turning inwards towards private and family life. After all, personal conflicts between the three generations were comparatively rare and apolitical by nature. Where disputes arose, they had less to do with the Nazi past and more to do with romantic choices, age of marriage, and career options. Jointly hushing up and sugar-coating the most recent past cut right across all social classes and levels of education.[98] There were both functional and emotional reasons for this silence. All three age groups were keen to keep family relationships open and financial transfers flowing from old to young, not to hurt one another, and to believe in each other's integrity. 'Intimacy through silence' kept relationships alive without poisoning them.

Thus, relations between the generations were far less fraught than the Sixty-Eighters' slogan 'Trust Nobody Over Thirty' would have us believe.

Incidentally, in 1975, as many as 70 per cent of young West Germans—and 89 per cent of those with a university education—disagreed with this line.[99] They were reacting both to the intermediary role that their parents played between grandparents and the young, and to the broad spectrum of political opinions held by older people. We need to overcome the pithy yet reductive view of 'the old' in conflict with 'the young'. For one thing, at least three generations were present in around 1968, with the middle age group of adults often building bridges between old and young. Secondly, a minority of the over-60s were part of the left-wing scene and endorsed the protests, particularly where they were targeting the Emergency Acts and the Vietnam War. The majority of the grandparents' generation did indeed, however, hold authoritarian and anti-consumerist views. Many of them had such a deep-seated fear of war, inflation, communism, and political violence that public protest rallies of any kind provoked intense disapproval.

5

The Female Sixty-Eight

The moment Professor Dr Dr Kölbel hurried into his seminar at the Bonn Pedagogical University on Thursday, 24 June 1971, he noticed a change in the atmosphere. The tutorial group seemed somewhat larger than usual. Even more of the female students than usual had brought their knitting with them, which surprised him. Their needles clacked busily—he might almost have said demonstratively. Paying this no further attention, Kölbel began, as always, to expound on his subject, the education of girls. Their emotional structure meant that girls were predestined for the 'natural sphere' of the family, he taught. 'Thus an education that prepares the female sex for the household and family life', he read from his notes, 'still largely corresponds to the needs of our society'. Feminine virtues could only unfold within marriage because 'a virgin who has not yet experienced the power of the man is, so to speak, a neutral entity'. Had he heard a restless grumbling in the room there? Kölbel looked around, but continued with a rhetorical question: 'Why should a girl in her best years, that is, at the age of nineteen to twenty, waste her time on academic work when that is the time when she can bear children most easily?' To the professor's amazement, a long-haired woman in the front row stood up in answer to his question and handed out a leaflet inviting 'feedback' on the seminar. She then enquired about the basis in psychological, sociological, or pedagogical research for his ideas. Another female participant backed her up: he was glorifying motherhood as a woman's destiny in exactly the way the Nazis had once done! The clicking knitting needles had fallen silent. More and more women were now demanding a discussion. Kölbel felt ambushed. He reached for his briefcase, declared the seminar over, and left the room. This was the first time that the women in Bonn's 'Emancipation Working Group' had busted a class.[1]

The '*Arbeitskreis Emanzipation*' (Emancipation Working Group, AKE for short) had been in existence for several years by then. Half a dozen female students had formed a discussion group in 1967 after meeting at a study event on Marx's *Das Kapital* run by the Bonn SDS, where 'we very soon realized that, as female students, we were just not taken all that seriously, and that, to put it crudely, we were only any use for making the coffee and typing the leaflets', said Florence Hervé. Their 'disquiet' at that led the SDS women to 'get together as women students'. At first, they met in private flats and read Simone de Beauvoir's *The Second Sex* together. The book was 'an aha experience' for Hervé: 'I felt taken seriously in my personal, very complicated situation' and understood that 'my disquiet was actually a product of society'. The circle subsequently discussed August Bebel's classic *Woman and Socialism*, and Clara Zetkin's writings on women's rights.[2] In April 1969, they resolved to put political theory into practice, gave themselves a name, and elected a coordinating committee. Speaking for around thirty members at that time, of whom a third were housewives or working, and the rest were students from all faculties, Hervé declared: 'We are working for women's emancipation, and we don't wish to take a hostile stance towards the men, but to work together with them, or at least with the more advanced among them.'[3]

One of the working group's first campaigns was a leaflet aimed at Bonn's female students, which enumerated their dreadful career prospects. A quarter of the university's students were women, yet they made up only 11 per cent of assistant professors, and 0.6 per cent of full professors. Only one woman student in six made it to graduation. Eight in ten professors were of the opinion that their female students had no serious academic aspirations and wanted 'to get married either way'. And once a woman had married, a tiny minority of husbands were prepared to help with the housework or childcare. 'Do not expect the situation to change by itself', the flyer urged its readers. 'It is only by democratizing the university that equality for female students...can be achieved.'[4]

It proved harder than expected, however, to win any solidarity from their male colleagues, as the working group realized when they tried to explain their aims in the Bonn student newspaper. In November 1969, the *akut* editorial department (then staffed by a conservative AStA) invited two AKE campaigners for an interview. Florence Hervé and psychology student Ursula-Regine Teiner accepted the invitation, only to be greeted by editors Gerd Langguth and Thomas G. Vetterlein, who remarked in surprise that they didn't look the least bit like the 'old bats' and 'suffragettes' they'd been expecting. Their report on the working group was quite something. Headlined 'Prostitution Under Phallic Gallows', it featured a photo of a naked woman lying face down in bed with a black tom cat on her legs. The mocking preamble noted sardonically that the women wanted 'no more prostitution under phallic gallows: here we go into future-oriented technical positions!' The front page offered a lurid teaser for the report. 'Going topless sets you free—emancipation today' it proclaimed, accompanied by a photograph of seven

Figure 5.1 Teaser for the report on the Emancipation Working Group in student newspaper *akut*, 7 November 1969

bare-breasted young women in a Hamburg courtroom (Figure 5.1). Anyone inclined to make a tenuous link with the content of the article on the AKE was welcome to do so.[5] When the women of the working group protested 'really very angrily' (Hervé) against the bizarre headlines and sexual imagery, *akut* went one better in the issue after next. The 'refreshingly bawdy caricatures' had actually been an effective advertising tool for the issue of equal rights. The 'oversensitive reaction' by the AKE was 'a typical example of the schizophrenia of left-wing criticism' of the student newspaper, for having gone over to the bourgeois camp. The AKE representatives, who had demanded a clarification, were given a few columns on page three. There, Teiner and Hervé wrote that there was an excessive focus on 'an exclusively sexual emancipation [which] only served as a distraction from true, comprehensive emancipation', and that the working group had specifically not called for a fight against men. Despite this, the newspaper illustrated their remarks with yet another suggestive photo: a naked young woman biting into a man's arm. Caption: 'Incensed AKE associate takes her grievance at *akut* reporting out on *akut* editor Leopold Lama.'[6]

The student members of the AKE were not alone in working towards sexual equality in Bonn in around 1968. In December 1967, the 'Monday Club for Political and Societal Contacts' had been formed. According to the Bonn *General-Anzeiger*, it was headed by 'attractive SPD MPs Annemarie Renger and Hannelore Fuchs'. The club had up to 400 members, 90 per cent of them female, and was moderately feminist in its thinking. It wanted to achieve its aims—overcoming clichéd gender roles, and greater representation of women in politics—by educational means, and through parliamentary reform, in close cooperation with all political parties, and especially the SPD. The lead figure, Hannelore Fuchs, was then in her late 30s, a trained journalist, housewife, and mother. She would later go on to be the women's representative in the SPD party leadership. The 'Monday Club', mainly university-educated, middle-class women from parliament, government ministries, and the media, now met on the first Monday of every month to listen to invited speakers and build networks. They were addressed by SPD politicians including Helmut Schmidt and Gerhard Jahn; journalists such as Rolf Zundel, Werner Höfer, and Klaus Mehnert; and social psychologists, among them Walter Jaide, Ursula Lehr, and Ingrid Tismer-Puschner. The last two were members of the Bolsa research team.[7] The 'Monday Club' saw itself as liberal and democratic, and strongly distanced itself from communism. This resulted in open conflict with Hervé's 'Emancipation Working Group', which in May 1970 accused the Monday women of pursuing an 'anti-communism dictated from the top', and thus of deliberately 'keeping women politically disenfranchised'. The women of the AKE considered themselves to be part of the New Left and wanted both a feminist and a socialist revolution.[8] Here, the traditional split within the German women's movement into bourgeois and radical wings was directly reflected in local events in late-sixties' Bonn. It was predominantly the radical, socialist wing, with its daring private experiments and provocative campaign methods, that would subsequently have a major impact on society.

Both the Emancipation Working Group and the reform-minded Monday Club are now all but forgotten. When the Bonn Stadtmuseum organized an exhibition, events programme, and catalogue to mark the fortieth anniversary of 1968, neither of the two women's groups was even mentioned. The museum curators did not seek out any of their founders, yet interviewed dozens of male former students, with whom they designed the exhibition. Florence Hervé wrote to the Stadtmuseum at the time, saying she considered it 'a pity' that 'one aspect of the activism had not been taken into account', especially as the Bonn working group had been 'one of the first groups in the new women's movement, alongside Berlin and Frankfurt'.[9] The feminine 1968 had long been relegated to the side lines, and was only commemorated in publications by the university equal opportunities officer and local women's historians.[10]

Just as with the history of the female Sixty-Eight in Bonn, the commemorative discourse in (West) Germany and beyond plays down the feminist element of the student protests, regarding it as secondary to the political, male-dominated Sixty-Eight. German books on the period mostly feature

96   THE OTHER '68

young men on the cover, especially Rudi Dutschke, Daniel Cohn-Bendit, Fritz Teufel, and Rainer Langhans.[11] Up until the fiftieth anniversary in 2018, television discussion programmes and newspaper interviews featured almost exclusively male veterans, who commented on the history of their own generation. Like the *akut* editors at the time, most modern historians push the women's movement into the margins. Here, there is a particularly striking contrast between their positive evaluation of the women's movement and their lack of engagement with it. There is talk of the 'undeniable record of success', and even of the 'century-defining triumph of female emancipation' (Hans-Ulrich Wehler), which profoundly altered society. Yet at the same time, accounts of the era focus overwhelmingly on the APO, the SDS, and on sons criticizing their fathers. Ulrich Herbert's complete overview of German twentieth century history, for example, concedes that of all the social movements of that time, the feminist movement was 'doubtless the most significant', and then goes on to omit it almost entirely. Eckart Conze's history of the Federal Republic devotes a whole three pages of almost a thousand to the topic.[12] The marginalization of the feminine Sixty-Eight is also true of the whole of Europe, the USA, and Mexico. Everywhere, the rebellions are considered from a male perspective, with terms defined so as to exclude the key women, the private sphere, and the fight against the patriarchy. A recent *Handbook of the Global Sixties* acknowledges in its preface that young women's 'caucuses, organizations and sisterhoods...over time created the most important social change that came out of the 1960s' but, yet again, relegates the topic to a few niche chapters. The international variations on Sixty-Eight are typically 'group portraits without the ladies'.[13] It is therefore somewhat surprising to a modern observer that, despite everything, a quarter of SDS members were women.[14]

Why are the women missing from our image of Sixty-Eight? There are several answers here. One is that female rebellion often occurred primarily within the private sphere. Another is that the fledgling women's movement was often reduced to questions of women's sexual autonomy, especially in relation to abortion and rape. Thirdly, many of the leading women shunned the limelight. It was only later that well-known spokeswomen emerged, such as Alice Schwarzer and her 'We've had Abortions' campaign in *Stern* magazine in 1971. Schwarzer was one of very few female journalists who could cover feminist protest events for the media. Even Helke Sander and Sigrid Damm-Rüger, the two SDS women who, in September 1968, heralded the fight for equal rights at an SDS congress in Frankfurt with a valiant speech, followed by tomatoes thrown at the male conference organizers, remained comparatively little known. Sigrid Damm-Rüger shied so far away from media appearances that her daughter Dorothee only learnt of 'my mother's importance to the new women's movement' on the day of her funeral: 'I first realized it when a few women...laid a wreath of tomatoes on my mother's grave and described her throwing [them] as the initial spark of the fledgling women's movement.'[15] The few campaigns that attracted public attention—Damm-Rüger's tomatoes, Alice Schwarzer's self-incrimination campaign, and the later demonstrations against paragraph 218 of the penal code, which outlawed abortion—were only the tip of the iceberg. The broad sweep of change remained hidden from many people at the time, as did the thousands of personal conflicts within families and marriages, which spread like wildfire after 1968.

Young women were then beginning, with increasing self-confidence, to carry demands for equal rights and personal fulfilment into their private lives—and meeting with resistance. They posed everyday questions such as who should do the dishes, supervise children, and care for elderly parents, as well as whose career should take priority. Private concerns of this kind became political because they sparked discussions of fundamental principles up and down the country, leaving relationships with partners, mothers, and fathers strained and altered. It is only when we shine a light into the dark corners of familial privacy that we can fully make out the long-term impact of Sixty-Eight.

Although the (75 per cent male) students' political protest movement sporadically dominated the media, little remained of their goals. The campaign against the Emergency Acts, and for a socialist revolution, dried up once the emergency constitution was passed in May 1968, and after the social-liberal coalition came to power in October 1969. The extra-parliamentary opposition and the SDS disbanded. The communist cadre groups, which continued to wage their campaign against capitalism into the 1970s, remained ineffectual because they never won popularity among the West German population.[16] Things were very different, however, with the comparatively quiet women's revolution, which only received mass media coverage much later. In the short-term, Helke Sander's speech and Sigrid Damm-Rüger's tomatoes acted like a bolt of lightning, forcing public awareness of something that, from the very beginning, spread underground beyond the university, recruiting women from all social classes and every region, at breath-taking speed. The uptake was enormous. In the *Frankfurter Weiberrat* (Frankfurt Women's Council), for example, 'everything [went] incredibly fast...it expanded very quickly...It was like, if you had a cold for two days, you ended up feeling that you'd lost touch with the spirit of the world', recalled activist Silvia

Bovenschen.[17] Sander reported from West Berlin in September 1968: 'We've got such a massive influx that we can barely cope with the organization of it all.' The significance of women's advance remained underestimated because commentators of all persuasions did not then recognize female concerns, private matters, as political, or see that they would change society. Helke Sander reproached the men in the SDS in these terms:

> When we started six months ago, most [male] comrades reacted with mockery…How slow you lot are on the uptake, because you can't see that suddenly, without your help, people that you never even thought about are getting organized, and in numbers that you'd see as the break of a [red] dawn if they were from the working classes.[18]

It could be argued that the private confrontations around women's liberation were simply a matter of course—a kind of backdrop to the 'real' Sixty-Eight. This is not the case, because engaging with female activism throws up numerous questions that have the potential to radically subvert our assessment of the era. We might ask, for example, whether we should continue to characterize the uprising as a generational conflict. Did arguments within families over female lifestyles really pit young women against old women, daughters against their mothers or mothers-in-law? Or was there, by contrast, an intergenerational female solidarity, where women of whatever age pushed back against the demands of men with a patriarchal mindset? Equally urgent questions arise from our understanding of the Sixty-Eighters as a political generation. Could women be Sixty-Eighters too and, if so, what defined them? We may have to come to a new understanding of 1968 as a historical event if we rank the private sphere equally alongside public life. How weighty are the classical political motivations for the protest movement—a protest against the ongoing taint of Nazism; a critique of capitalism, consumer society, the Vietnam War, and imperialism—compared to women's attempts to alter gender roles, the course of their lives, and their families? It is no coincidence that 1968 in West Germany has already frequently been cast as a 'lifestyle revolution', against which the misfired political uprisings fade into insignificance. Norbert Frei's book, for example, summarizes the lasting achievements of the West German protest movement with these images: 'a somewhat longer-haired tradesman pushing a pram through a Swabian village without his partner was certainly not the rule from then on, but he was a possibility, as was a young woman from a small town in Hesse, an office clerk, holidaying alone in Spain'. The things that Frei characterizes

THE FEMALE SIXTY-EIGHT   99

here as a change in the 'face and mentality of the Republic' are new ways of
'doing gender'—i.e. the ways in which women and men express their gender
identities in everyday life, and how they negotiate with each other. Despite
this, Frei has very little to say about disputes around sexual morality, and
his book barely mentions conflicts relating to gender roles.[19]

What if we were to turn the tables for once and start from the premise that
women's groups were, in the long-term, more important than the men in the
SDS? It would then be Helke Sander and Sigrid Damm-Rüger, not Rudi
Dutschke or Daniel Cohn-Bendit, who were the flag-bearers on the long
march that changed the Republic, and that took place less in political institutions than in the nation's fitted kitchens. Florence Hervé, not Hannes Heer,
who led the protest movement in Bonn. And Gretchen, rather than Rudi
Dutschke, would represent the legacy of Sixty-Eight in West Germany. After
all, Gretchen's fight for equal rights was destined to have a greater long-term
historical effect than Rudi's espousal of an anti-authoritarian, socialist society.

Gretchen Dutschke-Klotz saw herself as an activist and considered it 'awful'
that 'so many people saw me only as "Rudi's wife"' and were 'only interested
in Rudi'. It was her idea to form communes on the American model that was
later picked up by Dieter Kunzelmann.[20] She also made a conscious effort to
implement the 'struggle for a better society in our own home', in the Dutschke
family's everyday life. Yet her avant-garde wishes ran up against—highly
typical—boundaries. Gretchen saw herself and her marriage as a prime
example of the women's movement in around 1968:

> We women were trying to live out our thirst for independence, even if we
> didn't want to leave our boyfriends or husbands, and children. It stirred up a
> degree of contradictions, for me, at any rate. I wanted to be my own person,
> not to let my life and my identity be determined by Rudi.... Obviously, I
> didn't realize at the time how much he misunderstood my behaviour.

After Rudi's death, Gretchen read his diaries, which left her speechless:

> He didn't even mention the birth of his first child [in January 1968]. I find
> that strange because for me it was a milestone in life... When Rudi describes
> the course of his day, you'd think he lived alone... Rudi had problems with
> our life... and thought that too much concentration on the domestic would
> lead to reformism instead of revolution.... I was not always happy about that
> because it meant that I was responsible for the household... It remained a
> point of friction between us... He listened to my complaints and recognized

that there was something wrong. He saw that I wanted a certain independence for myself, but what that meant and how it could be achieved remained a mystery to him.[21]

Gretchen was annoyed by Rudi's frequent absences, his disparagement of housework, and 'by the arrogance of the people who came to our flat to visit Rudi and left everything in a mess'.[22] It also rankled with her that Rudi initially only perceived his children 'as screaming nappy-fillers'. It wasn't until they learnt to speak that he took an interest in them as subjects to be educated. 'But at least he cleaned up the shit and changed the nappies without grumbling… The only problem was that he was so seldom there.'[23]

The Dutschkes were not the average German family, and Gretchen Dutschke-Klotz, who had grown up in North America, was by no means typical of West German women of her age. At that time, there were worlds of difference between female students and other young middle- and working-class women. In the 1960s, young women typically continued to be heavily dependent on their parents into their mid-20s. Sixty per cent of those who had come of age, i.e. those over 21, were still living with their parents. Most of them—seven in ten—first moved out of the parental home when they married. Admittedly, almost half of these young women had married by the age of 23, and a further 14 per cent were engaged by then. Young men, on the other hand, generally did not marry until their mid- to late-20s. At that time, both sexes considered it expressly desirable for the husband to be older than his wife. Ninety-two per cent of young women, whether unskilled workers or students, preferred a 'more mature' partner, who could take the leading role in the marriage. This attitude was based on traditional norms: daughters grew up with the objective of finding a good husband and fitting in with him. Girls were also prepared for their later married lives in material terms, in that parents and relatives would give them bed linen, crockery, and other household goods as Christmas and birthday presents. As late as 1964, every second bride went into her marriage with a regular trousseau, and surveys found large majorities in agreement with the view that a well-filled bottom drawer was more important to a young woman than a good vocational education. As an example, the daughter of a master plumber in Harburg, who was not yet engaged at the age of 23, reported that she had acquired over the years twelve bedsheets, eighteen pillows, thirty-two towels, silver cutlery for six, and a set of stainless-steel cutlery for twenty-four people.[24]

A certain emphasis on partnership in marriage and family life had gained acceptance in public discourse by the sixties. Unvarnished displays of patriarchal power were considered old-fashioned, and decision-making through discussion and conversation was the order of the day. People called publicly for better education for girls. Daughters were now more frequently prepared for a dual role as both housewife and working woman. Young women should be educated and gainfully employed, so long as this didn't conflict with their familial role.[25] Part-time work, in particular, which was then spreading rapidly, increased many women's room for manoeuvre.[26] In practice, however, the traditional gender order had barely even been rattled. The majority, even of the young, thought in patriarchal terms. A poll of 800 young people from Hamburg, born in 1941, conducted in October 1964 found them almost unanimous (up to 95 per cent agreement) that 'the husband should continue to be the provider in the family' and that the wife should only earn extra money temporarily and in an emergency situation, especially in the early, child-free years. In line with this, 88 per cent of childless young women were working, followed by 43 per cent of mothers with one child, and only 14 per cent of mothers with two children. The pollsters stated that 'the old saying: "the woman's place is in the home" lives on in an amended form: "the mother's place is with her children"'. Norms were changing only slowly, and primarily among educated people. It is notable that the only group of interviewees who could imagine a long-term professional life, even after marriage, were one in three of the female students.[27]

But taking responsibility for planning their own lives was still an unfamiliar experiment, even for women students in the late 1960s, and one that invited self-doubt. The traditional orientation towards marriage had, after all, freed young women from responsibility: a happy life depended on men and not on themselves. 'Love, and a good husband. This ranked at the top, in the background to every concern, in a supressed yet self-evident way', recalled Elke Regehr, who was then a young artist and a member of the Berlin SDS.

> The image of women that I had absorbed from my East Prussian family was one I couldn't accept. You had to be the one who served. Men, love and the family ought to be the main thing for a woman. I found the constriction bound up with this unbearable, but the thought of marriage and a child was still there in the back of my mind as a default goal for a long time.

Similarly, Berlin student Karin Adrian had 'not been brought up to see a woman as having equal rights. Conformity was considered a positive attribute for a woman'. Helke Sander was struggling with the same internalized norms, and 'simply had no experience of anything but women being inferior'.[28] It was

102   THE OTHER '68

no coincidence that everyday speech, the media, and even academic publications frequently referred to unmarried women as 'girls'.[29]

Thus equipped for a life as a wife and mother, students in and around 1968 found it difficult to assert themselves publicly in academia. None of them had learnt to take the stage self-confidently, and role models were rare. PhD student Elsa Rassbach's experience...

> ...of university at that time was that it was a very intimidating atmosphere. There were very few female professors. There were constant intimidating remarks...In my first year in the department of philosophy, I was supposed to give a paper on Kierkegaard but I was so scared of the men that, in the end, I didn't turn up. Back then, I'd certainly never have dared speak in a political plenary meeting of the Freie Universität, where the SDS's great theoreticians used to debate.

Art student Sarah Haffner was also plagued by self-doubt 'whenever I sat in the main lecture hall and these [male] students propounded their abstract theories and their reams of sociological gobbledegook'. But despite her criticism, she kept silent because 'it was so deeply ingrained in you that as a woman, you had to subordinate yourself and that there are certain things that you actually can't even do'. Commune member Dagmar Seehuber condemned the general 'attitude on the left' that 'women could certainly sit in [on a discussion] but that they weren't expected to contribute'. 'The men often laughed' the moment a woman started to speak, said Gretchen Dutschke-Klotz bitterly. There came a point when she found both this and the intellectual 'cant' used by the speakers 'simply unbearable'.[30] Beatrix Novy said of the University of Cologne: 'Everywhere, there was this huge gap where the [male] comrades always talked a lot, and very loudly, and the women said very little.'[31]

Discomfort with the theoretical language of the SDS was widespread among female students. Christel Bookhagen of Kommune 2 experienced this 'dreadfully stilted language' as downright 'oppressive' and 'far too abstract': 'it scared me and was totally not on my wavelength'. 'Incomprehensible stuff', said Elke Regehr; all the same, her 'great woe' was 'that I didn't dare speak' when 'the same old "revolutionary cadres" continually held forth for hours'.[32] It would be years yet before the women's movement point-blank denounced both the intellectual language of the sociologists and philosophers, and everyday speech as essentially patriarchal and began to develop a language of their own in response.[33] Inga Buhmann would later judge that sociological jargon had been 'an arrogant instrument of power, [wielded] mainly against women'.

The SDS had cultivated 'repressive communication structures', concurred Mona Steffen, a 25-year-old sociology student in Frankfurt. In September 1968, Helke Sander made a famous speech, accusing the men in the SDS of suppressing female voices: 'we demand a discussion of our substantive issues here, we will no longer settle for women being permitted to say a word now and then...before going back to business as usual'.[34]

Helke Sander's speech acted as a rallying cry at the time, and almost every publication now cites it as a key event at the outset of the 'second wave' of the German women's movement.[35] Sander created a stir merely by speaking at the SDS Conference of Delegates—very few women had ever done so. But it was the well-aimed tomato thrown at SDS functionary Hans-Jürgen Krahl by Sigrid Damm-Rüger, who had been involved in Berlin student politics since 1964, that gave the speech its drama and media impact. The heavily pregnant Damm-Rüger pulled 'two pounds of soup tomatoes,...at seventy pfennigs a pound' out of her string shopping bag and methodically 'flung them, one after another' towards the speakers' podium, 'in total silence at first, and then amid a tumult'. According to Helke Sander:

> She wanted to force the discussion and then spoke up once the assembly had reconvened, to say something to the effect that if the SDS wasn't prepared to have this discussion, it deserved to be treated the same way that it treated the establishment. She was very articulate and was clear and self-assured and stood there with her green dress and her red hair and her round belly, and looked wonderful.

The daily and weekly press all reported on the sensation, especially *Der Spiegel*.[36] Meanwhile, eighteen months before her descent into the terrorist underground, Ulrike Meinhof was a columnist at *konkret* magazine, widely read in student circles; she offered a blazing commentary, interpreting the incident as a decisive breakthrough. She called on women everywhere now to use up 'entire goods trains of tomatoes' in public so that something would finally 'dawn on' men:

> The woman who threw the tomatoes, and the one who provided the reason for doing so, were not speaking on the basis of borrowed, laboriously medi-ated experience, they were speaking and acting, while speaking for countless women, for themselves. And they didn't give a monkey's whether or not what they had to say was at the very high theoretical level that is generally to be found in the SDS...These women from Berlin in Frankfurt don't want to

104   THE OTHER '68

play anymore, seeing that the entire burden of bringing up children falls on them... They no longer want to be looked down on because, for the sake of bringing up children, they've been badly educated, had no education at all, or broken off their studies, or not been able to pursue their profession.... When the men refused to take any interest in this, they copped tomatoes to the head.[37]

Ulrike Meinhof had not thrown herself into the breach on behalf of the pro-testing SDS women by chance. Newly divorced and mother to 5-year-old twins, she was caught in the same 'private' dilemma that drove Helke Sander, Florence Hervé, Sarah Haffner, and Karin Adrian to get involved in politics. They were all mothers of young children who, despite their studies, had been saddled with the brunt of the childcare by the fathers. The emergence of the new women's movement, the first self-organized groups, and public campaigns were all inextricably linked with this family situation. The first leaflets directly addressed young mothers who had been prevented from studying. The West Berlin flyers used precise and direct language, with titles such as: 'To All Women', 'We Are Envious and We Have Been Sad' and 'First Attempt at Finding the Right Questions'. The Bonn leaflets were headlined 'Pamphlet for Women Students: Why Are You Studying?' and 'Once a Year: Mother's Day Flowers—And What Else?'.[38] The Berlin 'Aktionsrat zur Befreiung der Frauen' (Action Committee for the Liberation of Women), launched by Helke Sander and Marianne Herzog, began with the immediate and urgent question of childcare. At its very first meeting, they were advised to set up five Kinderläden, 'as a practical response for the women to the tiresome issue of time'.[39] This was the start of the wave of self-run playgroups, which were then rolled out at high speed.

The beginnings of the new women's movement were so closely bound up with childcare issues because there was a distinct lack of day nurseries in the late sixties. There were kindergarten places for only 30 per cent of 3- to 6-year-olds, and no provision at all for younger children to be cared for outside the family. Long waiting lists and over-subscribed nursery groups were the rule. There were fifty children to every preschool teacher. This is a primary reason for the tone in the vast majority of kindergartens being one of command, and strictly regimented daily routines. There were considerably fewer childcare places in West Germany than in neighbouring countries such as Italy, France, and Belgium.[40] Meanwhile, most women were still marrying in their early- to mid-20s and having their first child soon afterwards. As a consequence, the first pregnancy practically forced young married couples to ask which of them would take care of the baby and therefore neglect or abandon their career or their studies. It was generally decided, without a great deal of discussion, to ditch the woman's career aspirations. In those days, even young people considered it natural for the wife only to work temporarily and only to have a profession in the early days, so as to help with the expensive process of setting up home. Opinion polls found only 13 per cent of West German 23-year-olds in favour of long-term employment for married women. As soon as the children came along, the women would withdraw from the work-force and concentrate on childcare, in which, incidentally, only one new father in five was involved.[41]

Women students were hit particularly hard by this dilemma because the duration of German degree courses meant that they were generally still in the middle of their studies when expecting their first child. At that time, one in nine male students was married, and this held true for the SDS members and the politically active too. Meanwhile, 15 per cent of female students were married.[42] Judith Olek, née Ramm, who was studying chemistry in Bonn, had been an independent member of the student parliament since 1966. But when she married in late 1968, she had to give up politics so that she could at least complete her degree and later become a chemistry teacher. 'In '69 I had my first child and that was that, of course.... I graduated, got my degree in chemistry, but no more chance of a doctorate.' At first, she took her baby son along to seminars. 'I...left him out in the foyer in the chemistry department...and a secretary to one of the professors would often [look after him] during the lectures...in the outer office.' Later on, she was 'only at uni when he [slept]', and her husband helped out for a few hours at a time. As a result, it took her an additional four years to get her degree. A crèche was not an option for her.[43] In 1970, the university crèche in Bonn had a grand total of twenty places when there were 600 children to married students. Even the four *Kinderläden* set up there in November 1969, which were partially subsidized by the AStA, were merely a drop in the ocean.[44] Florence Hervé of the Emancipation Working Group had two small children at that time, and could only afford a babysitter twice a week 'just to run to seminars and back again'. Quite apart from the difficulty of carving out time for herself, in her experience 'professors and students were utterly opposed to you studying as a mother'. When she wanted to take a psychology class, she went to speak to the lecturer who 'just said right out:...Please, as the mother of two children, there's no way you can manage this...You can't be part of my seminar group.' In the end, Hervé was only able to graduate and gain a doctorate by switching to a correspondence course from a French university and getting places for her children at an American preschool in Bonn—they had US citizenship through their father. Anke Brunn, one of the co-founders of the university kindergarten in Cologne, had a similar experience. She described 'the professor, who asked me during my exams whether I wanted to do a PhD, and when I asked if there was a funded position, he answered: What on earth for? You're married. And that really enraged me.'[45]

It is striking how many of these feminist activists came from a transnational background. They compared their situation as young mothers in West Germany to those in their countries of origin or other places that they had lived. The FRG seemed backwards to them, and they imported ideas for improving conditions. Florence Hervé was French and found things in West Germany simply 'oppressive'. 'There was an everyday hostility to children or to women who worked or studied, which felt really bad to me. These little everyday discriminations, this disdain...you would have been best off hiding the fact that you had children.' Everywhere she went, on the tram, in the market, in cafés, she'd been given to understand: 'This is not your place, your place as mother and child is at home!' Children, but not dogs, were banned from playing in the Hofgarten meadows, and her landlord scolded her because her children ran up and down the flat too much. Helke Sander had also experienced better childcare options in Finland, and had been trying in vain since 1966 to transplant the Scandinavian idea of *Parktanten* ('park aunts': women who kept an eye on children as they played in public parks after school) to West Berlin. The will for change was driven by these experiences abroad.[46]

For Helke Sander, a student at the Filmakademie in West Berlin, everyday life with her young son was 'hard' because 'the day-care centres were so gruesome I didn't want to stick him in them. And the kindergartens were totally over-subscribed, the teachers were constantly overwhelmed.' Hanna B., aged 26, from Berlin tried to continue with her studies despite having a child, but she too experienced a constant lack of time, poor conditions in the crèches she visited, and frequent arguments with her husband. Although he supported her in principle, 'there were differences between us, about the little things, you know', because he didn't help with the washing up, paying the bills, or doing the shopping.[47] For many women, it therefore seemed wiser just to give up their studies. As the *Studentenwerk* (students welfare office) stated in 1967, many female students would drop out despite good prospects for success, 'because there was no possible way of accommodating their child during lectures, seminars, tutorials and practicals.'[48] Sarah Haffner (Figure 5.2) said: 'I was at the art college from seventeen to twenty, but then I got pregnant, had my son, and, as you did at that time, I left the college...By contrast,

Figure 5.2 Sarah Haffner in the studio with her son David, 1966

my ex-husband continued his studies as a matter of course.' Her fellow student Karin Adrian took a semester's leave in mid-1968, 'to be able to take care of the baby. It never even occurred to him to do the same.' Sociology student and member of the Berlin SDS, Frigga Haug, gave up on completing her examination thesis 'after my daughter had been around just a few weeks' and moved to Cologne for the sake of her husband's career.

> Before the baby, I thought studying would be endless, that I'd always be able to learn and do what I liked... And suddenly, I was a housewife! I was living in a villa in the countryside with the baby, until I was half mad, drinking martinis in the mornings and other terrible stuff like that... I ended up not even knowing why I was getting up in the morning... Back then, it felt like being buried alive.[49]

Forced against their will into an existence as a wife and mother, former students experienced everyday life as a 'trap' (Haug) from which, because of the children, there seemed to be no way out. By the late sixties, 80 or 90 per cent of families had a washing machine and a fridge, yet housework remained time-consuming, lonely, repetitive—and a matter for women.[50] Even among younger couples, the distribution of household tasks was highly unequal, as a Hamburg survey showed. In 93 per cent of cases, the women took on nine tenths, or more, of all the jobs to be done. Young wives did the shopping, prepared meals, cleaned, washed, ironed, tidied, made beds, and looked after the children. If their husbands did get involved, they devoted themselves to the less traditionally housewifely tasks, such as interactions with the authorities, and paying the rent. But even here, only one man in three took an active role. Among married students, things were a little different, as one male

108 THE OTHER '68

student in three took on at least a quarter of the household duties.[51] Even so, the arrival of a child changed this dynamic. As Karin Adrian recalled, 'you were simply caught up in the classic female role that you knew from home'; after her daughter was born, she too initially drew on the patterns of her parental home:

> There was no alternative model because my mother was just like most women. As a result, I started by taking on that template and doing everything the way I remembered it from home. I cooked, washed the socks and shirts, ironed the shirts, and imitated doing the housework, just like I did when I was playing with dolls. But there came a point when that started to get on my nerves.

Moving into a commune seemed like a potential solution. The collective offered an opportunity to 'live differently', not in the 'isolated and very self-contained' way that their parents had done, and to do away with the 'great divide' between 'public and private' (as Beatrix Novy, a student in Cologne, put it). Even so, the tiresome problems of housework were far from overcome. Communes held weekly meetings to discuss problems and the 'main issue' raised 'everywhere was that, yet again, nobody had done any cleaning'.[52] Hedda Kuschel from the Wieland commune said: 'I noticed, for example, how often the men dodged the housework. They would have very important meetings and discussions instead, and yet again it was the women who had to get most of the work done.'[53] Over the years, the women began to fight back. 'There were endless arguments in young families and the first communes alike about washing up, cleaning, cooking, shopping.' Helke Sander lived in shared accommodation with ten rooms, and the women once locked up their male housemates in a room for a night until they promised that they too would occasionally clean the toilet.[54] Although the communes were originally set up with the aim of trying out alternatives to the classic, bourgeois distribution of family gender roles, in practice this came up against limits. It was easier to reach gender parity in childcare and cooking than with the cleaning or protesting. After all, cleaning had feminine connotations, while brainwork and public political activity were seen as masculine.

Susanne Schunter-Kleemann was a key member of the Berlin SDS and the circle of friends around Kommune 1 (although she never lived there). In 1968, she found that the men would not take her studies seriously and teased her over her hard work. 'After breakfast in K1, I...would leave to work on my thesis. I'd often be rewarded with sneers like: "Oh! Plomsuse's off to work again!".

Fritz [Teufel] nicknamed me that, which was short for *Diplom* [degree] Susanne.' The same thing happened to Karin Adrian: 'I needed to cram for an exam and all guys from the commune would say was: "Oh, you, and your bourgeois degree shit!" ' On another occasion, when Kommune 2 were planning a political campaign and the question arose of who should stay at home with the children, Eike Hemmer told his girlfriend and fellow-communard Christel Bookhagen: 'obviously, it's more important politically for me to be there than you'. Christel was 'seriously peeved', but went along with it.[55] It was evidently not just the men in the SDS who found it hard to imagine a female revolutionary. Women arrested at demonstrations or happenings were often quickly released by the police.[56] True militants simply had to be men. Moreover, to be political, an act must be done in public and aimed at masculine revolutionary subjects. The Berlin Action Committee for the Liberation of Women, for example, was frustrated by the men in the New Left being 'so totally fixated on the *male* working class'.[57] Overthrowing the situation within the family, the home, and the private sphere could not really be important. There was a line of argument on the left which distinguished between the 'principal contradiction' and the 'side contradiction'. This made the prevailing self-evidence of patriarchal thinking abundantly clear: revolution to overthrow capitalism (the principal contradiction) was necessary before side issues such as women's rights, parenting, or gay rights could be addressed. Former activist Lutz von Werder summed this up as follows:

> So their general attitude was one of arguing 'we'll leave that bit out, we'll do all that after the revolution', and seen like that, it obviously just so happened that the whole *Kinderladen* movement was very soon shunted off to the side, ... and so was the women's movement.[58]

Even decades later, SDS veterans tended to classify the women's movement as 'cultural' and to see it as an apolitical issue on the fringes of Sixty-Eight, as the minutes of a discussion event involving 300 ex-SDS members in 1985 show. There was a heated argument over how to handle 'this funny foundling, the women's movement'.[59]

The radical women's groups founded after 1967 initially recruited from the immediate vicinity of the SDS. Many of the early activists had learnt political activism in the SDS, and they also adopted its forms of protest such as direct action and symbolic provocation, now investing them with gender-specific symbolism from the home, childcare, and feminine professions. Sigrid Damm-Rüger threw tomatoes sold for making soup. When a 'go-in' targeted *Stern*

110 THE OTHER '68

magazine, Annette Schwarzenau smeared the contents of full nappies from a *Kinderladen* on the walls of its publishing house. 'Kommune 99' in Steglitz organized a children's demonstration with balloons and a Punch and Judy show. SDS women drew leaflets in a picture-book style calling on kindergarten teachers to strike. They also supported nurses in the '*Haubenkampf*—their fight not to have to wear caps over their hair.[60]

For all the agreement between the men and women in the SDS, there were still areas of friction. As the women were not taken seriously, they elected early on to have single sex meetings, excluding the men. Many left-wing women also subsequently criticized the pressure the SDS men had put on them in the name of the sexual revolution.[61] Meanwhile, a fully blown row grew up between men and women on the left over the approach to take to the *Kinderläden*. These alternative nurseries had been started by women as a practical way of freeing up time for the mothers, but the men now realized their ideological potential and sought to take control. As nurseries sprang up all over the place, the Action Committee for the Liberation of Women in West Berlin found itself in dispute with the '*Zentralrat der sozialistischen Kinderläden*' (Central Council of Socialist Nurseries), founded by men. The *Zentralrat* saw the nurseries as a historic chance to raise the next generation as New Humans. A revolutionary upbringing should equip the children to break the bonds of capitalism, a competitive society, and the bourgeois family.[62] After these time-consuming ideological conflicts, however, a more pragmatic model soon asserted itself in the burgeoning *Kinderladen* movement. The nursery set up in late 1969 in Dransdorf, Bonn, for example, after a few initial experiments settled on a structured daily routine and numerous rules that differed very little from those in an ordinary kindergarten.[63]

The relationship between the emerging women's movement and the SDS was also impaired because the women were working to deconstruct the internalized patriarchal template of the masculine revolutionary and the feminine assistant and companion. They objected to the fact 'that it was only ever the men who made the big speeches and the women who typed the leaflets.[64] According to Sigrid Damm-Rüger, 'the traditional low regard for the female intellect' created 'an unmistakable male dominance'. 'It was the men who talked, theorized and made decisions; the female members essentially limited themselves to listening and learning.'[65] For Sarah Haffner, 'a great awakening' began slowly, giving the example of the West Berlin *Aktionsrat* in 1969: 'If people today talk about us back then as "leaflet typists" or "so-and-so's girlfriend", I have to admit that it wasn't just men who made these classifications. We had them in our own heads.' Typing was far from the only task seen as women's work. Female students sewed banners, translated correspondence, decorated conference halls, designed badges and placards.[66] The women also kept the revolutionaries fed. The Bonn SDS 'had its HQ there in Herwarthstraße, and that was kind of the Holy of Holies', a former student recalled. He was less welcome in the SDS office than his wife, who 'was allowed in more often [because] she used to pass them a bit of supper' while the men were in there preparing 'the great battles'.[67] Most SDS women were perceived as nameless 'accessories' and 'essentially seen as their comrade's arm candy'. Even those like Sigrid Fronius and Susanne Schunter-Kleemann, who sat on academic or SDS committees, were pigeonholed as 'brides of the Revolution'. Schunter-Kleemann rebelled against this label: 'as if we'd just been the revolutionaries' "brides"...In actual fact, we were key players ourselves and not just hangers-on to anyone.'[68]

Questioning traditional patterns of perception was difficult because they were reproduced all over the media and in debates everywhere at that time.[69] It was easiest to imagine a woman either as an asexual mother and housewife or as a sex object, along the same lines as the traditional Madonna or whore distinction. A prime example can be seen in the highly popular West German family sit-com *Ein Herz und eine Seele* (A Heart and a Soul), which ran in the early 1970s, based on the British series *Till Death Do Us Part* (*All in the Family* in the USA). It starred the patriarch 'Ekel Alfred' in the Alf Garnett role. The two main female characters were the inane, houseproud housewife Else and their sexy yet non-political and dependent daughter Rita, who constantly cleaned up after her left-wing husband without complaining.[70] We can find the same polarization of women's roles in late-sixties' reporting on the student movement. Uschi Obermaier, the attractive girlfriend of Berlin communard Rainer Langhans, was marketed to the media as a sex bomb. She was photographed topless for the cover of *Stern* magazine and her (utterly atypical) uninhibited life as the 'it girl' on the rock music scene meant that she could always be relied on for lascivious headlines. As the rebellion's pin-up, she conveyed an image of the female Sixty-Eighter that ran entirely counter to the feminists' aims.[71] For the media and the alpha males of the SDS alike, women were of most interest as sex objects. In early reports on the new women's movement, the glossy magazines could manage nothing more original than mocking the 'bleary-eyed brides of the revolution', and concentrating not on their ideas, but on anything linked to female bodies and feminine sexuality. Even a political magazine like *Der Spiegel* was more inclined to poke fun at contraceptive-pill-guzzling, intercourse-refusing, penis-envying, heavily

112 THE OTHER '68

made-up 'nightshadow plants' with tampons in their handbags than to engage with the female students' arguments.[72]

To make any lasting headway against general principles of this kind, the women's movement needed theoretical ammunition. The central role of ideas can be seen, for example, in the Soviet Union, where no feminist discourse was ever able to develop. Women experienced decades of full equality in the working world there yet, throughout the course of the twentieth century, this could not in itself bring about fundamental change to the role of women in the family.[73] In West Germany after 1967, many women sought to free themselves from patriarchal thinking via the well-trodden path of discussing feminist reading matter with others. A theoretical approach could open the eyes of those who had yet to recognize when they were suffering discrimination.[74] As yet, however, such texts were thin on the ground. 'Books about the women's movement, they were out of the question back then, even in the early seventies you could still carry all of them around with you in a small box, when you set up a book table', recalled Sibylle Plogstedt of the Berlin SDS.[75] Many of the new women's groups at that time lacked knowledge even of the 'first' German women's movement, which had fought for the right to vote.[76] Another problem was that they still did not have the words to describe their own situation. 'In those days we had no labels for what we now term sexism, or for the large number of variants on what you could call patriarchalism', said Silvia Bovenschen of the *Frankfurter Weiberrat*. 'We were relatively badly equipped... The bourgeois women's movement had been very much buried and forgotten... we had no theory of feminism.'[77]

On the search for ideas and historical role models, the emerging women's groups split into two wings in 1969. One, like the West Berlin *Aktionsrat* headed by Helke Sander, addressed women's everyday needs. They were concerned with childcare, housework, prevailing norms of childrearing, and the undervaluing of women's intellects. They read socialist classics, as well as Simone de Beauvoir's *The Second Sex*, Doris Lessing's *The Golden Notebook*, and Betty Friedan's reckoning with the image of woman as housewife in *The Feminine Mystique*.[78] By contrast, the socialist women's reading groups in Frankfurt and West Berlin began with the 'principal contradiction' of capital and labour. They mainly ploughed through Marx, Engels, August Bebel, and Clara Zetkin, so as to emulate the men in the New Left. These groups followed the party line so closely that they initially rejected the word 'patriarchal' and it was only after considerable controversy that they could bring themselves to join the protests against the anti-abortion paragraph 218 in the 1970s.[79] Fellow campaigners such as Bovenschen and Sander felt that the sudden inclination towards dogma on the part of the 'indoctrination faction' represented 'a deep betrayal'.[80]

The question at the heart of the split into 'indoctrination' and 'motherhood' factions was that of whether the women's groups saw themselves as an independent movement or as part of the student-socialist wing of Sixty-Eight. Did the fight against capitalism ultimately distort the ability to see patriarchal structures in private life and their own psyche?[81] For many women, a dawning feminist awareness was the gateway to overthrowing their private lives and a personal revolution, while most men continued to focus entirely on revolutionizing high-level politics. Here, a rift opened up between the sexes. Elke Regehr judged her male colleagues harshly: 'It was just so easy; you could blame everything on capitalism or the "system". You never had to take a concrete look at anyone, least of all yourself.' 'The men . . . wielded revolutionary slogans and looked past themselves', agreed Hedda Kuschel. Dagmar Seehuber went as far as to see Kommune 1 as an environment where the patriarchal character of society was 'expressed more strongly': 'because the men totally disavowed the need to change anything about themselves'.[82] Whereas it was possible for male Sixty-Eighters to rebel against abstract opponents, their female counterparts had to take on actual opposition in their own close circle: (boy)friends, husbands, fathers.

It was precisely because the men were slow to adapt their expectations to the women's new plans for their lives, and because the support networks of state-run childcare provision were as yet underdeveloped, that when the women took an uncompromising attitude towards emancipation this often provoked painful crises within relationships and families. Sociologist Rosemarie Nave-Herz had good reason to write, as early as 1981, of 'the experiences of failure' and sometimes 'high mental "costs" to everyone involved in the women's movement'.[83] In those years, many feminists went through separation, divorce, and feelings of guilt towards their children and partners, which had developed, at least in part, out of their striving to revolutionize traditional gender roles. Those who adhered to the primacy of self-determination—by prioritizing their careers or being more successful professionally than their husbands—would often find themselves single and, where they had children, bringing them up alone.[84] Let us take Regine Walter-Lehmann as an example: she was active in the Berlin women's movement and the New Left in the 1970s, and was later editor of the *tageszeitung*. She had been married to Joachim Lehmann since her student days and had, while heavily pregnant, typed up his degree thesis for him. He would go on to write that he had become 'the sluggish object of a re-education campaign, instructed

114   THE OTHER '68

by Regine, in relation to childcare, kitchen, and cleaning duties'. They lived together in a flat in Charlottenburg, which Regine experienced as a 'prison', especially after she resigned, at her husband's insistence, from a highly interesting but badly paid job as a dramaturgical assistant at the theatre. He felt overburdened with caring for a child and earning money at the same time, but was also jealous of Regine's career. Regine recorded the ensuing crisis in her diary. 'I will never in my whole life forgive myself for the fact that I gave up such a madly coveted job and one that I loved so madly. It nags + nags...Instead, I played the crazed wife and let myself have a little fling. Sadly typical. And damn stupid too.' Afterwards, Regine began to work half-days in a women's collective bookshop, to travel alone, and to toy with plans for moving out. Although she loved her husband, she felt confined within the family:

> It's hard to believe, yet plain to see, how sick I am of this nuclear family life...Daughter puts it in a nutshell: she formulates her wishes with a provoking conservatism. Mama, Pappa, Baby, all together! Of course she can sense my flight tendencies very acutely and she's aggressive and afraid. If it carries on like this for another couple of years, I will lose myself. I have to do something new, something different!

She had found herself trapped in this 'stuffy wifely perspective' without any action on her own part: 'I never wanted this!' But at the same time, she 'felt utterly wretched in advance' when she imagined how her daughter would react. 'If she freaks out if I say that I want to move out and she'll have to share the 4-days-of-Mama and 3-days-of-Pappa a week, or vice versa, like loads of her classmates at the *Schülerladen*. Holy Mary!' In the end, Regine did indeed move out for a few years, became a three-day-a-week mother, and fulfilled her professional ambitions.[85]

The Walter-Lehmann family was not unusual on the left-wing, alternative scene in major cities in the 1970s, as Regine's reference to the many children of divorced parents at the '*Schülerladen*' (a self-organized centre providing care for primary school children outside of school hours) indicates. Regine's daughter had previously attended a *Kinderladen* where there would 'soon be only two children, whose parents hadn't split up'.[86] Similarly, a report from 1969 on the work of the Berlin *Kinderladen*, co-founded by Kommune 2, noted: 'From the beginning and without exception, there were severe tensions between the parents in all the nuclear families involved in the *Kinderladen*. As we worked together in the *Kinderladen*, it really became clear to everyone that these marriages were no longer sustainable.'[87] Disdain for bourgeois family

THE FEMALE SIXTY-EIGHT   115

life, experimentation with new roles, and desire for sexual liberation created strains that many partnerships could not stand. Art student Karin Adrian, for example, found that her love for the father of her daughter foundered amid the circle of parents at the Technical University of Berlin's 'repression-free *Kinderladen*': 'All around us, relationships were breaking up by the dozen... the sleeping around led to jealousies, and I think each of the men slept with the kindergarten teacher Freda at one time or another, mine included, and I was livid with her.'[88] Contemporary observers liked to describe the '*Beziehungskisten*' (difficult relationships) on the alternative scene in the seventies and early eighties as 'a merry-go-round of dramas', 'a relationship trap', or simply as 'everyday feuding'.[89] This was the experience of Regine's husband Joachim, who was wandering around a minefield of cleaning duty, laundry duty, earning money, and self-expression, and who rode out the 'kitchen table controversies around female and male perception, ways of thinking and writing, that dragged on into the early hours of the morning', when in his eyes, 'an understanding could [never] be reached'.[90] Demographic statistics from that time show an increase in cohabitations and short-term partnerships and a markedly higher divorce rate. The lonely-hearts columns in left-leaning city listings magazines frowned upon marriage as a goal. Better to portray yourself as sensitive and expressive, and to stress a longing for autonomy and a rejection of 'ownership' of each other.[91] In 1977, *Die Zeit* newspaper was concerned that this tendency was no longer confined to the alternative milieu and was breaking through into wider sections of society:

> It is an increasingly common experience at marriage counselling centres in the Federal Republic: conflicts that break the lifelong bond are arising from women's wishes and desires for independence. Even young mothers of tod-dlers are determinedly tucking their offspring under their arms and trying to go it alone. 72 per cent of divorces are not filed by the husbands, but by their 'better halves'.[92]

A less commonly chosen alternative to leaving their husbands was for women to leave their children in pursuit of emancipation. Ulrike Meinhof and Gudrun Ensslin became the subjects of major media attention when they abandoned their children and joined the terrorist underground. Nessim and Grischa, two young children who had been foisted off onto Kommune 2 by their parents and were brought up there by the collective (their reaction to this being 'deeply disturbed'), were another well-known case.[93] Other women fled the maternal role away from the glare of the media. Annette Schwarzenau, a nurse and active member of the Berlin SDS, had 'this basic attitude of not wanting to play the wife any longer' and left both her husband and her son.

> It was awful for me and for him too...For me, back then, it was more important to realize my political aspirations instead of being a single mother like millions of other women...The price for that is an incredibly guilty conscience, which I still feel to this day.

In extreme instances, this striving for autonomy resulted in both parents underhandedly passing the buck for the children onto each other. Hedda Kuschel described an occasion in 1968 when she visited her ex-husband at the former family home:

> When I came back because I wanted to see the children again, my husband took advantage of me being there to flee the flat. By then, he'd realized that he was totally out of his depth caring for the children. Then I had all three children for a while.[94]

The shock waves unleashed by the break from the traditional family could only be partially absorbed by groups and communes. Solidarity among women was far from a given in around 1968 and its desirability was only gradually recognized over the following decades, due to some extent to the search for new visions of womanhood. Many activists were still tentatively feeling their way towards their own identities as women and saw their fellow campaigners as threatening rivals, and as embodying 'wrong' expressions of femininity. Misunderstood self-doubt or self-loathing sometimes erupted as aggression towards other women, as Luisa Passerini has shown with reference to female Sixty-Eighters in Italy.[95] Helke Sander remembered how quite a few fellow women students 'constantly hinted to our male colleagues that they had nothing to do with us [feminists]'. Dagmar Seehuber was 'often a bit concerned, even, about being lumped in with the feminists'.[96] Bonn psychology student and SDS activist Heidrun Lotz offers another salient example of this ambivalent stance. Although Lotz had similar pro-communist views to the AKE, she kept her distance from the working group on emancipation. Looking back, Lotz viewed the women's dedication, which had involved 'a great deal of legwork and a great deal of work to raise awareness', as 'absolutely crucial' to Sixty-Eight in West Germany. All the same, she expressed scepticism about the 'feminists' era, whatever one may think about that', and in a biographical interview, she aggressively distanced herself from two of her female contemporaries. One was an unnamed fellow student who had later turned to terrorism. The other was radical feminist Karin Struck, also from Bonn, whom Lotz described like a witch: 'a redhead, a very wild person [...] I didn't like her...she was like this orator, kept climbing on the table'. Struck's book *Die Mutter* (The Mother), about the yearning for a new maternalism, struck Lotz as 'verging on National Socialist'.[97]

As they searched for new female role models, many women also found it helpful to differentiate themselves from their own mothers. Most young women whose mothers had been homemakers insisted that they could never live in a way that was so 'resigned to fate' and 'determined by others'. More than a few female Sixty-Eighters remembered their mothers as 'depressed' housewives, who had lived 'under the thumb' of their husbands.[98] 'We no longer wanted to live like our mothers, who only ever took their cue from the man, where all they ever did was to keep the family breadwinner satisfied at all times', stated Münster student Mechtild Düsing. 'That was the really horrifying image, your own mother!'[99] Yet while they clearly distanced themselves from their mothers' lifestyles, they did not openly criticize them: sympathy, not confrontation, was the order of the day. Even when, as in Frigga Haug's case, the mother had been a convinced Nazi, they did not argue. Frigga overlooked her mother's remarks, however openly anti-Semitic and racist, on the grounds that her father had been killed in the war. 'When you have a mother who has to struggle to support her four children, there isn't such a fight for independence as you get in complete families, where there's a father there too. I felt more like my mother's protector.' In the families of these 1960s' feminists, we consistently see the same pattern of mutually hushing up the past as we did with the sons. Angelika Lehndorff-Felsko was a student in Cologne, whose mother criticized her harshly whenever she got involved in politics; despite this, she could not speak to her mother about the Nazi period:

> That was what you might call a modus vivendi that we'd found...Talking about it didn't work; whenever I broached the subject, it'd be 'you weren't around in those days, you've got no idea what we went through'...That was the issue we shied away from because my mother said 'you just want a row'.[100]

The mothers were also more rarely perceived as having been politically active than the fathers, and this made it easier to classify them mentally as victims of the regime. This tendency went hand in hand with the prevailing imagery of the *Trümmerfrau* (the woman clearing up the bombsite rubble),

118 THE OTHER '68

or the war widow, both of which emphasized the feminine traits of self-sacrifice and self-denial. Consequently, their mothers' Nazi pasts had far less bearing on the female Sixty-Eighters' self-image than was the case for their male counterparts.

There was certainly no unbridled generational conflict between women in around 1968. Although daughters no longer saw their mothers as suitable role models, they retained their trust in them and talked to them.[101] In a survey carried out in Hamburg, almost a third of 23-year-old women described their mother as their closest confidante, while another fifth cited both parents. This held true both for students and for working women.[102] Four young people in five said that, in their experience, their mothers were 'approachable' and 'emotionally positive'. 'In contrast to their fathers, the twenty-three-year-olds found their mothers less authoritative, much more emotional, more consistent and more approachable…Inflexibility and coldness were rarely attributed to the mothers.' The families of clerical staff, civil servants, and academics were particularly likely to describe their mothers as loving.[103] This contradicts current stereotypes of unfeeling disciplinarians, who had raised their offspring—the Sixty-Eighter generation—with an iron hand. This cohort is sometimes portrayed as 'Hitler's willing mothers' (Sabine Bode). An array of bestsellers published since around 2004 have argued that discipline-obsessed and loveless, overwhelmed mothers scarred the wartime generation's fatherless daughters for life. The only evidence for this falsification of history comes from anecdotal accounts of individual cases.[104]

What was the mother–daughter relationship generally like in the late sixties? What did the mothers and grandmothers of 1968 think about their daughters' and granddaughters' goals, expectations, role models, and parenting styles? Where were the limits to their tolerance when younger women's behaviour did not conform to traditional gender norms? Many voices were answering these questions in the summer of 1968 and, moreover, doing so with the help of a mother–daughter team in a family garden in Cologne. Helga Merker was Hans Thomae's PhD student in Bonn; her mother had broken her ankle, and would spend weeks lying among the flowers in a deckchair, with the bulky reel-to-reel tape recorder at her side. As a favour to her daughter, she was listening to dozens of recorded interviews and painstakingly transcribing them by hand. Her daughter Helga sat upstairs and typed up the transcripts on a portable typewriter. This created 'mountains of written material'—around 4,000 pages—which Helga Merker then categorized, ready for her statistical analysis. Merker considered this 'a pig of a job', but from our modern perspective, her efforts are a boon. The conversations that have come down to us as a result offer unusual insight into the family lives of this intermediate generation. The transcripts include thirty-nine interviews with women aged between 35 and 56, almost all of whom had children who fell into the Sixty-Eighter age bracket. These middle-aged mothers came 'mainly...from the middle social class'. About half of them had elementary schooling to age 14, and the other half had gone on to some further education.[105]

These interviews, which were held in the Cologne-Bonn area between May 1967 and August 1968, took place too early for the women to express their views on the feminist movement. But they spoke in detail about their relationships with their adolescent or adult daughters. Many everyday decisions were negotiated jointly. A mother of two girls wanted to be a 'friend' to them:

> I allow my children a very great deal. After all, I want to hold onto my girls...They get some wishes that we wouldn't have had in the past...And nowadays they go out dancing such a great deal, and they get their hands on a lot of money, which we didn't have.

A woman of 41 compared her family to a democratic forum, where the teenagers were allowed to have a voice, whereas she had not been allowed 'to say a word' as a child:

> In the old days, there was this *Führer* principle...the father is the master of the house. Nowadays in a democracy, there are plenty of masters in the house and young people...today are brought up so that they just speak up, and basically, I don't think that's a bad thing.

The mother of a 25-year-old who was studying at the Pedagogical University stressed that her children were allowed to pick out 'what they wanted to wear...when we just had to be obedient'. Because after all, 'the business of their personal freedom' was very important to teenagers. A Frau Faust, who had been widowed at a young age, also compared her parenting style, which favoured independence and trust, to her own parents' strictness and distantness. 'I am raising my children to be self-reliant. They should learn to deal with problems at a young age, whereas we relied on our parents' advice.' She wanted 'a close and trusting relationship...and to be able to discuss anything with the children. My parents thought that as children it was none of our business.' Frau Seifert, aged 45, urged that 'a child needs freedom too...I leave decisions to my children, I don't give them orders'.[106]

120   THE OTHER '68

All these 35- to 56-year-olds remarked that their own upbringings had been extremely strict. They almost unanimously criticized their parents for how stern they had been. A 44-year-old said:

> Talking now about my youth, I wasn't allowed much, for instance, I didn't have much in my youth except work. My mother kept me pretty strictly, I wasn't allowed to go out either, when I think about our Rita, she's allowed so much more than I was at 18...she goes to the cinema, she goes to parties now and then, which I wasn't allowed to do.

Frau Banse described her own childhood as 'scared, in terms of upbringing': 'Our day just demanded obedience, just don't make a mistake, don't talk back at work, while in comparison young people today get to have a say sometimes.' She had been told point-blank what to wear and when to be home, whereas she liked to let her daughter have a little fun sometimes: 'Today, if my daughter rings and says *Mutti*, I'm having such fun, I'll be late home. Well, why not? I'm fairly generous about that kind of thing. Because that's how the others handle things too.' Similarly, Frau Eichhorn, born in 1925, portrayed her parental home as uncompromising. Her father was in charge, the post and cupboards were supervised, and pocket money was as unimaginable as answering back. There was

> never any conversation at the table. The children had to be quiet...You know, my parents were enthroned, while [today] we sit with the children...We had to ask for everything. And then we were either allowed it or not allowed it. Our children say, I'm going there today, or I'm doing this or I'm doing that...We talk to the children. That's the big difference...And the older children aren't regarded as children anymore, but as adults with equal rights.[107]

Many of them mentioned that their mothers had never played with them and had had no more to do with them than strictly necessary.[108] Once Helga Merker had read all the interviews, she sat down at her little typewriter and wrote: 'Many...study participants criticized the fact that their parents had had too little time for them as children, that it was not uncommon for there to be a major emotional distance between them and their parents, and that they had often felt misunderstood.'

And the results of Helga Merker's statistical analysis of the questionnaires filled in by the interviewees pointed in the same direction. While those aged over 60 preferred strict, controlling childrearing techniques and parental dominance, the group aged 35 to 56 favoured a more partnership-based relationship with their children. The middle generation tended to reject attempts to break a child's self-will, and to veto aggressive behaviour, while most of the over-60s argued for authoritarian intervention.[109] There was a strikingly wide gap between the parenting styles that the different age groups had experienced and those they preferred. The older respondents stated that their own upbringings had been strict, and that they had brought their children up relatively strictly, whereas only 5 per cent of the intermediate generation took a severe approach to parenting their own children.[110]

The middle and older generations were particularly likely to disagree in their views on young people when it came to sexuality and girls' outward appearance. The Sixty-Eighters' grandparents judged them by far stricter standards than their parents.[111] Yet short skirts, fashionable hair styles, smoking, drinking, and partying were the signals that young women in the 1960s used to proclaim their modern attitudes and allegiance to new lifestyles. Almost all the mothers interviewed in Bonn and Cologne talked about discussions along these lines. Their families negotiated compromises that ascribed importance to respectability and frugality, while allowing the daughters a degree of choice within defined limits. Here, their mothers actively differentiated themselves from the grandmothers. 'The parents may still understand that, they can still keep up with them putting on mini-skirts ... but I think the grandparents probably can't go along with that ... after all, that was just impossible in their day', said a 37-year-old mother of two. Frau Fischer stressed what she would 'do differently' from her parents back then: 'well, I'd never tell my children, "you must, you must", in external things that is. I'd give them a bit more free rein, when it comes to clothes, for example, or what they're doing these days with haircuts and all that.' Frau Zabel, a shop assistant and cleaner, sympathized with girls in mini-skirts: 'well, yes, that's how it goes, we always followed the fashions too'. She felt that long hair on men was acceptable too, just so long as it was 'often cut'. She envied the young women of the day, who got all dressed up to go dancing, for their carefree youth, not least because she herself had been raped by Soviet soldiers when she was 19.

> I was born in '25 you know, we went through so much ... so, for me personally there was the business with the Russians, and that happened to lots of others too, so I wouldn't wish that on my children, no way ... If only I could've gone dancing, but like that ... Oh, I'd really have loved to make myself smart.

Frau Hahn, aged 49, declared: 'Well, if I had lovely legs, I'd wear a mini-skirt too. They should wear what they like.' Frau Rottorf spoke fondly of her daughter and her friends: 'They can dress to their own tastes, to the latest fashion. We weren't allowed to [do] what we liked, our parents were stricter. You'd never have been allowed to go out in a short mini-skirt like that.'[112]

There were certainly arguments over the age at which varying degrees of freedom could be allowed, or when girls could start styling themselves with clothes and make-up. Some mothers were stricter than others, such as Frau Langer, whose 15-year-old daughter was not yet allowed to wear perfume. Yet for the most part, these things were negotiated not dictated. Frau Hirsch sewed her daughters' mini-dresses herself, and let them stay out until ten, provided they 'behaved decently' and did not 'slob around'. The 13-year-old daughter of a Frau Angermann was not allowed to 'paint her lips bright red' or 'wear spindly high-heels'. All the same, Frau Angermann was 'much more accommodating' towards her daughter

> in many things than my mother was. My mother would have had a fit if we'd come home with nail polish on when we were 22. I let mine do it because she came and said: I can't shape my fingernails (she plays the violin), all the other kids can shape their fingernails! So I say: well have a go with nail polish then. Well, my mother would never have done a deal like that, she'd have been stubborn.[113]

As a matter of fact, very few young people in those days felt entirely patronized at home. Surveys from the sixties show that in their view, arguments were mainly about how late they were allowed to stay out in the evening. Parents and adolescents might have disagreed over matters of detail, but there was already a prevailing culture of negotiation.[114]

Despite the fact that the Sixty-Eighters' parents were meeting their children halfway, they still had a tendency to express outrage at the abstract 'youth of today' that they knew of from hearsay, or off the television (Figure 5.3). Many parents were haunted by the spectre of big-city 'beatniks', and viewed their own children favourably in comparison.[115] The middle-aged women of Cologne and Bonn were sometimes extremely critical of female apprentices or schoolgirls whom they had encountered only fleetingly. A woman of 56 complained about the trainees in her business: 'you hear about some girls who drink six, seven glasses of beer in the evening.... they have no (other) interests at all, just going out, getting together with boys, smoking'. But she made an exception for a 20-year-old woman and her own son, whom she

Figure 5.3 A young woman in hot pants and a mini-skirted member of the middle generation: on Maximilianstraße, Bonn, 1970

knew better. Frau Anz was just as horrified by 'the stuff that goes on in those beat clubs, they show that on TV sometimes, it doesn't bear looking at, it's shameful, truly shameful, the way those girls behave'. Despite this, she added: 'well, thank God they're not all like that' before bringing up the example of her own daughter, a primary school teacher, who had turned out exceptionally well.[116]

The closer the personal contact, the greater the tolerance. Mothers whose own children were in their 20s were far more inclined than single women or those aged over 60 to be forgiving of the young. Elderly men who had little contact with teenagers were the most prejudiced against them.[117]

The mothers of the Sixty-Eighter generation were thus living in a grey area between traditional and modern lifestyles when it came to fashion, consumerism, and parenting. But how firmly were they still clinging to the housewifely ideal? We know that in families with several children born around 1940, sons were given preferential treatment in everyday life, and also had to deal with greater pressure from educational expectations. In three quarters of families, boys had to help out considerably less with the housework than girls. Almost every young man at that time considered this a 'natural' privilege, but only one young woman in four shared that view.[118] When

124 THE OTHER '68

the Bonn survey asked the mothers who treated their children so unequally 'should boys and girls be brought up differently?', they tended to give highly inconsistent answers. They would almost always initially insist that you should not differentiate, but then go on to suggest that girls should be prepared for domesticity, and boys for the competition of professional life. Frau Russ, for example, said: 'No, I don't think I'd make a big difference there... Yes, for a boy, I'd definitely attach more importance to him getting trained for a good job if he had the opportunity. I mean, a girl can always get through life without an *Abitur*.'[119] According to Frau Zabel, a boy needed more pocket money than a girl, and could come home later, so that he'd be able to ask a girlfriend out to a café now and then. By contrast, a girl needed to 'help out with the drying up because she'll need to do that later in life' (or so said Frau Märker). Frau Gröpsch expected 'a girl to isolate herself more, there's no worry about a boy having a bit more freedom' and 'a girl to be clean and tidy, where [you can] let that pass a bit more with a boy'.[120] The vast majority of mothers questioned emphasized that young women needed stronger encouragement in moderation, thrift, and helping out at home. Despite this, they no longer wanted to direct their daughters solely towards a future within the family. When these middle-aged women filled in a questionnaire on the role of the housewife, they were already significantly less likely than the over-60s to defend it. The younger the woman questioned, the less she agreed with statements such as 'too many women forget that a mother's place is at home'.[121]

The 35- to 56-year-olds' aspirations for their daughters included training for a career that would enable them to earn a little extra money, while not disputing the husband's role as the main breadwinner. Frau Anz's view was typical:

So long as they don't have children, I'm in favour of them working, but as soon as the children come along, you shouldn't leave them to somebody else, just to earn money. That always has an effect later on. Otherwise, a girl nowadays should definitely have a profession, that's a necessity. The husband can easily have an accident these days, with cars, or some such thing, and then the wife won't be dependent, then she can earn her own living.

Having a profession was important in case of emergency, agreed Frau Weser, whose 'own experience' had taught her 'that you often end up with a very urgent need for the trade you learnt'. All the same, she qualified this by saying that 'if you can't manage it financially... then the boy should definitely get the better training in terms of a profession'.[122] The Sixty-Eighters' mothers saw paid employment as an additional role that they wanted to be open to their daughters at certain phases in their lives, on top of their work within the family. Within certain limits, these mothers welcomed half-day working, but dismissed the idea of women with children having a full-time job. This held true even of those who worked full-time themselves, or who looked back on their own years in work as the best time of their lives.[123]

It is thus hardly surprising that, even in the late sixties, one young woman in eight still complained of feeling patronized over her choice of profession.[124] The differences between women in different age groups in those days were enormous. Women born before 1910 had seldom had a clear professional ambition on leaving school (only 7 per cent). Their choices were almost entirely limited to a few, very similar jobs, generally related to caring or the home, and thus reputed to improve their marriage prospects. These included working as a nursery teacher, dry nurse or nanny, laundress, dressmaker, or seamstress, or doing ironing. Similarly, only around 10 per cent of the next age group, those born between 1910 and 1930, had a clear idea of their future working lives. These women, however, could at least contemplate a broader spectrum of options, including teaching and working as a laboratory assistant, office clerk, or sales assistant. By contrast, the situation for the women born after 1938, which included the Sixty-Eighters, was completely different. Choosing a profession was 'taken for granted when planning their futures, either as a transitional phase before marriage, or even seen as their purpose in life'. For 43 per cent of them, a detailed career plan had emerged during their final school year. Meanwhile, 60 per cent had been given complete freedom of choice by their parents, compared to only 10 per cent of women then aged over 50.[125]

Many young women in the Sixty-Eighter generation experienced arguments at home over their educational and professional goals, especially if they aspired to higher education. Their accounts suggest that they generally had to overcome their fathers' scepticism with their mothers' assistance. Dagmar Seehuber, for example, was one of four children to a metalworker: 'My father's view was that it would be better for me to learn a trade than to move to the *Realschule*, given that girls would end up getting married anyway. But my mother was at least able to get him to agree to me going to a *Mittelschule*.' Frau Neuer, born in 1940, was one of five children whose parents owned their own farm. 'My father in particular assumed that I would marry and therefore didn't need any better education. I had to fight my way through, and it really was a fight. My father even said that he hoped I failed the exams.'[126] A Frau Kasten, who was born in 1948, got to university despite her father, and with help from her mother. 'My mother didn't go to university, which she always very much regretted... My father had four children... When it came to me, he thought I didn't need a profession, that he might be able to save himself that [cost].'[127] In better-off families with a tradition of university education, this path was seen as more natural for the daughters, but even here, the father sometimes applied the brakes. Karin Adrian's 'father was opposed to me studying fine art, so I opted for art history, as a kind of compromise'. All the same, Adrian complained that her father continued to denigrate educated women as 'butch' and 'bluestockings' and continually 'blocked' her 'independent thoughts'.[128]

The mothers often backed their adolescent daughters because of their own lack of educational opportunities. A member of the *Frankfurter Weiberrat* emphasized that her mother, a housewife who had left school at the age of 14, 'absolutely' wanted her to get a good education. 'She had always really regretted that she hadn't been able to do that.'[129] Missed chances were a major issue for the mothers interviewed in Bonn too. When asked what she would do differently from her own parents, Frau Krause, born 1912, said: 'Well, I'd have given my children the opportunity to have a longer education than I did.' She felt that her lack of education was a 'deficit' and 'rather a bitter pill'. Her parents would probably have had the means, but not the vision to encourage her. Frau Gröpsch also felt that she had had 'a very bad youth': 'I didn't get a trade, which I'd have liked to learn.' Instead, she had only 'learnt to run a household'.[130] 'Parents used to say that a girl doesn't need higher education... whereas I told myself that a girl needs to go to secondary school too', said 50-year-old Frau Weser.[131] Frau Esser, aged 42, enjoyed doing homework with her daughter Rosi on the grounds that 'I'm learning along with her. You'd have liked to do that in the past too. But it just wasn't like that, that wasn't an option.' Meanwhile, Frau Gutsche argued that even a housewife needed 'a good education... to be able to help her children':

> In the old days, if you told your mother that a girl is training as a secondary school teacher or wants to go to university, they used to say: girls don't study, girls get married. Yes, nowadays, that's taken for granted. And it's exactly the same if a girl these days says: education is just as important. That's my opinion, too.[132]

In the 1960s, Bonn psychologist Ursula Lehr conducted 500 biographical interviews, asking women about their working lives. She found that 24 per cent of women who had left school at 14, and even 37 per cent of those who had passed their middle-school leaving exams, regretted not having attended a higher-level school.[133] In 1968, many mothers' sense of having been cheated of their schooling, collided with a society where education for girls already had wide political support and public demand. Families on an average income could now afford to support several children through their *Abitur* or even a university degree. With the wind of social change in their sails, young women could now often (but not always) learn a profession or study at university despite their fathers' or grandparents' conservative views.[134]

The fact that young women in around 1968 had often had a longer period in education and recourse to better professions gave them the chance to define their own lives, independently of their families. This set them clearly apart from their mothers and grandmothers. Deferring their own needs to the good of the family was a dominant theme in biographical interviews with women aged over 60, as the team at the Bonn Department of Psychology soon discovered during their study of ageing. The catalogue of psychological response patterns (*Daseinstechniken*), developed by principal investigator Hans Thomae, initially contained no match for this behaviour. The Bolsa team had to draw up a distinct additional characteristic, which they nicknamed the 'Assisi category'—alluding to the self-denial and altruistic love for which Saint Francis of Assisi was canonized.[135] The women on the team had pushed for this change. Twenty-nine-year-old Ingrid Tismer-Puschner was spending time face-to-face with the old ladies in the Bonn interview rooms, and she recalled the way she 'fought for it, for what we called the Assisi category, cutting back on your own needs for the benefit of others', to be recognized as a new response pattern. She had 'strongly defended' the need to make this addition to the catalogue of behaviours 'because [she] had spoken to so many women' who always acted unselfishly 'in familial situations'. Tismer was impressed by the 'humility' of the old women she talked to: 'very many of them,...who often didn't have a lot of schooling...seriously impressed me' precisely because they took a back seat and 'accepted' their limited opportunities in life.[136]

This tendency not to obtrude often resulted in the generation of grandmothers holding back on political matters in everyday life. While the husbands enjoyed debating with their friends and colleagues, and allowed themselves to have opinions, the wives would retreat. Housework meant that the old women had less free time than the retired men. They were less likely to read the newspapers, less interested in the news, and went to church more often.[137] During the 'exploration' of 71-year-old Eugenie Theiler, wife of a lower-level civil servant, Bonn psychologist Maria Renner noted that 'she appeared very modest and reticent'. She was not at all interested in world events or politics: 'I prefer to leave all that to my husband.' Hanna Hahnert, a housewife born in 1895, even wanted to repeal women's suffrage: 'I'd leave voting to the men. I'd exclude the women altogether...Politically, they're just not educated to be able to judge.' Overall, the women aged over 60 had considerably less interest in politics than the men of the same age.[138] There was also a clear divide between women of different ages in this respect. An opinion poll found that as many as 43 per cent of women over 60 agreed with the statement that 'politics is men's work', compared to only 28 per cent of women under 30.[139] This apolitical stance among the elderly may have been rooted both in conscious deference to the husbands, and in a lack of self-confidence.

The older the respondents, the more they were inclined to criticize their fellow women for perceived poor public behaviour. In a 1966 poll on manners, the age differences were stark. Over two thirds of those aged 60 and above disapproved of women who went shopping in shorts, cuddled up to the driver in a car, or smoked. Only 37 per cent of 16- to 29-year-olds shared those views. Fifty-eight per cent of the elderly disliked mini-skirts, compared to only 23 per cent of young people. On all these issues of behaviour, the opinions of the two intermediate age groups (those aged 30 to 44, and the 45- to 59-year-olds) were in a range almost exactly at the mid-point between those of the grandparents' and grandchildren's generations.[140]

The Sixty-Eighters' parents were thus considerably less strict on lifestyle questions than their grandparents. Nevertheless, many young women criticized their mothers for their ritualistic diffidence. They blamed their mothers for a level of self-effacement that they perceived as servility and depersonalization. To Helke Sander of the Berlin *Aktionsrat* 'our mothers were creepy...There was something submissive about women that we didn't like...We began to hate that humility.'[141] Dagmar Seehuber found her mother 'utterly indifferent to politics'[142] and Karin Adrian's 'mother didn't even actually exist as a personality because she did everything that my father said.'[143] Similarly, Theresia Weiner-Rat, born in 1953, criticized her mother for 'the model that entrusts everything to the men, right, and then no longer criticizes [anything] and predominantly says "yes"'.[144]

At that time, the principal difference between the life goals of mothers and daughters lay in the shift from 'existing for others' to the search for 'a life of one's own'.[145] The value women placed on a career was changing. Women's lives were becoming 'professionalized'; that is, women born after around 1940 were increasingly likely to interpret and narrate their life stories through a timeline of education, career, and retirement. On top of this, increasing

THE FEMALE SIXTY-EIGHT   129

numbers of women worked throughout their lives, rather than just for certain periods.[146] For the Sixty-Eighters in particular, this change went hand in hand with their explicit dissociation from their mothers' examples. For them, wanting to do things 'differently from mum' meant turning away from external control and submissiveness. 'I needed role models. My mother couldn't have been one for me; I didn't want to live the way she did', explained Erika Runge, born 1939. Runge's book, for which she interviewed seventeen German women about their life stories, went on to sell a sensational 66,000 copies between 1969 and 1978. Her aim had been to 'collect examples of successful emancipation' so as to 'encourage' other women to leave the path trodden by their mothers.[147]

Social scientist Christine Thon interviewed grandmothers, mothers, and daughters from West German families after the turn of the millennium. These conversations show how deeply this message penetrated into society. The Sixty-Eighters she spoke to continually compared themselves to their mothers. Marlies Arndt, for example, who was born 1947, had 'internalized [a need] for some kind of employment' by the time she left school:

> At any rate, I knew what I didn't want…I didn't want to turn out like my mother. I was pretty clear about that; that I didn't want to sit around at home and…look after the children and wait for a husband to eventually get back in the evening.

Similarly, Monika Cadenberg, born in 1949, dismissed her mother as 'just a mum' and resolved: 'You're never doing that…that role…she had to do all that and never got so much as a thank you.' For that generation, the housewife-and-mother acted as the epitome of the traditional gender-specific expectations that they sought to shake off.[148] All the same, this negative foil was considerably exaggerated because, in reality, the contrast between mothers and daughters was rather more graduated. Monika Cadenberg, for example, was glossing over the fact that she herself had taken a career break of over ten years because of her children, and that she had changed jobs partly on family grounds. Meanwhile, her mother, Grete Claussen, had in fact worked at different points, having been a cook, a Red Cross nurse, and worked in agriculture. But she had played this employment down, so as not to cast doubt on her husband's ability. She never described her contribution as an individual achievement, but always as part of ensuring the livelihood of the family unit—a euphemistic interpretation that her daughter took at face value. In the same way, in her interview, Marlies Arndt drew a contrast between her mother's family life and her own professional career, largely overlooking the fact that she had also been a housewife when her children were young, while her mother, Gertrud Aschauer, had worked several years as an accountant and supermarket branch manager.[149]

Thus, the switch towards seeing a working life as compatible with a family had begun a generation before the protests, yet the Sixty-Eighters' mothers had refrained from going on the offensive with demands. Instead, they had only cautiously increased the scope of their professional options without breaking away from the idealized 'breadwinner' model of marriage. The grandmother generation frequently strove to give their daughters certain resources to take along on the road to emancipation: by advocating partnership as a basis for family relations, for example, or urging improved schooling or professional education for them.[150] As our snapshot from 1967/68 shows, the next generation of mothers and daughters frequently compromised in matters of dress and leisure activities, and the mothers were far less strict than their own upbringing had been. Having suffered the curtailment of their own educational or professional options, they wanted to make it possible for their daughters to have a dual role with a family and a career. All the same, the majority of this middle generation still embraced a gender-specific model of phased employment in the course of life, which involved leaving the workforce on the birth of children. This means that the in-between generation was already halfway to equal rights.

The female Sixty-Eight was shaped by women who clearly distinguished themselves from their mothers in public, yet mustered understanding for them in private. Young women saw their mothers as a symbol of an enforced existence as housewives, of self-sacrifice and depersonalization, of domination by authoritarian fathers, of the impositions made by unpaid and unrecognized caregiving work—yet the image that they constructed in this way did not actually correspond precisely to their own mothers. And while the Sixty-Eighters carefully cultivated a contrast with their mothers (while practically never referring to Nazism), subconsciously they had more in common with the generation before them than they wanted to admit. Even the cohort born around and after 1940 lived the model of phased working, and had the traditional rites of female modesty deeply ingrained within them.

One reason why the women's movement's part in Sixty-Eight in West Germany remained so scantly regarded for decades is that almost all the women involved habitually trivialized their role as the vanguard of the historic change in values. Where many men worked diligently on myth-making, and achieved a high level of media exposure, almost all the women deliberately relativized their contribution. Asked whether they saw themselves as Sixty-Eighters, former activists tended to give negative or doubtful answers. Annette Schwarzenau, for instance, stressed that she was 'never a feminist'; she knew that she did not 'represent the Sixty-Eighters' because of her 'lack of theoretical knowledge'. Anke Brunn insisted that she had 'not been actively involved' in Sixty-Eight in Cologne because she was driven by a critique of the image of the family that 'was easy pickings. That has relatively little to do with Sixty-Eight. Sixty-Eight in the narrower sense was a purely male movement.'[151] SDS women downplayed the women's rebellion as a 'phenomenon' of a 'white-collar culture' (Annemarie Tröger) and 'more of a hobby than a field of work' (Georgia Tornow).[152] Women's yearbooks frequently anonymized the contributions of individual authors—a sure-fire way of preventing them from ascending from trailblazers to stars.[153] At a panel discussion held in June 1988 on the role of women in the rebellion, chair Halina Bendkowski declared that although the newspapers were selling feminism as the sole major outcome of the student revolt, 'the protagonists of the women's movement were the only ones who were less than pleased about that'. The women on the panel, all champions of the movement, agreed with her. Silvia Bovenschen deplored 'these peculiar acrobatics of memory that are now demanded of us', and admitted to a 'strong tendency to run away' from public appearances. Sigrid Damm-Rüger turned 'against the mythologizing of the volley of tomatoes and the women's movement at that time'. Sibylle Plogstedt regretted that they had 'never even attempted to arrange a meet-up of former SDS women where we could work through our own history'. The media had never 'discovered a retrospective interest in the women' and nor had they 'themselves ever again formulated an interest in telling their own history'.[154]

By effacing themselves in the approved, feminine, Assisi manner, the protagonists of the women's movement further enlarged the blind spots in the media narrative around Sixty-Eight. They left the myth-making to the men and witnessed male ringleaders such as Dutschke being given celebrity status while 'the women suddenly disappeared, despite being forcefully involved'. 'I'm sure that we gave others guidance. But we certainly acted less conceitedly than some of the men', said Susanne Schunter-Kleemann. As a result, women such as Sigrid Fronius and Sigrid Damm-Rüger 'no longer even appear in the index' to books on this period, despite the fact that, until 1967, they were better known at the Freie Universität Berlin than Dutschke.[155]

The mass media's narrow focus on key figures like Dutschke, Krahl, and Cohn-Bendit meant that the feminist awakening in the late sixties went underestimated by contemporary observers and historians alike. It was

132   THE OTHER '68

considered in isolation, or viewed as an inessential by-product of the rebellion. There are also repeated arguments over whether the 'second wave' of the German women's movement has its origins in 1968: were the women's groups of that time really significant enough to have inspired the rapidly burgeoning feminist movement of the 1970s that shifted the focus onto new areas? The internal divisions within the feminist camp and the fact that the early women's groups were still naïve in terms of theory, and comparatively socially exclusive, also go some way towards explaining the row over the Sixty-Eight origin myth.[156]

In fact, the women's movement in West Germany readjusted itself after 1971. Inspired by ideas from abroad, they now set their sights on women's bodily and sexual autonomy, and on campaigning against the ban on abortion, a shift that guaranteed major media attention. After her 'We've had Abortions' magazine campaign in 1971, activist Alice Schwarzer became the star of the West German women's movement. In 1975, she upped the ante with her book on 'The Small Difference and its Big Consequences', which spoke clearly on the sexual exploitation and dissatisfaction of women. Now the media did develop an intense interest in the women's movement, although they focused more on sexuality than on the feminists' demands. The first longer article on Alice Schwarzer in *Der Spiegel*, for example, informed the reader that she had been deflowered at the age of 19, that she had not masturbated as a girl, and that she'd been attacked as 'Miss Hängetitt' (Miss Slopy Tit) and 'Schwanzab-Schwarzer' (Dick-Off Schwarzer). Her aims were merely mentioned in passing. News magazine stories on the movement merited bare breasts on the covers and headlines such as 'Great Erotic Mother' or 'Women Loving Women'. Articles on lesbians or the quest for the vaginal orgasm were clearly better sellers than debates on gender pay gaps, unequal division of childcare, and men ducking household chores.[157]

Furthermore, this new concentration on the campaign for abortion rights allowed the women's movement to work in temporary solidarity with women's groups and associations from beyond the New Left. Millions of women of every age and from every social background were suffering under the ban on abortion. Reform-minded and moderate women were therefore now working together with those who were more radical. From 1971 in Bonn, for example, the AKE, a new 'women's forum', and a group close to the Monday Club called the 'Bad Godesberg Working Group for Emancipation and Equal Rights' organized joint actions against paragraph 218.[158] In the mid-seventies, the Monday Club also invited more radical speakers, such as Jutta Menschik and Alice Schwarzer. When Schwarzer went on a reading tour with her book, the

Monday Club invited her to speak at the Bonn-Bad Godesberg civic centre, and every seat in the house was sold. The moderate Hannelore Fuchs of the Monday Club found Schwarzer's particular emphasis on women's sexual oppression somehow 'scandalous', yet 'also emboldening'. Fuchs criticized Schwarzer for 'smashing everything to pieces'. In turn, Schwarzer would have found the Monday Club under Fuchs's leadership too soft. Yet despite these internal tensions, by the mid-seventies, they were working together.[159] Likewise, it was only then that more stable feminist institutions began to develop. In Bonn, for instance, women's shelter initiatives, a women's bookshop, a women's band, and a women's *Stammtisch* (a group meeting regularly to discuss ideas over a beer) grew up from 1977 onwards; as of 1978, there was a women's café; as of 1979, a women's theatre group and a lesbians' group, while the women's shelter also finally came into existence that year.[160]

So was it in fact the seventies, rather than Sixty-Eight, that represented the feminist structural break in the history of West German society, as is sometimes claimed? Were the female Sixty-Eighters only the 'non-essential beginning' of a women's movement that would not find its 'essential' issue until 1971? Even in the anniversary year of 2018, *Emma* magazine (editor-in-chief Alice Schwarzer) argued that the tomato-throwing and the women's groups of the late 1960s could only be considered a 'pre-spring' that had reached nobody beyond the 'exceptional women' in the 'student ghetto'. The movement's 'avalanche' had only been set in motion in 1971.[161] It is worth noting that this dispute over the timing of the emergence of the Women's Liberation Movement and the relationship between feminist activism and Sixty-Eight is mirrored in debates over the movement in France and Western Europe more widely. In these settings, too, the dispute is centred on such questions as whether this wave of feminism arose as part of, or from the ashes of 1968; whether it arose because of, despite of, or in opposition to 1968.[162] Although historians tend to distance themselves from 'a competitive struggle to identify the first, or the truest, feminists',[163] it is nevertheless important not to obscure the concurrence and interdependency of developments within the West German students' and women's movements.

It was undoubtedly not until the 1970s that the feminist movement achieved a huge social reach and broad media echo in the Federal Republic. It gained greater theoretical nuance, more diverse groupings, and greater numbers of campaigns and institutions. Yet the central scope of the new women's movement had already been formulated in around 1968: the utopian desire for change, the expansion of politics to take in the private sphere, and the establishment of women as political players. Similarly, the provocative methods of protest, the informal, separatist women's groups, and the *Kinderläden*, which were later emulated everywhere, date back to Sixty-Eight.[164] There is no reason to assume that the so-called second wave of the women's movement in Germany only began in 1971.

The female Sixty-Eight brought something qualitatively new into the revolt: it revolutionized gender roles and empowered women to take independent decisions about their own lives. The objectives of the male-led, mass-mediated revolt—the struggle against authoritarianism, fascism, capitalism, and imperialism, and the striving for greater participation from below—aligned in part with those of the women, as did its forms of protest. But while the male-dominated, traditionally political side of the revolt came to nothing in the long term, the female Sixty-Eight gained momentum and potency by changing the self-perception and ways of life of women in every social class. This broad and widespread impact was due to the accelerated change in gender roles. Ideological, radical, and often painful experiments, aimed at breaking the boundaries of the bourgeois family and breadwinner model of marriage, created learning curves and led over time to gradual change in everyday family life. Women went on the march through the institutions of marriage, the family, and work, aiming for a less gender-specific division of tasks. Their undertaking was not wholly new. It was built on the partial successes of preceding generations, and decades of increasing employment and improving education for women. But the female Sixty-Eighters formed an advance guard, accelerating and radicalizing the existing developments, because women now dared to step into the limelight and arm themselves with theory. Feminist ideas became the wind in the movement's sails.

The angry young women, both inside and outside the SDS, who met in Berlin, Frankfurt, Bonn, Cologne, and elsewhere to discuss the oppression of women belong to the political generation of the Sixty-Eighters. They would later speak considerably less than the men about their generational identity, and the media never hyped them up as a generation. All the same, they were the founders of the 'new' West German women's movement, which then expanded in the 1970s, taking in new groups and taking up new issues.

For this reason, we need to redefine the historiographical concept of the political generation. Until now, scholars have thought of political generations as masculine, elitist, and highly educated—whether the Sixty-Eighters are being cast in distinction to the Forty-Fivers, 'Thirty-Three-ers', or 'Wilhelmines'. The formative experience that creates a generation has generally been traced back to shared, public political action, yet it is in fact bestowed retrospectively by media discussion of these experiences—a process of working together on the myth, a public and collective defence of a particular interpretation that gives meaning to countless individual biographies.[165] The media discourse on generational experiences typically narrows the focus onto recognizable idols and patterns, all of which have masculine connotations: father–son conflict, the male revolutionary, Nazi and anti-Nazi, pioneer, Sixty-Eighter. By contrast, if we turn our attention to the women, a more adequate concept of the political generation emerges: one that is formed directly by life-changing experiences. These experiences can be equally well located in the private sphere, and do not need to be limited to the educated upper classes. The lived experience, not the discussion, of the long sixties then takes centre stage; media discourse loses importance. Eva-Maria Silies has recently argued that the 'pill' was a 'quiet' experience, yet one that defined a generation, which unified a 'majority of young women in the sixties and seventies, and thus a much larger proportion of the cohort in comparison' to the men that we generally think of as Sixty-Eighters.[166] It was not just the 'pill', however; the many private battles for a more equal life made the female Sixty-Eighters part of a political generation. Given that the private became political, the Sixty-Eighters were the first political generation in German history that included men *and* women. Many men became Sixty-Eighters by participating in media debates and thus constructing their own biographies around a generational myth. Many women became Sixty-Eighters by changing themselves, their families, and thus their society.

6

Variations on Sexual Liberation

It was a muggy, rainy Wednesday afternoon in April 1968 and a large group of elderly people were being served coffee from chrome pots, apple cake, and cream. The rubber trees, net curtains, and antique-style wall paintings in the Konditorei Müller (Figure 6.1) clearly suited the ladies and gentlemen down to the ground. They had just finished their sessions in the Department of Psychology, directly opposite the café. Just as the Bolsianers were settling down to enjoy their cakes, a schoolboy and his friends came in to buy sweet palmier pastries from the counter. Seven-year-old Holger lived around the corner and passed the Konditorei on his way home from school. He was making polite conversation with Frau Müller, who sent her very best regards to his mother. Barely ten years later, the café and patisserie would close to make way for a 'Dr. Müllers Sexshop', part of the Beate Uhse chain; this time the homeward journey for Holger and his friends, then studying for the *Abitur*, featured wisecracks: what on earth had got into the Müllers in their old age?[1]

One of the old ladies seated on the bench had been paying careful attention to the conversation with the schoolboy. Children *did* still have very polite and respectful manners, nodded 72-year-old Frau Tänzer appreciatively. She considered 'young people as a whole' perfectly nice, yes 'a hundred per cent, actually', just 'not that drop-out rubbish'. This seemed to reanimate the group. Everyone present had just had to go through a barrage of psychological tests, including questionnaires on parenting styles and the youth of the day. Now everyone had something to say. 'We never used to see the things they get to see these days...in the cinema...on the television...on the street...In the old days you'd never have seen a young couple kissing right there on the street', insisted Frau Eugel. She pitied the young people for their lack of emotional security: 'Advertising for example...it's constantly crashing in on them, isn't it.' A 74-year-old Frau Mutschmann, who lived in a residential home, got quite agitated: 'When I watch [them] in the park by us, they're not embarrassed by anyone...It doesn't always stop at sport between boys and girls, to put it bluntly, things are terrible these days.' Now the men got involved too. Herr Stapel, a skilled worker who was approaching 80, looked out from behind the sports section of the *BILD* newspaper: in the old days, really

Figure 6.1 Interior of the Konditorei Müller, c. 1960

nobody had 'canoodled' on the street. 'That never used to happen, really very young couples and girls walking down the street arm in arm in broad daylight', agreed Herr Konstantin, who had been a senior construction supervisor. Television was corrupting the youngsters with 'these films and that sexual education'. And as for the magazines, fulminated former civil servant August Brackenbusch: 'What they're selling is all about sex. And young people aren't exactly blocks of ice, they tell themselves that's how it has to be.' There was even 'a publisher that sends out pictures of naked people—they have the nastiest stuff on offer'. Sitting beside him was retired cobbler Herr Wieder, who backed him up. 'These days they're smart, know the facts of life, from 16 up, but they don't know all the consequences', he boomed. 'When we were that age, nobody even talked about that stuff', and the girls were 'all buttoned right up'. But he whispered enviously to the man beside him: 'compared to us, young people these days are living in paradise...they get a load more out of life than us'.[2]

While the older ladies and gentlemen were chatting over apple cake in this genteel ambience, the young psychologists were only a few metres away, across the street, working on the interviews they had just conducted. Ms Tismer-Puschner was handwriting a character study of Frau Mutschmann, who had been preceded by 'something of a reputation'. The Bolsa team had been 'rather looking forward to her appearance' because the lady had set her old people's home in a tizzy and split it into two camps as a result of a libel suit. The young psychology graduate described 'a slight, delicate, simply-dressed, little old lady', wearing 'meticulously looked-after, old-fashioned clothing with old family jewels—her hair was put up into a tiny little bun, topped by a very correct, but ladylike, diminutive summer hat'. The old woman had immediately started to speak about the trial and the strain associated with it, but had asked her 'to turn off the tape so that nobody else could hear it'.

One of her friends in the home had been 'attacked' in the corridor one evening, but the lady had been unable to see the attacker. But it had definitely been 'the Jewess from downstairs'. 'This lady with "curly black hair", who always "dressed herself up to the nines", kept visiting the man in the room next door and often staying until the early hours. "That's just not right", especially, "the noises you hear"', she objected. As the couple were not married, you 'really couldn't . . . stand by and watch!' Frau Mutschmann was a spinster but liked to 'list a whole series of admirers—even now, she was in contact with a gentleman from her teenage dance class, he still admired her and sent her little gifts', of which she was visibly proud. She claimed that the only reason she had never married was that she had been unable to choose.[3]

Sitting in the office next door was Tismer-Puschner's colleague Manfred Schreiner, spooling forward and back through his tape to ensure that the transcript of his conversation with August Brackenbusch was accurate to the word. Brackenbusch, who was in his late 60s, had become so emotional while sketching out his life story that it had been entirely impossible to make notes. Schreiner too had been shaken by his volunteer's sudden surge of emotion. This was why he was now spending the afternoon on a multi-page transcript that was not immediately necessary for the Bolsa investigations. In his youth, Herr Brackenbusch had entered a Roman Catholic monastery but had later left because he did not wish to take a lifetime vow of chastity. He had subsequently worked for various government agencies, and eventually found a wife through an ad. The relationship proved a fiasco that ended in illness for both, and separation ('the marriage was a disaster from the first day—couldn't satisfy her sexually on the wedding night. She cried hysterically, demanded too much sexually'). In answer to Schreiner asking if anything in his life had been a particular obstacle to him, Brackenbusch said:

I could say that, but I wouldn't like to speak about it. These are such intimate things...I'm ashamed of myself...I've been approached on the subject mainly in these last years. A tenant caused me such difficulties about it that I gave her notice. I couldn't put up with it any longer, all over the neighbourhood, people were saying and suspecting that I might be a 175er. That got me so down. That is the reason that I've become very reticent in everything, that I don't get involved with anything anymore. I feel like a second-class human being...It's really terrible, really awful. I feel it in my own body, the way they look at one. I get told that by my son's wife...I've always bottled that up inside me, I could only talk about it at confession. I'm utterly convinced that some people might still be alive if it wasn't for that paragraph [175 of the criminal code, which criminalized sex between men]. I can't tell that to just anyone, I have to carry that all myself, but I hear people saying I'm a 175er. That's why [I] ended up deciding not to care about anyone anymore. Now I'm permanently left on my own.

A doctor called me perverted. He told me I should get myself a girl... Grandfather and Grandmother were cousins, I'm the victim, the fact that I'm not sexually inclined the way I ought to be...It's good that I had a religious upbringing, or I wouldn't have been able to bear it. Father confessor says, bear your cross in patience. Why am I inclined that way? I can't help it. Carried this cross all my life. My body is nothing but a burden to me. I despise my body. I'll be glad when it's over. If I hadn't had religion, I'd already have made an end to it.[4]

The word 'homosexual' was never spoken that afternoon, nor was any term such as 'gay', yet both interviewer and interviewee knew exactly what it was about. The overall character study that the 27-year-old researcher would later compile on Herr Brackenbusch was sympathetic. Schreiner described his subject as 'seriously depressed', lonely, hard of hearing, and plagued by heart problems. His life had been 'nothing but disappointment' as a result of his 'suffering and cross [to bear], homosexuality' and his failed marriage. His Catholic faith had been his 'only support'. He felt cast out of society: 'he believes his neighbours to be gossiping about him, saying that he is homosexual. A charge against which he cannot defend himself.'[5]

The Bolsa study was designed to omit everything pertaining to sexuality. The conversation guidelines, questionnaires, and encoding instructions consistently skipped the subject.[6] All the same, people forged ahead with telling their personal accounts—and fascinated the young psychologists, whose handwritten notes often talked about the participants' sexual morality. On Wednesday afternoons in the year 1967/68, the Bolsianers were asked to talk about their attitudes towards young people. And almost all of them took this as an invitation to discuss the timing of sex education and first relationships. Most of the older men and women initially resorted to the kind of stereotypical remarks that they'd shared over apple cake at Café Müller. In the group, they reassured each other of the disgracefulness of an excess of nudity in the media and on the street. They felt shocked by public displays of affection. There was something almost mantra-like about their insistence on respectability in appearance, as far as clothes, physical posture, and hairstyles were concerned. Yet the pensioners responded differently when they were in the consultation room, alone with the investigator. Here, in hours of conversation, they admitted to private concerns that, for all their adherence to a strict code of sexual morals, also hinted at the personal suffering and familial conflicts that lay behind the façade. Like Frau Mutschmann and Herr Brackenbusch, they could only imagine sex within marriage, and saw it as indispensable to its fulfilment—yet this had not necessarily made them happy. Some, like Herr Weider, were sure that the youth of today learnt the facts of life far too young. Yet there were discernible hints of how difficult it had been to manage their first encounters without the necessary prior knowledge. They also often disclosed, with sadness, that children or grandchildren had had shotgun weddings, with a baby on the way.

Spring and summer 1968 have gone down in the history books as the period of the attempted assassination of Rudi Dutschke, the Easter riots this prompted, and the increasing radicalization of the New Left in the universities. This same period is consistently described as the initial spark for the 'sexual revolution'. This is classically seen as a 'turning point', whereby the fifties were stuffy and repressed, and it was only the late sixties and their wild hedonism that ushered in fresh air, tolerance, and liberation. Pre-marital sex, adultery, gayness, porn, nudes in magazines, the 'pill', and frequent changes of partner were suddenly said to be permitted and even 'hip'. The Sixty-Eighters' attack on bourgeois morality supposedly led to the seventies as the high point of sexual liberation, in the course of which such traditional values as religion, marriage, and the family crumbled irretrievably. Within a few years, West German legislators and courts decriminalized homosexuality and abortion, made divorce easier, and gave up on prohibiting the commercial sales of pornography and contraceptives. While one side complained about the loss of morals and decency, the other celebrated the increase in pleasure and liberalization.[7]

More recent historical scholarship has, however, explored the links between Sixty-Eight and the sexual revolution in West Germany more closely, and appended large question marks to the catchy narrative of the stuffy morality of the 1950s and revolutionary mores of the 1960s. Dagmar Herzog, Sybille Steinbacher, Elizabeth Heineman, and others have highlighted the ways in which mass consumerism, market forces, and American sexological research began to impact on lived sexuality across society at large well before the rise of late-1960s activism. 'The massive transformation of the sexual landscape of Europe in the 1960s-1970s' extended beyond Germany and had multiple roots.[8] But how was the generational conflict in around 1968 linked to disagreement over morals and decency? Did divergent attitudes towards sexuality fan the flames of political discord between old and young? We can take Bonn as an instance where it is possible to compare the views of three generations—young students, their parents, and their grandparents—on sexual matters.

As late as July 1968, sex and politics were clearly distinct concerns for Bonn's students. When the University of Bonn celebrated its 150th anniversary on 10 July, the politics took place on the first floor of the main building, while the petting happened on the ground floor. Upstairs, there were scuffles between the police and demonstrators, led by Hannes Heer. The SDS staged a sit-in, aimed at blocking entry to the Greek guests of honour, invited to the celebrations by the Rector, after which they took a battering ram to the doors to the banqueting hall. Around thirty to forty activists targeted the representatives of the Greek military dictatorship with slogans such as: '*Faschistenschweine groß und klein geben sich ein Stelldichein*' (Fascist pigs some small, some big, on a date with uni prigs). In response, conservative students chanted 'SDS out'. Meanwhile downstairs at the student party (entry fee three marks), the bass was pounding (Figure 6.2). Student H. Lindner reported to the UniNachrichtenstelle (University's press office):

> 21.10 The first rams on the doors, while the beat hammers in the background....21.34 Massive police operation begins...21.44 A few steps away, the dancers stamp and twirl, 'If I were a rich man'...22.20 The light is tinged with pink, the hovering beat fills the room, stifling heat prevails, they've shut the windows, probably out of fear that the police might throw a demonstrator or two out of them....23.30 (last work-related note) Lots of dark corridors, there's some serious fumbling going on all over the place! Enthusiastic stamping...the revolution that was in session only a few metres from here has long been forgotten...long live the beat![9]

Figure 6.2 Dancing to the beat at the university summer party on 10 July 1968

The 'serious fumbling', as the student reporter put it, was then known as 'petting', and was a 'widespread sexual experience' for young men and women, or so sexologists Hans Giese and Günter Schmidt concluded in 1968 from a survey of 3,666 students at twelve universities, Bonn included. People's first experience of petting generally happened between the ages of 15 and 21, and around 70 per cent of students had experienced it by 25. By contrast, only about half of students had had full sexual intercourse. In Bonn, that was true of 63 per cent of the men and 52 per cent of the women.[10] There were plenty of reasons for holding back at that time—not least a lack of opportunity. 'You had landladies, you know, who paid attention to what time you got home, and who you were seen alone with', recalled one female student. On the occasion of the university jubilee, the Bonn local newspaper praised all the 'student mothers', lodging-house landladies who 'fondly clean the young gentlemen's shoes, make their beds, spirit away the rows of bottles with a shake of the head, and empty the overflowing ashtrays in their rooms'.[11] It glossed right over the fact that this arrangement also entailed a large dash of social control:

until 1973, the *Kuppeleiparagraph* (procuration law, paragraphs 180–181 of the criminal code) applied in West Germany, by which parents or landlords who allowed unmarried couples to spend the night together were risking up to five years in jail. Anyone who so much as gave a couple the opportunity for private hanky-panky without the benefit of a marriage certificate was aiding and abetting fornication, and leaving themselves liable to prosecution.[12]

By the late sixties, this situation was resulting in certain contortions. Young women reached 'compromises' with their parents, whereby their boyfriends might not be allowed to park their cars on the street, but were allowed to stay over at the weekends: 'that was progress in itself, the fact that the parents accepted it up to a point, in a world where that was still punishable'. Bonn physics student Bernd Ramm said, with a shake of his head: 'They really ought to have charged my parents with serious procuration. My girlfriend, she was always round at our house, and in my bedroom with me, it was totally insane.'[13] Men were given notice on their rooms because their fiancées had been seen entering them, and a couple were not allowed to go travelling together without a marriage certificate. Angelika Lehndorff-Felsko, a student in Cologne, asked her parents' permission before going on holiday to France: 'Well, nobody realized that my boyfriend was there too…By then you had the pill and then you got on with it, and so long as your parents didn't find out, it was OK.'[14] Similarly, students living in halls of residence could only have visitors of the opposite sex in secret. In 1966, a case from 'Newman-Haus' in Bonn hit the headlines.

The management had kicked out a Black resident because a cleaning lady had walked in unannounced, and found herself witness to a scene of an erotic nature. There were similar occurrences in halls of residence in Marburg and Erlangen, where the wardens liked to check under the ground floor windows every morning for footprints from unauthorized overnight guests. A porter at a women's hall of residence in Cologne would note down the name of every male visitor along with the time of his arrival, and enforced a 10 p.m. curfew.[15] Consequently, the dark hallways of the main university building were a welcome alternative.

The penal code might condemn pre-marital sex, but students were almost unanimous in defending it. 'These "violations" of traditional morality occur without any sense of transgressing the norm', Giese and Schmidt concluded on the basis of their data gathered in 1966.[16] This concurs with surveys among the wider population. Even in 1963, only 12 per cent of men and 25 per cent of women of any age asserted that they had never had any pre-marital relations. And blue-collar workers began to have sexual intercourse at a

144   THE OTHER '68

considerably younger age than the students because they were earning sooner, and had access to their own accommodation.[17] Nobody was unaware that marriage was often a 'necessity': a child was already on the way by the time that one in two weddings took place in the early sixties.[18] In the circumstances, the strict moral precepts of the church struck most young people as no more than cant. This applied both to sex outside marriage and to the use of contraceptives. The 'pill', which had been on the market in West Germany since 1961, but which was only dispensed to married women with a doctor's prescription, set passions running particularly high. In 1966, as many as 98 per cent of students advocated the use of contraception. Even among religious and conservative students, 'the question of the moral legitimacy of contraceptives was no longer seriously being discussed'.[19] Although most doctors and both the Roman Catholic and Protestant churches repeatedly expressed their opposition to the use of the pill over the course of the sixties, people simply ignored those qualms. Between 1964 and 1972, the number of women who were on the pill rose from around 215,000 to 3.8 million—almost a third of those aged 15 to 44. Even the Catholic laity attending the German *Katholikentag* festival in September 1968 rebelled openly against the papal ban on any kind of 'artificial' birth control.[20]

The Universities of Bonn and Cologne had a high percentage of Catholic students, and contraceptives were a big issue here too. The student faculty committee for the humanities departments in Cologne was doing 'a great deal of advisory work because at that time it was [mainly women] coming to the student council...who wanted the pill...and so I had a list of doctors who'd prescribe it', student member Angelika Lehndorff-Felsko reported. Similarly, the centre-right Bonn AStA, which held office under Rudolf Pörtner from May 1967 to March 1968, gained a great deal of popularity by running a 'pill project'. It distributed for free the address of a dentist in Bamberg who would send anyone a prescription on request, including unmarried women students. The AStA even placed a classified ad in the *Frankfurter Rundschau* to find doctors who were willing to prescribe it, unleashing a nationwide media response.[21] Central to the 'pill project' were the speaker of the student parliament, Jürgen Rosorius of the RCDS, and the AStA social officer, Eckehart Ehrenberg, who had links to the SPD. The latter had previously spent a semester abroad in Manchester, UK, where he had first experienced student discussion evenings on the subject of sex and society. He had doubted the theoretical propositions, but been impressed by the 'factual findings presented', as he later recalled. 'My first ever television interview related to the AStA procuring the "pill", and I gave it together, and in agreement with, the chair of the

Christian RCDS.'[22] Not even the membership of the conservative RCDS were at all prudish. As the cameras rolled, Jürgen Rosorius announced that 'it is a well-known fact that 90 per cent of students are in favour of free love, and also practise it.'[23]

Here, Rosorius was exaggerating. Almost half of all students lived a celibate life, many of them because they were afraid of pregnancy. This was an understandable fear, considering that the birth of a child generally meant that the woman had to break off her studies, and that many young people had had insufficient sex education. Moreover, couples in over 50 per cent of relationships were using relatively unreliable birth control techniques, such as the withdrawal method and temperature measurement.[24] Young women of this generation were still familiar with shaking with nerves once a month, and with the panic of suspecting they might be pregnant, because the pill only became truly widely used after the turn of the seventies.[25]

The example of Bonn shows that the vast majority of students of every stripe in around 1968 were in favour of pre-marital sex, access to contraceptives, and private spaces for intimate encounters. There was also a clear demand for basic information on sexuality and fertility. Back in January 1967, the Bonn student parliament—not yet divided into political factions—had resolved to establish a series of lectures on sex 'for students from all faculties'. The AStA chair, Madeleine Hackspiel, asked the Rector to find speakers from the medical teaching staff who could lay out 'the most important facts in the area of sexual education'. The Rector agreed, but then played for time before eventually letting the AStA (which was by then left-leaning, under Bernhelm Booß's leadership) know that it would have to organize the 'sexual problems lectures' itself. Booß's successor, Rudolf Pörtner, then announced a 'series of talks on the problem of birth control' for the winter semester 1967/68, 'with particular emphasis on contraceptives'. He said that here, as with giving out the addresses 'of doctors who would also prescribe the pill to unmarried women students', the AStA was concerned with practical solutions, and not with politics. It simply wanted to treat 'previously taboo subjects with an appropriate level of objectivity'. On this issue the student representatives were all pulling in the same direction, whether they represented social democratic (Hackspiel), socialist (Booß), moderate conservative (Pörtner), or conservative (Rosorius) thought.[26]

Protests by more sexually conservative students were rare. They generally focused on the visual 'educational work' conducted by the Bonn student newspaper *akut*, which had been wooing readers since December 1966 with suggestive pictures of semi-naked women. In October 1968, the paper even hired its own '*akut* Kolle', in imitation of the West German sex education guru Oswalt Kolle. Philosophy student Mathias Jung, who described himself as a 'pacifistically-minded pupil of the Jesuits, in solidarity with Beate Uhse', henceforth filled a smug series of columns with his 'Philosophy of Shagging' ('Coito ergo sum'). Sales figures increased and letters from readers were overwhelmingly positive. An anonymous reader, signing as 'an upright pornographer', offered satirical thanks to the Kolle of Bonn 'with the German salute Shag-Heil'. Even the national press paid attention, with the tabloid *Express*, and *Der Spiegel* magazine happy to take the opportunity to reprint the lewdest photos from *akut* and other West German student newspapers (Figure 6.3). Bare breasts and attractive bottoms abounded not only in *akut*, but also in the Stuttgart, Hamburg, Karlsruhe, and Marburg university rags. According to *Der Spiegel* 'Germany's young academics are also part of this, the *Playboy*-reading world'.[27]

The student press had jumped on a bandwagon. The battle for moral propriety in the West German media had been lost long before 1968. Mass-market glossy magazines such as the *Neue Revue* had seen a massive increase in circulation after 1963 with Oswalt Kolle's prissy sex education articles ('Your Husband, an Unfamiliar Being'). *Jasmin*, *Bravo*, *Quick*, and now

Figure 6.3 Controversial nude in the Bonn student newspaper *akut* from November 1966. 'Courrèges? / No—Honnefer Model'. Fashion designer André Courrèges was famous for his very short mini-skirts; the 'Honnefer Model' was the name given to state student grants up to 1971

student journalism followed in the wake of this third post-war sex wave, bringing salacious 'sex education' to millions of readers in the name of progress. The first wave had rolled in after the currency reform of 1948, with erotic pamphlets being sold from newspaper kiosks, while the second wave was shaped after 1954 by media debates on Alfred C. Kinsey's research on human sexual behaviour. Meanwhile, the massive expansion of the mail-order erotica companies Beate Uhse and 'Gisela' attests to the contemporaneous commercialization of sex. In 1962, at least half of West German homes had ordered condoms, marriage advice manuals, or other intimate articles by post. Sex was now a consumer good and a leisure activity. 170,000 copies of Kinsey's academic study of the sexual behaviour of women were sold in West Germany between 1963 and 1968 alone. Oswalt Kolle made eight sex education films, including *Das Wunder der Liebe* (The Miracle of Love), which lured an audience of 26 million to West German cinemas alone between 1968 and 1973.[28]

Although West Germany's moral guardians in politics, the police, and the justice system had had to accept constant setbacks over the course of the decade, contemporary observers in 1968 did not yet realize how comprehensively the sexual conservatives had already been defeated. Paragraphs 175 and 218 were still in force, sex between men, and abortion were still prosecuted. As recently as 1962, the Federal government had put forward an illiberal redraft of the law on sexual offences, which adhered to the culpability of adultery, pornography, striptease, partner-swapping, male homosexuality, and divorce— yet it encountered sharp criticism and eventually fizzled out in the Bundestag.[29] Attitudes among the general public were changing fast.

The events playing out at provincial universities such as Bonn merely mirrored those happening nationwide, across all social classes. The overwhelming majority favoured a basic version of the sexual revolution that had begun its triumphal march by the mid-sixties at the latest. This version included the permissibility of pre-marital sex, the free availability of contraceptives, and the provision of sexual education to all. There was also a consensus (among students and young people in general) that the commercialization and publication of heterosexuality was acceptable. Opinion polls dating back to 1963 already showed clear majorities of the population for pre-marital relations, and contraception, and these would increase still further. By 1972, there was a two thirds majority in favour of introducing sex education as a school subject.[30] Kissing on the street, super-short skirts, and conversations within relationships about sex should now be just as permissible as nude advertising photos, erotic reports in newspapers, and porn films at the cinema. Approval of this basic sexual 'revolution' was not dependent on being young or left-wing, or on any theory. You could remain faithful to the church, and there was no need for difficulties with parents. Eckehart Ehrenberg, the social officer of Bonn's AStA responsible for procuring contraceptives, 'had a church wedding'. The *akut* editor Hans Günter Jürgensmeier married in 1969, but also had an official engagement period, at his parents' insistence:

> So there we were, bang in the middle between what our parents wanted and what our youth culture wanted...you know, it's square to sleep with the same girl twice and all that...Then we made an engagement card saying we wanted to found an individual commune [Figure 6.4]. That's pretty schizophrenic really, an individual commune.[31]

A considerable majority of students only demanded tolerance for 'sexual relationships with a single partner, within a loving relationship, and whom you would like to marry'. Promiscuity of the kind publicly preached by Kommune 1 in Berlin did not feature in this basic variety. Adultery was outside its scope for 60 per cent of students and up to three quarters of the general population.[32]

There were two further manifestations of the sexual revolution, which did not (yet) command a majority as of 1968. The first was around the politicization of sex: sex and porn at the service of the socialist revolution. The second related to the emancipation of sexual minorities—both in terms of gay and lesbian rights, and as a critique of the patriarchal character of heterosexuality. Challenges to male dominance referred to the neglect of female desire, and to victims of sexual violence, especially of rape. There was practically no trace of

Figure 6.4 Engagement as founding an 'individual commune': announcement by Hans Günter Jürgensmeier and Helga Nägler in February 1968

either the emancipatory or the political expansion of the sexual revolution in the microcosm of late-sixties' Bonn.

The Bonn student newspaper, for example, devoted not a single line to the emancipation of sexual minorities between 1967 and 1969, while both the SDS and the student parliament remained silent on the subject. The local 'Emancipation Working Group', which campaigned for equality for women, came only very late to issues related to the repression of the female body. Co-founder Florence Hervé observed with retrospect that 'the question of the body' and 'sexist violence against women' barely featured: 'we just weren't a self-awareness group'.[33] In Bonn, as elsewhere, public perception was dominated by a male perspective, where everything was centred on penetration and his orgasm. It was only in the 1970s, influenced not least by developments in the USA, that female desire was discovered as an end in itself, and became the topic of wide-ranging debates, such as that on the myth of the vaginal orgasm.[34]

Things were similar with the emancipation of LGBT minorities. Within the broader population, gay people continued to suffer discrimination or persecution throughout the sixties. Between 1950 and 1965, West German courts sentenced around 45,000 gay men simply for living out their sexuality. Meanwhile, in the mid-sixties, considerably more than 80 per cent of West Germans, including around 60 per cent of students, still considered homosexuality to be an impermissible vice, or permissible only within restrictions. The glossy magazines primarily portrayed gays as criminal or sick, with the disease model slowly gaining ground against the notion of a crime. In December 1968, a relative majority of the population was opposed to legalizing sex between men (although 48 per cent of those aged under 30 were in favour). It was not until the mid-seventies that these attitudes began to change on a broader scale.[35] The LGBT movement cannot be traced back directly to the student protest movement, even if many of their activists later cooperated with the socialist and communist cadre groups. The first, hesitant gay rights groups began to form from December 1970 onwards, in Bochum and Münster. A subsequent wave followed in 1971 to 1973, after Rosa von Praunheim's controversial docudrama *It Is Not the Homosexual Who Is Perverse, But the Society in Which He Lives* was screened. Only then were similar action groups founded in Bonn and Cologne.[36]

In many respects, the situation in Bonn was more typical of West German society than the left-wing academic scene in West Berlin, which subscribed to a politicized version of the sexual revolution in the years around 1968. In the heartlands of the protest movement—Berlin and Frankfurt—a numerically small advance guard of the New Left was forming, which believed in the

150   THE OTHER '68

liberating power of pornography, nudity, and sexual intercourse. This group argued volubly that a state of sexual emergency prevailed among the general population, and especially among those aged over 30: the omnipresent repression of natural urges led inevitably to neuroses, anal fixation, violence, an authoritarian character, and ultimately to fascism. Here, the New Left appropriated selective psychological and sociological theories from Wilhelm Reich, Herbert Marcuse, Theodor Adorno, and Max Horkheimer, from which they cobbled together a logic whereby upfront nudity could have a liberating effect and set their political opponents on the defensive. Wild, hedonistic sex would act as an immunization against fascist ideas, and therapy for uptight souls, and would undermine the capitalist principle of achievement. Even toddlers needed to be brought up with the 'freedom from repression' that would allow them to live out their anal and sexual urges, and thus to shake off the straitjacket of bourgeois-fascistic family values.[37]

These ideas are particularly embodied by Kommune 1 and 2 in Berlin, such authors as Hubert Bacia, Klaus Theweleit, and Arno Plack, the 'Sexpol groups', and some of the first wave of Berlin *Kinderläden*. They were soon put into writing and circulated through the alternative milieu via magazines including *konkret*, *Kursbuch*, and *Agit 883*. Kommune 1's poster couple, Rainer Langhans and his photo model girlfriend Uschi Obermaier, offered the mass media a prime example of what Langhans called 'a political experience' and an 'enlightenment sexuality' on the journey towards the 'new man'. The politicized variant of the sexual revolution linked the Nazi past to sexual repression, a link constructed in ignorance of the historical realities.[38] Consequently, nudity was deployed as an aggressive assault on a capitalist, post-fascist, and protofascist society of fellow travellers—in the well-known nude group photo of Kommune 1, printed in *Der Spiegel* in 1967, for example, or the incident, later known as the '*Busenattentat*' (topless ambush), when bare-breasted women students drove Frankfurt sociologist Adorno to flee the hall where he was lecturing. Intimate encounters between nursery-age children and teachers that today carry a whiff of paedophilia were then seen as a reasonable consequence of a desire for political liberation.[39]

This politicized variant of the sexual revolution found expression in numerous written sources, and continued to have an effect on the left-leaning, alternative youth scene through the seventies and eighties. As a result, it has been of serious interest to historians.[40] Thus, the misconception that the Sixty-Eighters had liberated society through their own unbounded sexual practice became ingrained in the public mind. On the one hand, however, there were critics within the New Left, such as Rudi Dutschke and Reimut Reiche, who expressed scepticism towards the communards' flirtation with promiscuity and pornography.[41] Meanwhile, on the other hand, sexuality in metropolitan student movement circles was more uptight than the prurient gaze of the mass media wanted to believe. While the magazines stared in fascination at the Berlin 'sex communes' and projected all kinds of vivid pornographic fantasies onto them, these residential communities were far more intensely concerned with political theory than with sexual practice. Rather than wild orgies, they held hours of 'psychological discussions', aimed at airing the most intimate of subjects in public. This wordy psychologizing went together with deep inhibitions in bed: 'Nobody could have guessed that all of us were actually a pretty repressed bunch', said Dagmar Seehuber, looking back at life in Kommune 1.[42] The utopian, politicized form of revolutionary sexuality to which this avant-garde aspired was not much less regimented than traditional morality, while for many it ended in the frustrating merry-go-round of crises that afflicted alternative relationships in the 1970s, and, above all, perpetuated the dominance of male-penetrative heterosexuality.[43]

More than a few SDS women felt coerced into sex under the guise of nobly serving the revolution. Where the revolution was still defined as masculine, sexuality in its service could only benefit the men. The women around the first communes and the West Berlin SDS consistently reported that promiscuity primarily applied to the men, and that their sexual liberation was 'absolutely at the women's expense'—'always with the sense that if you don't play along, you're totally bourgeois!'[44] Angelika Lehndorff-Felsko described the situation in Cologne: 'Well, there was groping from the left-wing students too, and plenty of it.' During the 1970s this experience, which was widespread internationally, would feed the change of focus in the new women's movement towards issues around sexual autonomy for women.[45] But loud female protest against the urge for conquest among the macho SDS men was still very rare in the late sixties. The famous leaflet entitled 'Free the Socialist Eminences from their Bourgeois Dicks!', distributed at an SDS conference in November 1968 by the *Frankfurter Weiberrat* (Frankfurt women's council), remained a one-off, and actually upset some of the women.[46] Even female Sixty-Eighters had yet to discover the emancipatory version of the sexual revolution for themselves, and it was only later, in the course of the seventies, that they began to actively demand sexual self-determination for women, and the discovery of female desire.

It was thus more by coincidence than design that the sexual and political protest movements both occurred around 1968, and this coincidence was more 'atmospheric' than substantial in its significance.[47] The Sixty-Eighters were 'razing a castle that was no more than a ruin in any case', said Sven Reichardt: ' "sexual modernization" was already in full swing across all social classes when the student movement activists hoisted their own banner, laying

152   THE OTHER '68

claim to this development with a sometimes pompous gesture.[48] Only a few thousand young, middle-class university students linked sex to anti-capitalist and anti-fascist rebellion. The West Berlin bohemians who politicized the sexual revolution were anything but representative of most people's thinking or practice. They were not even setting the tone for young people or students as a whole, as the example of Bonn shows. Taking a look at the alternative nurseries in Bonn and elsewhere also shows how quickly most young parents adopted a pragmatic line and dropped the theory that a sexually liberated early childhood would benefit the revolution. The *Kinderladen* founded in the Dransdorf area of Bonn in November 1969 might have cited Wilhelm Reich's theories, but it barely followed them in practice.[49]

We can see then that young people at that time were enthusiastic participants in the basic sexual revolution, yet only small, avant-garde groups flirted with the politicization of sexuality, while the majority of them rejected the emancipation of sexual minorities. So how were they distinct from the older generations? What did love have to do with the generational conflict surrounding 1968?

On the same afternoon that Holger bought pastries on the way home from school and the pensioners chatted over cake in the Café Müller, student Gerda Andresen walked up the steps to the Department of Psychology opposite the *Konditorei*. She was carrying a bulky, beige case, which held a portable UHER tape recorder. It still weighed a whole eight kilos. In a second bag, she had a dozen reel-to-reel tapes. Gerda Andresen had a meeting with PhD student Helga Merker, for whom she had spent months recording numerous conversations with middle-aged men, working through questions around the differences between young people then and now, and about changes in parenting styles. As the student heaved the device onto Merker's desk, somewhat out of breath, she began to tell her about her experiences, and the way some of the men, aged 33 to 58, had reacted to a pretty, young interviewer. A business owner in his early 50s had told her in all seriousness that she should drop her studies: 'Don't take this the wrong way', he had said, 'female students, I think there are too many...they might know about all kinds of things that happened 4,000 years ago, but if they need to boil an egg or make some coffee for a change, then they're standing there with two left hands.' When the man had had a student daughter himself, and he'd moaned that she couldn't even wash the dishes properly! But the one who'd really taken the biscuit had been a *Herr Doktor* in his late 30s whom she'd met at Shrove Tuesday and recruited for the study. 'At Carnival, he told me he was a bachelor. But he's married and has two sons.' In general, she was astonished that almost all the conversation had come round very quickly to sex.[50] This last remark was particularly interesting to Helga Merker as she had spent recent weeks typing up a good many transcripts of taped conversations with middle-aged women. They too had, unasked, expressed themselves at length on the subject of sexual taboos. Attitudes towards sexuality were probably one of the most significant areas of difference between the generations, mused the PhD student. She would need to look into that more closely once she had assembled all the interviews—and of course compare the men and the women.[51]

In fact, after weeks and months of transcription and stamping punch-cards, Helga Merker established that the over-60s talked more frequently about sexual morality than the middle-aged participants, and that the women consistently did so more often than the men. About a tenth of quantifiable remarks in the 364 interviews related to young people's sexual behaviour.[52] Merker's sense that 'morality' was a key area where the generations were at odds with each other had not been mistaken. After dividing all the statements into those that made neutral, positive, or negative judgements, a clear picture emerged. The grandparents' generation were vociferous critics of the youth of 1968 when it came to their sexual behaviour and outward appearance. A majority of the parents' generation, on the other hand, had a neutral attitude: they cited a change in mores without expressly welcoming it. The starkest differences between the middle and older generations appeared when the talk was of sexuality, clothing, and hairstyles. In many other areas (not reflected in the table below) the elderly and middle-aged were in greater agreement in their opinion of the young: when it came to young people's attitudes towards money, or their liberty, interests, and open-mindedness, for example.[53]

Description of the social behaviour and nature of the youth of today in interviews

		Middle-aged adults (N = 120)	Over-60s from the Bolsa sample (N = 184)
Total of *all* statements		(3,212)	(4,160)
	Of which positive (%)	20	15
	Of which negative (%)	38	55
	Of which neutral (%)	42	30
Statements relating to sexual matters		(221)	(435)
	Of which positive (%)	8	5
	Of which negative (%)	16	67
	Of which neutral (%)	76	29
Statements relating to outward appearance		(278)	(457)
	Of which positive (%)	7	10
	Of which negative (%)	23	69
	Of which neutral (%)	69	22

154   THE OTHER '68

Listening to the conversations in greater detail, the centrality of sexual education, contraception, and pre-marital relationships is astonishing. Frau Borchert, a sales assistant and mother of two was interviewed by Gerda Andresen in May 1968; her immediate response to the very first question—'How are young people today different from young people in your day?'—was to say:

> I think that actually, young people know more of the facts of life than young people did in my day. Back then... it was all very different, with sex education before marriage, and everything that goes along with that. It was rare for a teenager to be told about that at all. Today, they either learn the facts of life from their parents or in school, I consider... that better than in our day.

She was happy for her nieces and nephews, who all had boyfriends and girlfriends already. By contrast, she herself 'might have overheard bits and pieces on the street', but had not learnt anything (about sex) from her parents and had even 'not been allowed to speak about anything even at the age of 14 or 15... people like us really were stupid'. Although she disapproved of 'the way the drop-outs do things, with this person one day and that person the next', she still considerably preferred the new approach to the old ways. So she too would talk to her children about sex while they were still young.[54]

Frau Borchert was typical of the mid-30s to mid-50s age group. Both men and women emphasized the extent to which they'd struggled with their parents' rigid morals. 'I spent long, long years suffering', said 42-year-old Herr Russ, from having been 'educated out of... this perfectly casual and natural togetherness' of the sexes. Herr Anschütz, who was only a few years older, thought that the strict separation of girls and boys had only resulted in 'anxieties and inhibitions'. In Weimar-era Berlin, wanting to get to the bottom of the secret, he had had the idea of 'going kerb-crawling and chatting to the hookers', i.e. asking the prostitutes for information. Others talked about having been let in on the secret by older friends and cousins, or by teachers 'because our parents hadn't told us a thing. Effectively nothing.' 'My mother would have died of embarrassment if she'd even breathed the merest word to us about that stuff.'[55] They also almost never saw their parents naked. 'Our parents hid from us. If they went into the bathroom, if at all possible, they'd lock the bathroom door!... I'd never do that.' Herr Hahn and Herr Lochny admitted that sheer curiosity had led them to '[peek] through the keyhole' at home,

VARIATIONS ON SEXUAL LIBERATION   155

or wait for the cows to calve.[56] Only two of the eighty-nine middle-aged inter-viewees reported that their parents had put them fully in the picture.[57]

The others criticized their mothers and fathers, sometimes sharply, for their prudery. As a 10- or 12-year-old, Herr Arnhold had been hit 'on the back of the neck' for asking questions, and silenced. A father of three adult daughters had been given no information of any kind as a teenager: 'I've got six sisters myself and so I can see the effect that this wrong [kind of] upbring-ing had on the girls.' Some of his sisters' 'stupidities...could have been avoided if we'd been able to talk openly about it'. A barber and father of two young men agreed: 'Girls under 18 were never allowed out', and if they did still meet a boy, 'then they fell into a trap, then they had to get married'.[58] The older generation's strait-laced morality seemed like sheer hypocrisy to some men who had been in the war.

> When I hear how worked up some people get about the lack of morals among the youth of today. We grew up amid the *Lebensborn* campaign. I was even called upon to get involved in that...You ought to father a child for the state. Where's the morality in that?

Herr Hanke felt similarly: 'The parents of today went through the Second World War.' At the Front, morals had been 'utterly devoid of value'. Nobody who had experienced that could any longer advocate traditional norms 'with that kind of consistency' in the post-war era, or misrepresent younger people as immoral.[59]

The intermediate generation were largely unanimous that children needed early and comprehensive sexual education, including those who advocated conservative moral values (such as Herr Groth), called themselves Christians (such as Herr Kaym), or admitted that they found talking about these matters hard (such as Herr Lochny).[60] Many of them thought 'reading a good book' a helpful way of overcoming inhibitions. Frau Kloppe, who worked half-days and had an adult son, was audibly relieved at having learnt the necessary in this way, without recourse to those 'dreadful magazines':

> So, I'd like to recommend other parents...a book by Dr Graupner: *Our Sons and Daughters*, it's fabulous. And when the time comes, give it to the chil-dren to read too...And the facts of life specifically are described in this book, it's really nice for parents to have a thing like that to hand, it gives you a sense of security yourself, it's so clearly written...If you have this know-ledge, from this book, I don't need any more magazines.[61]

156   THE OTHER '68

As here, the mothers seemed to take the lead in most families. Fathers were particularly likely to be involved when there were sons to be taught.[62]

In addition, there seemed to be a consensus that using contraception was acceptable. None of the interviewees spoke out against birth control. If the 'contraceptive pill' was mentioned, as by Herr Anz for example, then it was as a welcome invention.[63] This is in line with other sources, according to which young, unmarried women of the Sixty-Eighter generation met with (often unexpected) sympathy from their mothers as soon as they needed their help to access the 'pill'.[64] Open discussions between adult children and their parents were still rare or non-existent because most of the parents were only half-way to having liberal sexual morals.[65] Young people in 1968 sensed that while their parents had provided them with a degree of basic information, they were still repressed in certain respects.

This left the middle generation, born between 1910 and 1935, divided on the matter of pre-marital relationships. The more liberal among them explicitly defended sex before marriage as widespread and natural. An accountant, for example, said: 'I'd be the last to demand that my daughter stays a virgin until her wedding day. With these earlier sexual relationships nowadays, it could happen...that one day she ends up as an unmarried mother. Though I don't actually wish for it.' In any case, she ought to be given a good professional education so that she would be able to 'provide well for her child'. Frau Hahn had similar thoughts:

> If the boy really came to me and said: OK, mum, this and that happened, there's this girl, and she's expecting, I'd say: fine, speak to her parents, and if they have a go at the girl and tell her to get out, which does still happen even these days, then I'd say: come on, bring her here. I wouldn't have a go at my boy, or my girl either...I'd say: come on, be pleased about your child...In this respect, we are different nowadays. My father would have gone wild.[66]

Both remarks reflect both how widespread unwanted pregnancies and consequent marriages were at that time, and how often parents still saw a 'fallen' girl as a social disgrace. A father of two daughters listed the calamities that he feared as 'an accident, a war, a child out of wedlock'.[67]

Sometimes this divide ran right through a family. Gerda Andresen's interview with Herr and Frau Anz in May 1968 (both aged around 50) left her more than a little surprised. Asked what you should be careful of when bringing up a girl, the housewife answered: 'That she holds herself up, that she doesn't let the boys drag her through the dirt.' The student played dumb and asked: 'What do you mean by "holds herself up"? I haven't heard that expression before.' Frau Anz replied: 'That she's not running around with this boy one day and that one the next... You can't just assume that any more these days, sadly. That she'll go into marriage pure.' But her husband had a different emphasis. 'Honestly real parents show themselves when their child is in trouble, whether married or not.' He'd told his 'baby daughter', a young teacher: 'Come what may, your parents' home will always be open to you, and especially if something's gone wrong.' The couple also argued over their 18-year-old son dating a girl on Saturdays. Frau Anz put up some resistance but could not prevail against her husband and children. Resignedly, she observed: 'Well, I'm old-fashioned there, I'm from the seventeenth century, I can't have a say any more.'[68]

The middle generation's attitude towards physical love was thus contradictory and divided. They were fully in favour of sex education and contraception, but only some of them approved of pre-marital sex. The stigma of a pregnancy outside marriage was crumbling, but only slowly. Most considered nudity within your own home or in glossy magazines acceptable, but not frequently swapping partners, or hardcore pornography. A father of two got to the heart of his generation's transitional stance:

> Yes, that's the question of morality as such, where I don't entirely go along with current tendencies. There's no doubt that our upbringing was prudish and not right when it came to sex, but I think that people today are falling into the opposite mistake, and that people today take freedom too far in all ways.[69]

Many of them cited 'drop-outs' and 'sex communes' as images of horror, representing untrammelled promiscuity. As none of the interviewees had ever met a drop-out or a communard, however, they were drawing on reports on the television or in the magazines.[70] In fact, many of them knew how vast the gap between reality and this projected depravity actually was. A man in his mid-40s, who spent a lot of time with young people 'aged 20 and up' at work and via his daughters, stressed 'that young people in general these days are better in every respect than the way they're generally portrayed'. The majority of older people 'only [saw] the extreme cases and so they judged wrongly': 'You read something about them getting high on LSD, and sex-parties, and things like that, and it all sounds really gruesome', but 'similar things happened in the past too'. Most long-haired youngsters were 'sensible all the same', said Herr Märker, also defending the youth against a charge of immorality. Some even compared the drop-outs with their own time in the Hitler Youth and concluded that they themselves had been 'hooligans just the same' or worse.[71] Apprentices, sons, daughters, and other—specific—young people they knew in person were viewed considerably more favourable than the youth in the 'abstract', whose alleged excesses were the stuff of voyeuristic media reports.[72]

A large majority of those born between 1910 and 1935 thus held views that in themselves went beyond the scope of the 'dirt and trash' debate of the immediate post-war period: a public struggle for 'decency' that had been raging in the decade after 1945, referring to the *Gesetz zur Bewahrung der Jugend vor Schund- und Schmutzschriften* (Law to Protect Youth from Trashy and Dirty Writings) passed during the Weimar Republic. Both ecclesiastical and civil moral apostles had made every endeavour to reassert the strict Wilhelmine moral laws. They had used paternalistic and anti-modern arguments in their (futile) campaign against trends towards liberalizing and commercializing sex. From the mid-fifties onwards, advocates of virtue and censorship found themselves on an increasingly lonely outpost. The general public had begun to claim their right to trash, and to see Western modernism not as a threat but as a promise of personal happiness. By the early- to mid-sixties, the major battles had already been fought, and the outcome had favoured the sexual revolution.[73]

The severity with which moral conservatism had been defeated can be clearly seen in the interviews with middle-aged adults from 1967 and 1968, who predominantly rejected its key messages. Only three of the fifty men, and two of the thirty-nine women suspected the crisis in sexual morality of coming from abroad, from the West, or from North America (that is, that it could be traced back to imported films, occupation soldiers, or academics such as Kinsey). Only eight of eighty-nine interviewees characterized the modern mass media as morally corruptive.[74] Only five men and four women can be considered downright conservative in their sexual morals, about a tenth of the study participants, as opposed to twelve decided liberals (eight men and four women).[75] The rest made up a large midfield whose views ranged from the liberal to liberal-conservative, or held contradictory positions.

Ninety per cent of these middle-aged adults, therefore, welcomed the sexual revolution, in its basic form, at least in part. But they went no further. Not a single interviewee put the case for any kind of politicization of sexuality, nor did anyone even mention either the situation of sexual minorities or the problem of sexual violence. The idea that a more liberated sexuality could act as therapy for warped personalities, or counteract social repression, was as

VARIATIONS ON SEXUAL LIBERATION   159

foreign to this generation as any questioning of the taboo around same-sex sexuality.[76]

All the same, this middle generation felt that the wind had changed during the sixties. The conservatives among them, who considered too much sex to be damaging, felt out of step with the times or, as Frau Anz put it, 'from the seventeenth century'. Frau Ruhle had grown up in a village and had a traditional mindset; she said that she felt almost 'slow-witted' when she talked about 'sexual matters' with her adult son. 'Sometimes I end up saying, son, I've never heard of any such thing in all my life, never even known about it, you know?'[77] The liberals were in tune with the zeitgeist, as countless complaints about the grandparents standing in the way of progress attest. Many of those in their mid-30s to mid-50s maintained that older people 'hadn't moved with the times...they'd stood still'. Only an 'ossified geriatric' could hold young people's moral liberty against them, said a man in his mid-50s.[78] A 35-year-old accused 'the older generation' of often being more worried about 'keeping up appearances' and of not even living by their own rules. When it came to sex education, old people couldn't keep up, said sales assistant Frau Borchert: 'If a teenager talked about that stuff in their presence, they'd stand up and walk out because they can't comprehend that people that young already know these things.'[79]

Were the elderly really as inflexible and prudish as the middle generation thought? The interviews with the Bolsa participants are clear. The 60- to 80-year-olds were asked the same questions as the middle-aged adults about the youth of the day. And although some were initially reluctant to talk about lust and love in so many words, the topic played an even greater role in their perceptions of young people's conduct than it did for the intermediate age group.[80] It was extremely common for the Bolsianers to express their outrage at public displays of affection, which left them feeling awkward. 'You feel set aside in some way', complained a 76-year-old man.[81] 'Well, it's terrible sometimes when you're just walking along. They stand there in the middle of the street, hugging or kissing, well, that's—we're just not used to it, us older folk. In the old days they at least used to wait for it to get dark', said a 68-year-old widow.[82] They even found a peck on the cheek as a greeting uncomfortable:

> It's a French thing, isn't it, this slobbering over each other...in our day that wouldn't have, oh, it'd have been out of the question. But they just go at it so freely and publicly on the street, they stop and kiss each other, they've got no inhibitions at all.

160   THE OTHER '68

A retired businessman who described himself as 'not exactly squeamish' reacted with shock: 'it's a disgrace, they're at it in broad daylight, canoodling away!' Public kissing seemed hard to tolerate because it awakened unwelcome emotions.[83]

A majority of the grandparent generation still supported the Wilhelmine decency norms that 90 per cent of the middle-aged interviewees rejected. Many pensioners contrasted their well-behaved pre-war youth with dissolute lifestyles after 1945. They were fond of blaming this 'slovenliness' and 'ultra-modernity' on foreigners in the West; mini-skirts, make-up, smooching, and all the rest of it had 'come over from America', thought Frau Tänzer. In the view of Herr Bohe, aged 66, the decline in decency was caused 'by the foreign soldiers, especially the Americans, having stayed in Germany so long' and their customs 'being aped by our youngsters'. Business and academia were also becoming 'more and more Americanized' and thus spreading an immoral 'negro culture' throughout Europe.[84] Others held the huge number of recent inventions, and especially television, responsible for the advance of erotica. 'The programmes are often unbearable. Young people learn the facts of life too young, in a negative way', said a retired switchboard operator.[85] Both Herr Speck and Herr Gebler warned that the youth were falling victim to modern 'excesses' because of a general lack of role models and discipline after defeat in the war. Their examples of undesirable developments ranged from 'porno-graphic films', the 'pill', and LSD, to 'the menace of rockers', 'beat clubs', and 'liberty as described by Kolle', to 'sexual education in the schools'.[86] Some of the interviewees even called for state intervention to put a stop to immorality. The CDU government should restrict the freedom of the press, suggested Herr Dänhardt. Others proposed thrashings, police action, or arraigning fashion designers who promoted mini-skirts.[87] They seldom mentioned the 'pill', which could take the fear and stigma from pre-marital intercourse, but when they did, they tended to oppose it.[88]

The older generation objected not to sexuality in itself, but to displaying it publicly, or to talking about sex, especially to teenagers, children, or the opposite gender. As a result, they easily attracted accusations of hypocrisy: they clung to these taboos yet were incontrovertibly sexual beings themselves. Love affairs among the residents of Frau Mutschmann's old people's home led to arguments. Romances flourished and petty jealousies flared up within Frau Rahm's senior citizens' club. Some of the seniors had found lady friends in old age, while others boasted to the investigators about their conquests during the Second World War. Men who were struggling with impotence or whose wives had problems 'down below' (often resulting from the effects of a backstreet abortion), complained to the psychologists about their woes.[89] Meanwhile, pre-marital relations and contraceptives were certainly not news to this generation—they were already widespread in Germany long before 1914.[90]

More than a few of the old ladies hinted to the female researchers that they might in fact have wished for a little more room for manoeuvre in their own love lives, sometimes becoming quite emotional. 'Ah, such hard questions, my goodness', sighed the 67-year-old Frau Eugel on being asked about her upbringing. She didn't want to be 'ungrateful', but she had been properly 'unhappy and—inhibited', 'perhaps as a result of my mother's anxiety, anxiety that she had to compensate for by being strict'. 'It took me a dreadfully long time to find my way to myself and so I was very often squeezed into untruths, particularly towards my mother, because I wasn't allowed to say what I'd done, or where I was going, or what I wanted.' Frau Ziller also regretted having been clipped into extreme reserve on matters of morality because 'my mother brought me up as a kind of upper-class daughter, as the cartoons put it'. A woman aged 76 said that as a young girl she had married the wrong man because her mother and 'narrow-minded' aunts had been excessively prudish. 'Every step' in her youth had been watched through binoculars. She had not been allowed to greet male acquaintances on the street and had even been scolded for giving her future husband a kiss on their engagement. A woman who had trained as a bookkeeper had advised her own daughter to be sure to watch out for herself but 'well, not necessarily to be as demure as her mother was'.[91]

The love stories these older women told centred around the issue of relationships before marriage, and the risk of getting pregnant. For this generation, the invention and availability of the 'pill' had not yet weakened the taboo of a child out of wedlock, or an emergency wedding. The concern that their daughters and granddaughters might fall into the trap of motherhood too young was deep-seated: the family's social honour was at stake. A dressmaker, born to a metalworker in 1907, still felt the horror of her aunt bearing an illegitimate child in 1919, and recalled how the whole family had 'sunk into the ground with shame':

I was so ashamed that I wanted to sink into the ground too. I really thought everyone was giving me funny looks because of it... and I was convinced that it meant I'd never get a good husband. I thought, who'll take on a girl where illegitimate kids run in the family!

The trauma continued to have an impact on her choice of career and later romantic relationships.[92] The old women insisted that girls should not be given too much opportunity to stray, but should learn the facts of life early, so as to avoid the risk of illegitimate children. One former housemaid, for example, stressed that 'you can give boys more freedom than girls....You can let a rooster run, but you have to guard the hen.'[93] Elsa Gäbel, aged 65, talked a great deal about the 'many' women she knew who had borne a child out of wedlock in their youth, 'because we just didn't get educated like the youth of today'. But she thought that the young men of the day so often treated a young woman on a date 'like some cheap girl'. To spare her daughter from this, she'd filled her in at the age of 9. Although she'd been 'a bit shocked' because the daughter already seemed to know bits and pieces, she had not been deterred from buying a 'really educational book'. And 'then we read it, and after that my husband did too, eh', she remarked mischievously.[94]

Old women would mostly not speak directly about their own pre-marital experiences or their daughters' mistakes because they found the topic so shameful. They were more likely to get worked up about slatternly daughters-in-law, who had trapped their sons into marriage by way of a pregnancy. A widowed milliner, for example, fretted that her son's fiancée had already 'been intimate with' a man, and was thus going into the marriage sullied.[95]

The old gentlemen also insisted on purity before marriage, but were more likely to admit that there was a deep divide between aspirations and reality in their own circles. At least six of them made clear in conversation that they had married unwillingly. One interviewee said that his early marriage had 'handicapped' him, while another described the way that he and his fiancée had kept their child's existence a secret for two years.[96] Were such a thing to happen to their own daughters or granddaughters, it would still be a shock. A working man, born in 1894, said of his granddaughter: 'She had to get married. That depressed us a bit. We never had anything like that in our family. But it happened. She's got a good husband.' Despite this, he started later supporting her with considerable sums of money.[97] Things were different if a son 'had to' marry. In that case, the worries would be less about family honour and more about fear of the man's career and social mobility suffering from starting a family young.[98] As an example, a construction worker whose son had got a place at university found it regrettable that he had needed to walk down the aisle even before starting his studies. He viewed this as only a temporary setback though, and speculated about a second marriage: 'I didn't utter a word of complaint...You never know how it'll turn out for good. She's a simple girl. When my son's finished his studies, who knows who he'll end up with after that?'[99] Most of the men of this generation had first become fathers between the First World War and the Great Depression, and were still marked by the mass unemployment of that period. Looking back, many of them remarked that they had married too young and that this had had a negative effect on their professional training and future careers.[100]

For the over-60s, pre-marital sex was still wrong on principle. They might feel sympathy for 'fallen' girls, or for boys forced into marriage too young, but they were very far from prepared to defend perceived immorality. The balancing act between reality and moralistic taboos led to contortions once their own families were affected. A daughter's or granddaughter's unplanned pregnancy would be hushed up; they would press for an immediate wedding, but also frequently offer financial support. We can take Willi Nehmann as a typical example. He was a retired house painter aged 68, a home-loving man with a heart problem who liked to feed the pigeons on his weekly stroll through the town. He was annoyed that the young people 'in Berlin' walked 'down the street half-naked', and he called on the state to ban The Beatles. Now, in Bonn, he said that his youngest granddaughter had 'had to' get engaged. This bothered him, yet he was looking forward to the wedding. None of his moral views had changed ('I'm against early sex education—they learn that stuff anyway'). Rather, he took the situation as an immutable stroke of fate—and one that had befallen him too in his day. He confessed that he regretted his early marriage: 'There was a child on the way. [I'd] rather have stayed a bachelor a few [years]. The interviewer clearly did not share his opinions, as he deliberately put 'had to' in inverted commas.[101]

The older people often reacted harshly to moral failings when those involved were not their own family but 'merely' acquaintances or in-laws. Georg Bohe, who was 66, had a young subtenant ('a pretty blonde, slim'), who took her illegitimate son with her on an evening date in her lover's flat. When Bohe found out, he gave her notice and reported her to the welfare office; as a result, her 6-year-old son was put in a home. Yet at the same time, he spoke candidly about his own youth:

All the things we weren't allowed to do, we did, but secretly...Just take intercourse for example. Nowadays they take the view, a lot of the young people do, that: yes, you do that before marriage, it's better to, even, because you get to know whether you're a good match. Whereas we used to do that secretly. For God's sake, you couldn't let anyone know about it! But we all did it.[102]

164   THE OTHER '68

The statistics also show how much more deeply sexual taboos were ingrained in the older cohorts. Both groups of participants in Bonn filled in a questionnaire on the role of parents. Here, the older the interviewees, the more clearly they spoke up for complete non-discussion of sex, and for strict discipline within the family. The middle-aged adults diverged from this line, however: when asked to rank twenty-three attitude scales, all expressing authoritarian and traditionalist parenting standards, in order of preference, keeping sexuality taboo was by far the least popular option. Those aged 33 to 58 were considerably less likely to agree with putting sexual taboos in place when bringing up children than those aged over 60.[103] As many as 93 per cent of the older group were sufficiently inhibited that they agreed with the statement that 'Sexual problems are the most difficult to tackle in relation to children'. Sixty-eight per cent did not yet want to let young children 'hear anything about sexual matters'. No less than 43 per cent believed that children who joined in with physical play would grow up to be sex offenders. Old women tended to be more prudish than old men, and to think it particularly important that young boys and girls must not see each other naked. Those born before 1897 were consistently more uptight than the group born between 1898 and 1907.[104] These differences between the two age cohorts of pensioners cannot be explained by the influence of Nazism because all ages had been socialized as young people long before 1933, and had experienced the Third Reich as adults.

The age groups born before 1908 held views apparently frozen in the norms of the 1950s. Most of them rejected even the basic form of the sexual revolution that found widespread approval in West Germany in the years around 1968, considering it an impertinence on the part of Western modernity. Their calls for silence, censorship, and state intervention put the elderly sharply at odds with the two subsequent generations. They struggled with their children's sexual education, with talking about sexuality, and with public displays of either bare flesh or affection. Their inhibitions dated back to the turn of the century and had little to do with the National Socialist past. Admittedly, certain Bolsianers liked to associate sexual excesses with Jewish or Black people: Frau Mutschmann's nymphomaniac neighbour in the old people's home was 'Jewish', and Herr Bohe was afraid of the subversive effects of American 'negro culture' on morality. Anti-Semitic and racist mindsets such as these were a feature of Nazism, but also considerably pre-dated it. Clichés about Jewish pimps and sex-obsessed Black people were commonplace in around 1900, too.[105] Homophobia was equally deep-seated and unquestioned in the grandparents' generation, as the personal experience of Bonn study volunteer

August Brackenbusch shows.[106] Here, the difference with the younger people was more gradual.[107] The main areas of conflict between the elderly on one hand and the young or middle-aged adults on the other, however, were premarital relations, contraception, and nudity.

So, is it fair for Sixty-Eight to be treated as the spark for the sexual revolution? The conventional wisdom is to see the young rebels of that era as the vanguard of sexual liberation. This is not a tenable position, firstly, because the sexual 'revolution' was a longer-term process of liberalization that ran through the whole twentieth century, while occasionally accelerating. One such burst of speed had clearly begun prior to 1968, in the late fifties and early sixties, spelling defeat for both bourgeois and clerical moral guardians in West Germany. Yet contemporary observers only became aware of this breakthrough in 1966 or thereabouts. The 'pill' coincided with advances for sex education and pornography in the mass media, as a result of which the earlier wave of liberalization could now be clearly seen. The fact that sexual 'liberation' intensified and accelerated in the sixties thus had less to do with the protests and ideas of Sixty-Eight than with the rise of the media-driven consumer society. This is in line with the results of Sybille Steinbacher's and Elizabeth Heineman's studies of the history of sexuality.[108]

Secondly, the term sexual 'revolution' is misleading because it suggests a face-off between conservative and progressive ideas, a struggle between old and young, repression and an urge for freedom. In practice, the situation was more multifaceted. There were three generations involved, not two, with the adults in the middle taking on a crucial role as mediators between the other two age groups. While a majority of the over-60s held conservative views on sex, the middle generation favoured a basic version of liberalization. There were fewer differences in those days between young people and their parents (most of whom were relatively young) than we tend to think. The vast majority of the younger generation were not exactly radical on sexual matters. Even students, generally more liberal than the young working classes, were essentially as traditionally minded as their parents' generation, and predominantly rejected promiscuity and adultery. Sex no longer needed to focus on procreation, but should still 'be monogamous and result in marriage'. They were interested in 'bourgeois sexual reform' rather than a more radical sexual revolution.[109] The one issue that prompted almost unanimous agreement among young people in around 1968 was a need to remove the taboos around sexuality in the public and private spheres. This included uncensored mass media, revealing clothing, freer dialogue about sex within relationships and with children, a deregulated market for contraceptives and erotica, the

166 THE OTHER '68

popularization of sexological research, and tolerance for the widespread practice of pre-marital sex. I have termed this package the 'basic version' of the sexual revolution because it neither rocked the institution of marriage, nor encompassed a politicization of sexuality, or the emancipation of sexual minorities.

The aspects that we now, in 2024, consider fundamental legacies of the sexual revolution—the sexual emancipation of women and LGBT people, combatting sexual abuse and sexual violence—have little to do with Sixty-Eight. As it took until the seventies and eighties to make progress in this direction, it is sometimes argued that it was the 1970s that marked a structural break in the history of sexuality, and not Sixty-Eight.[110] Participants in the student revolts were not campaigning for gay sexual liberation, female desire, or rape victims' rights. Until the early seventies, the sexual 'revolution' was an essentially heterosexual, male, capitalist concern. This is equally true of the pragmatic majority of young people interested in sexual freedom, and of the small minority of the New Left who took a theoretical approach.

The New Left students began as a minority phenomenon in every respect. They were elitist, highly educated, and predominantly male, and congregated in only a few major cities, especially Frankfurt and West Berlin. Over the subsequent decade, this core developed into a 'left-wing alternative milieu', which accounted for about 10 to 15 per cent of young West Germans by 1980.[111] This scene had been guided, in part, since 1968 by a politicized version of the sexual revolution. Fully aware that they could break no more taboos merely by demanding free sex, its members turned towards a psychologically charged Marxism, which they burdened with anti-fascism. The alternative left saw restrictive sexual morality and bourgeois marriage and family alike as fascist, or a capitalist means of control. They argued that the repression of sexual urges had made the population neurotic, authoritarian, and violent, and thus that living these urges out would have a liberating effect on society. In this way, partner-swapping, pornography, nudity, and experiments with the sexuality of young children became a political manifesto. This fringe wing attempted to break the link between sex and fidelity, romantic love, and marriage, and was thus rejected not only by the parents' and grandparents' generations, but also by a large majority of young people and many women.

Thirdly, the language of revolution implies that the shift took place within the public, political arena. Yet the negotiation of sexual norms played out not only in the public sphere—to which both historians and contemporary observers have paid a great deal of attention—but also, and especially, in private. Partners, grandparents, parents, and children decided among themselves which societal norms they would abide by, and which they would not. Consensual non-compliance with official morality was commonplace, even before the 1960s. The Bonn interviewees' publicly proclaimed views were worlds apart from their private lives. The elderly might demonize pre-marital sex, but most of them had experienced it themselves. They gossiped about 'shotgun weddings', but if the worst came to the worst, they would support their children and grandchildren. Mothers might be reluctant to talk about sex, yet some would get hold of the pill for their unmarried daughters. They were harsh in judging the moral failings of young people in the abstract—the drop-outs and students they had seen on the television—yet hushed up similar lapses within their own families.

Given that the gulf between private practices and public norms was so wide, the familiar notion of Sixty-Eighters and their 'sex happenings' so beloved of the media is an equally distorted image. Isolated, symbolic incidents, in which members of the New Left used sex as a provocation, remain as recurring icons of this period. This goes both for the '*Busenattentat*' on Adorno in April 1969, and for the graphic castration leaflet put out by the *Frankfurter Weiberrat*. It also applies to the famous nude photo of the Kommune 1, first published for a mass audience in *Der Spiegel* in 1967. Similarly, the question ascribed to communard Dieter Kunzelmann, 'Why should I care about the Vietnam War if I'm having orgasm troubles?', immediately became part of the folklore of Sixty-Eight, despite the doubt as to whether he ever actually said it.[112] Such happenings were, and still are, highly entertaining for the media, but they paint a false picture of the role of the Sixty-Eighters, whether men or women, in the sexual revolution. They disregard both the exclusionary nature and narrow theoretical basis of their aims at the time, and the sizable majority of the public who favoured a basic form of sexual liberation, even before the protests of 1967 to 1969.

Thus, Sixty-Eight did not mark a turning point in the history of sexuality. The New Left's theories on sex and politics had very little impact on society. It would be similarly untrue to say that questions of sexual morality caused serious discord between old and young at that time. The situation was more complicated than that. In the late sixties, the foot soldiers of the sexual revolution—millions of the young and middle-aged—were picking up the pace on a march that had begun decades earlier. Meanwhile, a small, scattered group of Sixty-Eighters struck out leftwards, slipping away to the bushes, to fight in a few peripheral skirmishes with a small and long since vanquished band of elderly sexual conservatives.

7

Epilogue: What is Left of Sixty-Eight?

When this book first came out in the German original in February 2018, in time for the fiftieth anniversary of Sixty-Eight, I expected a rerun of the media circus of reminiscence that had accompanied previous anniversaries. I expected that, as in 1998 and 2008, the spotlight would be on a handful of male veterans; that they would do the rounds on talk shows and fill newspaper columns with interviews reasserting the central role of the SDS, the New Left, the theoretical debates, and the students' spectacular stunts, while claiming a conflict between anti-fascist sons and implicated fathers as the driving force behind the protests. And I suspected that the conservatives would also reappear to attack Sixty-Eight as a failed leftist revolution that had led to moral decline, and endangered marriage and the family. I thought we were due for a continuation of the unproductive arguments over Sixty-Eight that would, yet again, read the right–left camps of contemporary politics into the history of the 1960s and perpetuate old myths.

But I was wrong. In the wake of the #MeToo movement, which had gripped Germany too in the winter of 2017/18, the media suddenly became aware of the role of women Sixty-Eighters. Now I, as a published author, was invited to tour the TV magazine shows, talk shows, and radio stations, and my theses on the Other Sixty-Eight were also sparking dissent. Former activist Helke Sander was interviewed in *Der Spiegel* while Gretchen Dutschke-Klotz published an autobiography; both were now the subject of at least as much interest as such well-known SDS veterans as Wolfgang Kraushaar and Daniel Cohn-Bendit. When Frank-Walter Steinmeier, the President of the Federal Republic, invited various Sixty-Eighters, their former opponents, and historians to a shared dinner in July 2018 (in itself another sign that Sixty-Eight has become a cipher, a key marker of German national identity), male SDS representatives sat alongside assorted women, while younger historians joined contemporary observers at the table. New controversies flared up— particularly over the way intergenerational conflict related to gender conflict, but also relating to what stake the women's movement had in Sixty-Eight. Arguments now raged, as panellists and the press mused on whether there had been a feminine Sixty-Eight alongside the masculine version. In certain heated exchanges, Wolfgang Kraushaar and Axel Schildt denied my claim that 1968 had sparked the second wave of German feminism. While Kraushaar conceded that 'the female side was underrepresented in historical writing to date', he attacked what he saw as an attempt to rewrite the protest movement as a '*Studentinnenbewegung*', i.e. one belonging only to female students: 'The new women's movement first formed in 1971 in the context of the campaign against abortion laws...Prior to that there were tiny groups and circles, but no movement in the proper meaning of the word.' Likewise, Schildt acknowledged that 'the female aspect of the revolt had doubtlessly been marginalized in public perception', but criticized 'the backdating of the genesis of a new women's movement' and the inclusion of 'the SDS-heroines' "volleys of tomatoes" which have already been cited to death'. In trying to shift the women's movement into the 1970s, and thus to keep '1968' assigned to male protagonists, Kraushaar and Schildt were unintentionally reproducing the views of male New Leftists at the time, who saw women's struggle for equality as the 'minor contradiction'. They also reprised Alice Schwarzer's version of history in which the new feminist movement spawned from her own actions in 1971, relegating the women's groups of the late 1960s to the status of a 'pre-spring [*Vorfrühling*]'.[1]

In all the acrimony over the significance of the female Sixty-Eighters and the origin myth of the 'second wave' of feminism, my actual purpose in writing this study—expanding perspectives beyond an educated male elite at the universities, to take in the wider societal dimension of events—has often been pushed to the background. This book is an attempt to turn 1968 in West Germany inside out, to think of the personal as political. By referring to new sources, I have shone a light on the role of women, older and elderly people, and the working and middle classes. The atmosphere of protest in the years around 1968 reached far into the provinces, way beyond the strongholds of West Berlin and Frankfurt that were almost the sole focus of media attention. Fanning out from the university epicentres, it soon took in other societal institutions and realms of life: coupledom, families, schools, kindergartens, and offices.

The concern here is neither to deconstruct the icons of Sixty-Eight, nor to read evolutionary cultural change into them, to water them down beyond all recognition. The West German protest movement existed, and it had tangible results. Yet our skewed lens on events requires correction. It is only then that we can clearly make out the contours of another rebellion and another generation of Sixty-Eighters.

At heart, Sixty-Eight was a protest against traditional authorities and hierarchies, aiming to give individuals greater room for manoeuvre and to make new lifestyles possible. This upheaval went together with a sometimes-intoxicating sense that world history could be changed in the twinkling of an eye. Utopian thinking, often with a basis in theory, strengthened the belief that it was possible to create the new humanity, the new society, the new family, new institutions, or a new political system—and to do so right away. The utopian impulse behind Sixty-Eight—the assault on traditional hierarchies, the demand for wider dialogue, participation from below, and accelerated reform—played out in two separate arenas, which should be distinguished from one another. The first was the political and public sphere, while the second was the realm of private and family life. In both, there were quite distinct groups of protagonists, differing goals and variations on generational conflict, and differing levels of success in implementing reforms. All the same, the changes sparked in the private sphere proved more consequential in the long term than those in the public realm.

Let us begin with the public stage: the language of political discussions in the late sixties, not only at the universities, but also in parliament and the media, was male. Female problems and female protesters were ignored as irrelevant. From the outset, the activists were perceived as a masculine political generation. Moreover, subsequent debate was increasingly characterized by what might be termed Don Carlos Syndrome, after Friedrich Schiller's tragedy: the idea of father–son conflict over the Nazi past, extrapolated from a few individual cases, was superimposed on historical realities. Certainly, the charge of a tainted, Nazi past was ever-present in public life from 1966 to 1969; it was an effective weapon to deploy against political opponents, including professors and university rectors, police officers and judges, government ministers, and federal chancellors and presidents. All the same, the decisive point is that young critics only ever levied this charge as a means to an end, and only ever against the older generation in the abstract, unrelated to them. They would regularly turn a blind eye to the past of former Nazis they knew in person, especially if these were family members, however serious their involvement. In contrast, those who publicly criticized the protest movement were often accused of past Nazism, even though they were sometimes the wrong targets. Taking Bonn as an example, it is clear how little thorough research was done. Liberal professors were not accused, despite dubious pasts, while authoritarian rectors and deans were attacked as 'brown', even when they had a clean slate.

The public, political protest movement was predominantly made up of young people. While many of the middle generation, and a few older people, joined in with protests, particularly those against the Emergency Acts and the

Vietnam War, they rarely shared the utopian spirit that prevailed among the young. The handful of older people who protested alongside the young generation, and the many who, at least partly, assented passively to their protests, mostly had a background in the workers' movement, the SPD, or the trade unions. They shared their criticism of the sclerotic anti-communism of the fifties, and the fear that the Cold War might suddenly lurch into the carnage of war between East and West Germany. However, very few could comprehend some youngsters' flirtation with communism, or accept violent actions. The more the SDS emerged as opinion leaders among the students, the further many older people distanced themselves from them.

The status of the New Left as opinion leaders at the universities was always precarious though. It established itself briefly after the shooting of Benno Ohnesorg on 2 June 1967, aided by media-friendly direct actions, and was reanimated by the assassination attempt on Rudi Dutschke at Easter 1968, only to implode as the SDS was disbanded in 1970. Meanwhile, almost every university was dominated by a spirit of reform, even during the key phase of the revolts, from 1967 to 1969. The majority of the students favoured gradual change within West German democracy and rejected a socialist revolution. There was broad consensus among students—even including some conservatives—over incremental and specific changes, such as in anti-authoritarian university politics, or liberal sexual reform. The extent to which the upheaval of Sixty-Eight changed the ruling conservative party (CDU), enabled the electoral victory of the social-liberal coalition in 1969, and boosted the polarization of politics, on both the right and the left, in the 1970s is a strong argument for its indirect impact on the history of the Federal Republic.[2] It had a further, equally indirect effect, from the eighties onwards, as self-professed Sixty-Eighters became a powerful force in the political life of West Germany. This generation of Sixty-Eighters arose long after the student movement; it was a belated outcome, not a driver, of the unrest of that time. It was a political generation formed after the fact as its members discussed their interpretation of the protest movement, and their political mission, in the media. In this way, an agreement grew up between those men—because this was an almost exclusively male discourse—whose attempts to position themselves within a certain political camp resulted in a retrospective reframing of their life stories.

Secondly, Sixty-Eight played out in the private sphere, and thus within the family. In this arena, the protest against authority and tradition changed both families and relationships in the long term. Women's activism against patriarchal norms thus had a substantive impact on the historical effect of

172   THE OTHER '68

Sixty-Eight. This means that we should see the rebellion at least as much as a gender-based conflict as an intergenerational one. While public politics were dominated by an abstract, instrumentalized rhetoric of generational conflict, this was rare within families. It was not only about sons and fathers: three generations of families—grandparents, parents, and children—lived together in comparatively greater harmony than in previous decades, men and women alike. We should also note that the generation who dominated the Third Reich's functional elites was less the parents than the grandparents. All ages came together to hush up the Nazi past, and the Sixty-Eighters were just as active in this endeavour. The tape-recorded voices of grandparents, parents, and young adults from the late sixties point to a concord that largely masked the undoubted differences of opinion between the familial generations. Both 'intimacy at a distance' and 'intimacy through silence' kept the peace within households. Similarly, pensioners were in a better financial position following the introduction of index-linked pensions, and their consequent growing independence from children and grandchildren played a vital role in the generations being able to live together relatively peacefully.

The majority of the grandparents' generation did indeed turn against the student protests, sexual liberalization, and anti-authoritarian parenting. They remained wedded to a traditional culture of economic thrift and were concerned by the way young people had turned against nationalism and towards utopian thinking. All the same, the elderly generally directed their criticisms towards young people in the abstract: the students and drop-outs they saw on the television. Relationships with younger members of their own families were predominantly positive. They would, for example, tolerate pre-marital relations and support their grandchildren in their consumer desires so long as the appearance of outward respectability was maintained. In political terms, the old were converts to democracy, but most had been burnt several times in the past so were reluctant to get involved with party politics, and many (women in particular) retreated to a deeply apolitical stance. Many men (and some women) had experienced a long-lasting downgrading of social status during the years of denazification and, as a result, even the over-60s largely agreed that National Socialist ideas were undesirable and no longer socially acceptable.

The Sixty-Eighters' parents were clearly distinct from their grandparents; in many respects, they were a transitional generation. Parents in the 1960s were much more likely to meet their adult children halfway than the myth of 'being unlike your parents' cultivated by the self-defined Sixty-Eighters would have us believe. Many took a critical view of the tainted legacy of National Socialism and welcomed the Republic's transformation into a Western democracy, yet without picking fights with the elderly. They criticized the grandparents for their strictness and inflexibility. They advocated a collaborative approach to parenting and a basic version of the sexual revolution that accepted early sex education, contraception, and pre-marital sex. Many mothers supported their daughters in their fight for better educational opportunities and a freer choice of professions. Like their daughters, they were often already living out the phased model of temporary employment, yet did not yet dare question the image of marriage with a male breadwinner. Within families, we can thus often find an alliance between the young and middling generations in favour of reform, against the old.

The socialist revolution in West Germany that the radical students hoped for never came about. The failure of the political revolt was sealed when the Emergency Acts were passed in May 1968, if not earlier. Unlike in France or Italy, for example, Sixty-Eight in West Germany was no massive earthquake shaking up the state with involvement from the working classes.[3] Historians are keen to seize on the obvious differences when comparing Sixty-Eight in West Germany and other Western European examples. The Federal Republic was a particularly highly charged Cold War setting, a divided nation where a capitalist state faced a socialist other, and a post-fascist society in which perpetrators, bystanders, victims, and their children lived side by side. Scholars tend to draw on the first two of these specificities to explain the lack of desire for revolution among the workers. Meanwhile, the lasting legacy of Nazism is seen as the main factor in an intensified father–son generational conflict: the hushed-up guilt of ageing Nazis is said to be the distinguishing characteristic of the West German Sixty-Eight.[4] The question is, however, are we overstating these peculiarities? As I have shown, there was widespread silence about the Nazi past within families, and most Sixty-Eighters of both sexes played an active role in this. Yet if the generational conflict within families was much less virulent in practice than the conflict between the sexes, then a central tenet held to be specific to West Germany falls away.

It is therefore possible that these specificities are thus much less dominant than the parallels and links with events in other highly industrialized Western European countries. The tensions inherent to the many national master narratives of the 'Sixties in Upheaval' are similar in much of Western Europe— tensions between generational and gender-based conflict; familial and political generations; long-term shifts in cultural values and short-term attempts at political revolution; educated elites and the working classes; the male-dominated student movement and the 'second wave' of the women's movement; the 'political' and the 'private'; the centre and the periphery. For the most part, these patterns are still awaiting more detailed research and international comparative historiographical classification. Once we include gender, define 'the political' more broadly, and reject the paradigm of an apolitical 'cultural' revolution, the case of West Germany will probably come closer in many regards to other Western examples, such as those of France and Italy.[5]

Sixty-Eight was a watershed in the history of West Germany, but not in every respect. When it comes to dealing with the Nazi past, it represents no progress, and only indirect progress at most for the internal democratization of the Republic. Equally, Sixty-Eight does not represent any kind of breakthrough for the 'sexual revolution'; here, it was more of an expression and a by-product of longer-term developments. In around 1968, young people, even the students among them, wanted nothing beyond a basic liberalization of sexuality, which was fixated on marriage, heterosexuality, and bourgeois sexual reform, and was thus relatively traditional in outlook. The structural break in the history of the sexual revolution came about in the seventies, as the emancipation of women and same-sex sexuality came to the fore, along with the fight against sexual violence.

Yet the idea of Sixty-Eight as a watershed holds true in another sphere, that of gender roles and the politicization of the private. The new women's movement, the West German iteration of which originated in 1968, would in the long term permeate the whole of society and alter romantic relationships, families, and women's career paths. The change this unleashed was in line with the foundational ideas of Sixty-Eight: anti-authoritarianism, participation, utopia. The women attacked traditional patriarchal hierarchies from beneath in the name of anti-authoritarianism and participation. They ventured radical experiments in their private lives so as to break the bounds of female norms, and to allow the next generation to grow up as New Humans. Their activism intended to set gender relations, two-person relationships, and the family on new foundations. This utopian, anti-patriarchal spirit made the personal political and thus expanded the framework of what we now see as political.

I cannot agree with the commonplace that the movement was a 'political failure but a cultural success'.[6] For one thing, this assertion overestimates the cultural allure of Sixty-Eight. Many cultural processes that brought about change, such as the sexual revolution, changing parenting norms, and educational reform, had already begun before the revolts, and they were not borne by the younger generation alone, but also by elements of the generation in the middle. For another thing, this claim is based on an overly narrow view of politics. It obscures the fact that the trailblazers of the new women's movement politicized the family and gender relations. Sixty-Eight was a societal revolt against patriarchal authority that was carried both by the generations and by the sexes.

Lastly, we should also give new contours to the political generation of the Sixty-Eighters. There are the 'media Sixty-Eighters', the almost exclusively male and predominantly left-wing veterans of the movement, whose media appearances enabled them retrospectively to cobble together a generational myth based around themselves. Then there are the 'genuine' members of the generation, who carried the anti-authoritarian and utopian protests of the late sixties out of the political and into the private sphere, and were consequently changed themselves. They were women *and* men, revolutionaries *and* reformers. Because although the eye-catching actions of the SDS were immortalised in the media and thus branded into the long-term public memory, the protest movement extended far beyond the narrow circle of the New Left. Anyone who experimented on their own lives so as to create a freer, more equal society, against state and patriarchal authorities was and remains a Sixty-Eighter. There were left-liberal, liberal, and even a few conservative Sixty-Eighters— and not least among them were tens of thousands of women, who politicized their private lives and in so doing, rocked the authoritarian hierarchies to their core.

On Sources

The Bolsa (Bonn Longitudinal Study of Ageing) archive material had been forgotten until 2014, when I found it in the basement of the Psychological Institute, University of Heidelberg. It is now held in the Historical Data Centre at the University of Halle-Wittenberg. The holdings include almost 3,000 hours of conversation recorded onto reel-to-reel tape (*'Tonband'*, cited as TB), 20 metres of files (cited as BO), 300 illustrations, and raw statistical data. The Bolsa files and tapes have been digitized with funding from the Volkswagen Foundation and are now available to scholars via an online portal at https://bolsa.uni-halle.de.

The surviving tape recordings and transcripts are a unique source because it was not until twenty years later, as the oral history movement became established in West Germany, that historians began to interview ordinary people about their lives. I have cited files on the Bolsa study participants making use of the German abbreviations with which the Bolsa team structured their files. My citations consist of the participant number, the survey round (*'Durchgang'* or Dg.), and the relevant file section if applicable, for example: BO 1601, Dg. 3, Ex(ploration) 1. Such file sections include: Char (*Charakterbeschreibung*: character description), AGD (*Auseinandersetzung mit Grundsituationen des Daseins*: types of engagement with basic existential situations), GP (*Generationsproblem*: questioning on generational problems), TV (questioning on television use), VB (*Vergangenheitsbezug*: questioning on relationship with the past), ZEW (*Zukunftserwartungen*: questioning on expectations for the future), *Gesamtbeurteilung* (summary assessment), *Spontanbericht* (spontaneous report), *Tagesablauf* and *Wochenablauf* (daily or weekly schedule). General files relating to administration and implementation of the study are listed as 'A' and 'L' files, e.g.: BO A1. When I have quoted directly from a tape, I have given the tape number, participant number, and round of the study, e.g.: TB 308 (2701) Dg. 1. All the study participants' names are pseudonyms, which can be decoded with the help of a list held at the Historical Data Centre. Occasionally, biographical details such as profession, year of birth, or place of residence have been slightly altered to prevent individual study volunteers being identified. Where my text refers to 'Frau' or 'Herr', the last names given are pseudonyms.

178 ON SOURCES

The same anonymization method was used for the interviews with middle-aged adults conducted by Helga Merker's team. In 1967 and 1968, six students interviewed sixty women and sixty men aged 33 to 58 (born 1909–1934) in the Cologne-Bonn area. The study subjects were from working- and middle-class backgrounds, and over half had only primary education. Eighty-nine conversations, amounting to around 800 pages of typed transcripts are held in the Bolsa archive, file A17. Of these eighty-nine interviewees, fifty were men and thirty-nine were women, and all but one were aged 35 or over. Although Helga Merker's study questioned a total of 364 people, including thirty grandmothers, and 184 Bolsa participants aged from 60 to 78, only the eighty-nine transcripts described above survive in the archive.

Excerpts from my conversations with witnesses from Bonn are reproduced with their permission. This was either granted in advance and in full for the entire interview, or cleared with the speakers on a case-by-case basis for the particular section cited. I used the same method when I re-analysed conversations which had been taped or transcribed by others: the interviews conducted by Dr Horst-Pierre Bothien, curator at the Bonn Stadtmuseum, in 2005 and 2006 with former Bonn students who were then politically active (quoted as SMB conversations), and the interviews carried out from mid-2017 to mid-2018 for an exhibition at the Cologne Stadtmuseum (cited as KSM conversations). Twenty-one of Bothien's twenty-two conversations formed part of the Bonn exhibition and its accompanying catalogue. Sixteen of the twenty-one interviewees agreed to my secondary use of this material under their own names. Eight cleared their conversations completely for use, while another eight authorized the quotations used here. Where I calculated the frequencies of certain narrative or biographical patterns in the conversations, I also used Horst-Pierre Bothien's notes in his files which summarized the interviews as a whole. In the case of the ten interviews filmed in Cologne under the leadership of Stefan Lewejohann and Michaela Keim, I have evaluated the five featuring women in order to improve the gender balance of the interview sample. In the rare instances where I was unable to gain permission to quote specific passages from a conversation, I have used such passages only where they could be successfully anonymized.

Omissions are always clearly marked in quotations from oral sources. Transcription signs have not been used, for ease of reading.

Endnotes

Chapter 01

1. Bolsa (BO), Tonband (TB) 561 (2746) Dg. 3 (Investigator Reinhard Schmitz-Scherzer). TB 14 (1629) Dg. 3 (Investigator Manfred Schreiner). TB 607 (1738 – no connection with Bolsa). Stadtmuseum Bonn (SMB), conversation with Ulrich Rosenbaum of 11 April 2006.
2. On the figures, see Verheyen, *Diskussionslust*, p. 247; Kraushaar, *Achtundsechzig*, p. 58.
3. See Chapter 2. Michels, *Schahbesuch 1967*, p. 298, cf. p. 239 et seq. See also Gitlin, *The Whole World is Watching*; Vogel, *Unruhe im Fernsehen*; von Hodenberg, *Konsens und Krise*, p. 361 et seq.
4. Ex-activists such as Götz Aly, Peter Schneider, and Rainer Langhans took an active part in the reminiscence circus. Rohstock gives an overview of the literature published in 2008, *Von der 'Ordinarienuniversität'*, p. 10.
5. I discuss the debate around this book, originally published in German in 2018, in the final chapter. Works published by non-contemporary authors in the anniversary year include Vinen, *1968*; Siegfried, *1968 in der Bundesrepublik*; Großbölting, *1968 in Westfalen*; Michels, *Schahbesuch 1967*; Sedlmaier, *Konsum und Gewalt*. Works by contemporary authors: Kraushaar, *Die blinden Flecken*; Kraushaar, *1968*; Bude, *Adorno für Ruinenkinder*; Dutschke-Klotz, *1968*.
6. Cf. e.g. Frei, *1968*; Kraushaar, *Achtundsechzig*; Vogel, *Unruhe im Fernsehen*; Kraft, *Vom Hörsaal auf die Anklagebank*; Mercer, *Student Revolt in 1968*.
7. Cf. Ziemann, *Front und Heimat*, p. 39 et seq.; Verhey, *The Spirit of 1914*.
8. E.g. Großbölting, *1968 in Westfalen*, esp. p. 138 et seq.; Keim and Lewejohann, eds., *Köln 68!*; Nagel, *Die Provinz in Bewegung* (on Heidelberg); Bothien, *Protest und Provokation* (on Bonn). Siegfried (*1968 in der Bundesrepublik*) has recently granted the periphery more space than usual.
9. Cf. Michels, *Schahbesuch 1967*, p. 239 et seq.
10. Contemporary figures saw Bonn as both a provincial 'conglomeration of small and middle-sized towns and villages, and a cute university city'. *Merian* 9, 29 (1976): *Bonn*, p. 19 (Peter M. Bode) and p. 10 (Sebastian Haffner); figures from 1976 on p. 35 (Heinrich Lützeler). The population of Bonn in 1969 excluding the incorporated villages was only 138,012 (Müller-List, *Bonn als Bundeshauptstadt*, p. 685). *General-Anzeiger für Bonn und Umgegend* (hereafter *GA Bonn*) from 3 June 1967 (cockerel), 7 June 1967 (birthday), 4 May 1968 (wedding anniversary).
11. Cf. Moses, *German Intellectuals*; von Hodenberg, *Politische Generationen*, p. 270 et seq.; von Hodenberg, *Konsens und Krise*; Kersting, Reulecke, and Thamer, eds., *Die zweite Gründung*.
12. See e.g. Kohut, *A German Generation*, specifically p. 6 et seq.; Wehler, *Deutsche Gesellschaftsgeschichte 1949–1990*, pp. 310 et seq., 185 et seq.; Aly, *Unser Kampf 1968*.

180 ENDNOTES

13. Benninghaus, *Das Geschlecht der Generation*. See also Jureit, *Generationenforschung*; Weisbrod, *Generation und Generationalität*.

14. Cf. Frei, *1968*, p. 77 et seq.; Kohut, *A German Generation*.

15. Cf. for example: Klimke, *The Other Alliance*; Brown, *West Germany and the Global Sixties*; Gilcher-Holtey, ed., *1968: Vom Ereignis zum Gegenstand*; Kraft, *Vom Hörsaal auf die Anklagebank*; Rohstock, *Von der 'Ordinarienuniversität'*; Hacke, *Philosophie der Bürgerlichkeit*.

16. On professors cf. Moses, *German Intellectuals*; Wehrs, *Protest der Professoren*; on civilian service, Bernhard, *'Make Love not War'*.

17. Judt, *Postwar*, p. 417. Similarly: Ferree, *Varieties of Feminism*, p. 57.

18. Kohut, *A German Generation*, pp. 7–8, also p. 218 et seq. The same narrative: Kundnani, *Utopia or Auschwitz*; Wetterau, *68: Täterkinder und Rebellen*.

19. Frei, *1968*, pp. 222, 87, 84; Aly, *Unser Kampf 1968*, p. 80.

20. See Jian, Klimke, et al., eds., *The Routledge Handbook of the Global Sixties*; Klimke and Scharloth, eds., *1968 in Europe*; Fink, Gassert, et al., eds., *1968: The World Transformed*.

21. Ross, *May '68 and its Afterlives*; Zancarini-Fournel, *Le moment '68*; Jackson, *The Mystery of May 68*; Bracke, *One-Dimensional Conflict*, pp. 739–740.

22. Horn, *The Spirit of '68*, pp. 228–229.

23. Gildea and Mark, 'Introduction', pp. 6–7, 10–11.

24. von der Goltz, *The Other '68ers* (2021); see also von der Goltz and Waldschmidt-Nelson, eds., *Inventing the Silent Majority*.

25. Clifford, Gildea, and Warring, *Gender and Sexuality*, p. 239. See also Cornils, *Writing the Revolution*, ch. 5.

26. A notable exception is Italy, where Luisa Passerini's *Autobiography of a Generation* foregrounded women activists in the late 1980s. Quotation: Bracke, *Women's 1968*, p. 757. See also Bracke, *Women and the Reinvention of the Political*; Zellmer, *Töchter der Revolte*; Dehnavi, *Das politisierte Geschlecht*. See also a gendered take on the Black Freedom Movement: Howard, *Prairie Fires*.

27. For instance, Kershaw, *Roller-Coaster*, p. 237; Vinen, *1968*, ch. 8; Horn, *The Spirit of '68*, p. 217 et seq.; Mercer, *Student Revolt in 1968*, pp. 167–168, 288; Siegfried, *1968 in der Bundesrepublik*.

28. On gender bias in the cultural memory of 1968: Colvin and Karcher, eds., *Women*; Bracke, *Women's 1968*; von Hodenberg, *Writing Women's Agency*.

29. See Bracke, *Women's 1968*, p. 753; Jackson, *The Mystery of May 1968*, p. 632; Vinen, *1968*, p. 24; Horn, *The Spirit of '68*, p. 228; Marwick, *The Sixties*. Cf. Klimke and Nolan, *Introduction: The Globalization of the Sixties*, p. 5.

30. Siegfried, *Time is on My Side*, p. 9 et seq.; von Hodenberg and Siegfried, *Reform und Revolte*, p. 8; Schildt, Siegfried, and Lammers, eds., *Dynamische Zeiten*.

31. Often by way of critical contrast to Ronald Inglehart's influential idea of the 'Silent Revolution' (1977). Cf. Inglehart, *Silent Revolution*; Thome, *Value Change in Europe*; Dietz, Neumaier, and Rödder, eds., *Gab es den Wertewandel?*

32. More recent studies have interpreted the spread of everything from pizzerias or Balkan snack bars to Western pop music and Beatles hairstyles in this light. They

ENDNOTES 181

question if and when sexual freedom increased, whether or not a new culture of debate found its way into schools, the extent to which television changed the lives of wide social classes, and whether or when parents took a more collaborative approach to bringing up children. See Siegfried, *Time Is on My Side*; Möhring, *Fremdes Essen*; Seegers, ed., *Hot Stuff*; Levsen, *Autorität und Demokratie*; Herzog, *Sex after Fascism*; Steinbacher, *Wie der Sex nach Deutschland kam*; Silies, *Liebe, Lust und Last*; Verheyen, *Diskussionslust*, p. 275 et seq.; Gass-Bolm, *Das Gymnasium*; von Hodenberg, *Television's Moment*.

33. See Chapters 5 and 6, and Epilogue.

34. Ursula Lehr served as Federal Minister for Youth, Family, Women and Health from 1988 to 1991. Her student Andreas Kruse played a leading role in drawing up the German government's fifth to seventh Reports on the Situation of the Elderly (*Altenberichte*). See Chappel, *Old Volk*, pp. 806–807; Denninger, van Dyk, Lessenich, and Richter, *Leben im Ruhestand*, pp. 80–82.

35. On the sample cf. Schreiner, *Zur zukunftsbezogenen Zeitperspektive*, p. 269 et seq.; Renner, *Strukturen sozialer Teilhabe*, p. 35 et seq.

36. Additionally, thirty mothers and thirty grandmothers from the same families, and 184 Bolsianers were given the same questionnaire. The attitudes of the middle-aged and older cohorts were then compared with each other. Six female students, working on their examination theses, conducted the interviews and handed them over to Helga Merker. The outcomes are discussed in Merker, *Generations-Gegensätze*, esp. p. 40 et seq.; author interview with Helga Merker on 28 February 2017; surviving transcripts in folder BO A17. See also On Sources.

37. Bothien, born in 1955, had studied history in Bonn, with a focus on National Socialism and right-wing extremism in post-war Germany. Information given to the author by Horst-Pierre Bothien on 1 February 2017. See also the exhibition catalogue (Bothien, *Protest und Provokation*) and On Sources.

38. These include the 13 narratives based on edited interviews with West German women activists in *Die 68erinnen* ed. by Ute Kätzel, and the anonymized interview excerpts in Thon, *Frauenbewegung*; Dehnavi, *Das politisierte Geschlecht*; Silies, *Liebe, Lust und Last*.

39. Bonn and Cologne are near neighbours with a similar Catholic, Rhineland history; the cities grew together over the twentieth century to form a major conurbation, yet maintain separate universities, with their own traditions.

40. The team was led by Michaela Keim and Stefan Lewejohann. The quote is from Stefan Lewejohann in conversation with the author on 17 August 2020. The KSM team interviewed five men and five women; I have only assessed the women's interviews here. See also On Sources, and Keim and Lewejohann, eds., *Köln 68!*.

41. See Abrams, *Oral History Theory*.

42. With Katrin Moeller, Christoph Rott, and others: von Hodenberg and Moeller, *Die Stimmen der Alten*. For social science data, see https://www.ghil.ac.uk/research/project-hodenberg-2 (accessed 1 April 2021).

43. Using SPSS software.

182 ENDNOTES

Chapter 02

1. In this chapter I have constructed fictional everyday activities for the Bolsa volunteers, based on the available sources. There are extensive observations, transcripts, tape recordings, and photographs relating to the Langbeins, and the timetable for investigations in the week beginning 29 May 1967 has also survived. Pseudonyms have been used for all participants. The names of the academics have not been changed. Participant files BO 1709, Dg. 3, Wochenablauf; BO 2606, Dg. 3, AGD. Headlines from the *GA Bonn* for 29 May 1967. *Bonner Rundschau* quoted in Bothien, *Auf zur Demo*, p. 60; *GA Bonn*, 29 May 1967.

2. On the monument, see Derix, *Bebilderte Politik*, p. 143 et seq.

3. *GA Bonn*, 30 May 1967; AStA press release of 30 May 1967, in Bonn University Archive (UAB), folder 081/163; *akut* no. 32, May 1967, p. 8 et seq. See also Bothien, *Protest und Provokation*, p. 36 et seq. (including quotations from police report); Bothien , *Auf zur Demo*, p. 59.

4. *GA Bonn*, 31 May 1967. AStA press release of 30 May 1967, UAB 081/163. See also *GA Bonn*, 30 May 1967.

5. 'Bonn hat Gäste – die Polizei haut feste' (literally 'Bonn has guests, the police hit hard'), and 'Leben wir in einer Polizeistadt?'. *GA Bonn*, 30 May 1967 and 1 June 1967. On preceding events, see also the local history studies by Hillgruber, *Die Studentenrevolte*; von der Dollen, *'1968' an der Universität Bonn*; Fendrich, *Die Studentenproteste*; Pieper, *Die Studentenbewegung*.

6. Quote from BO A3, exhibition from 1977.

7. Erlemeier, born 1936, passed his *Abitur* in 1960 and studied at university from 1961 to 1966. Author interview with Norbert Erlemeier on 27 April 2016. On the timetable for 1967: Lehr and Thomae, *Stichprobe und Ablauf*, p. 10 et seq. See also Merker, *Generations-Gegensätze*, p. 310; Erlemeier, *Die Bolsa-Freitagsgruppe*.

8. BO 2604, Dg. 3, Char. BO 2605, Dg. 3, cover paper. On Frau Wellhöfer TB 59 (2604) Dg. 3. On Herr Langbein BO 1709, Dg. 3, Tagesablauf, Wochenablauf, Char. (Mitschrift Tismer). On Herr Tödtmann BO 1708, Dg. 3, Char., Spontanbericht. Cf. Schmitz-Scherzer CV in: Schmitz-Scherzer, *Freizeit und Alter*.

9. VW here means the Volkswagen Foundation, which financed the study. Handwritten poem by 1715, dated July 1967, BO A19 (emphasis in the original). Photos by Schubert in BO L1, letter of 21 December 1966, and BO A19. Quote from the behaviour description, BO 2710, Dg. 1.

10. Letter from the Deutsche Paritätische Wohlfahrtsverband Heidelberg, which provided the department with participants, to Ursula Lehr, 22 April 1965: BO A8. Home manager Maja Link to Hans Thomae, 10 January 1966, BO A19.

11. Cf. Olbrich, *Der ältere Mensch*, p. 77 et seq.

12. Letter from Schubert to Schmitz-Scherzer of 21 December 1966, BO L1, in which he calls him 'mein gestrenger und gründlicher Seelenforscher und Zerkleinerer'. Correspondence in Akte BO 1713: Postcard dated 28 December 1972, letters from 8 September 1971 and 21 December 1966, letter dated 17 December 1968.

13. Author interview with Georg Rudinger on 15 December 2014.

14. Author interview with Ursula Lehr on 15 December 2014. On the method and the researchers' training see Thomae, *Das Individuum und seine Welt*, 1st ed., p. 111 et seq.

ENDNOTES 183

15. Thomae, *Gerontologische Längsschnittstudien*, p. 5. On Thomae's move away from case histories towards statistics cf. the first and second editions of *Das Individuum und seine Welt*.

16. Thomae, *Das Individuum und seine Welt*, 1st ed.; summary in Kruse, *Personale Geschehensordnung*, and Kruse et al., *Der Beitrag der Psychologie*.

17. Cf. Kruse et al., *Der Beitrag der Psychologie* and Lehr, *Zur Geschichte der Entwicklungspsychologie der Lebensspanne*, pp. 9, 11; Olbrich and Pöhlmann, *Prozeß und Interaktion*, pp. 86, 90; Thomae, *Alltagsbelastungen*, p. 93 et seq.

18. On theories of activities and skills, see Lehr, *Psychologie des Alterns*, 1st ed.; Arbeitsgruppe Alternsforschung Bonn, *Altern psychologisch gesehen*. See also the rival idea of 'selective optimization with compensation': Baltes and Baltes, eds., *Successful Aging*.

19. All dissertations are listed in the complete Bolsa bibliography: Lehr and Thomae, eds., *Formen seelischen Alterns*, p. 287 et seq.

20. The VW funding periods spanned the years 1965 to 1970, 1976 to 1978, 1980 to 1982 and 1983/84. The 1972/73 round was funded by the German Research Foundation (DFG). Cf. correspondence with Thomae, BO A1.

21. Cf. Fooken, *Die Bonner Gerontologische Studie des Alterns*, and numerous contributions to Kruse and Schmitz-Scherzer, eds., *Psychologie der Lebensalter*. Author interview with Ingrid Tismer-Puschner on 4 August 2015.

22. Author interview with Ingrid Tismer-Puschner on 4 August 2015, and author interviews with Norbert Erlemeier on 27 April 2016, and Georg Rudinger and Ursula Lehr on 15 December 2014.

23. More detail on Thomae's past in Chapter 3. Cf. Stöwer, *Erich Rothacker*, p. 313 et seq.; Rudinger, *Hans Thomae als Wegbereiter*, p. 17; Rudinger and Stöwer, *Innenansichten*, p. 60 et seq.

24. The team regularly met in the Bear inn, cf. Erlemeier, *Die Bolsa-Freitagsgruppe*. The get-together on the evening of 29 May is fictional but based on the article in the *GA Bonn* of 9 June 1967 about Thomae's rejection of the post. Cf. CV in Tismer, *Untersuchungen zur Lebensthematik*; author interview with Ingrid Tismer-Puschner on 4 August 2015.

25. Photographs of the Hotel Löhndorf, Schafgans Archiv, Bonn; BO 1709, Dg. 3, Tagesablauf.

26. Cf. *GA Bonn*, 30 May, 31 May, and 1 June 1967.

27. TB 74 (2606) Dg. 3. TB 59 (2604) Dg. 3. BO 1709, Dg. 3, Wochenablauf.

28. BO 2605, BO 1709, BO 1755, Dg. 3: each a spontaneous report. Investigation guidelines in Merker, *Generations-Gegensätze*, p. 310 et seq.

29. *GA Bonn*, 31 May, 1 June, and 2 June 1967.

30. *GA Bonn*, 3 June and 5 June 1967; *Der Spiegel* no. 24, 5 June 1967, p. 42; *Welt am Sonntag*, 4 June 1967; *BILD*, 3 June 1967, Berlin edition. Kurras was not acting on behalf of the Stasi, cf. Michels, *Schahbesuch 1967*, p. 214 et seq.

31. Hans-Joachim Haubold, quoted in: *Der Spiegel* no. 26, 19 June 1967, p. 25.

32. *GA Bonn*, 7 June, 8 June, and 10/11 June 1967. Cf. Dutschke, *Die Tagebücher 1963–1979*, p. 44 et seq.

33. Silent marches and vigils took place on 7 June in cities including Marburg, Gießen, Bochum, Aachen, and Saarbrücken, and on 9 June in Freiburg, Konstanz, Stuttgart,

184 ENDNOTES

Heidelberg, Erlangen, Cologne, Darmstadt, and Munich. Cf. *GA Bonn* from 7 June, 9 June, and 10/11 June 1967; Michels, *Schahbesuch 1967*, p. 235 et seq.

34. The Provo movement was a Dutch youth counterculture in the mid-1960s.

35. *B. Z.* (Berlin) from 21 December 1966. *Welt am Sonntag*, 17 June 1967.

36. *Welt am Sonntag*, 17 June 1967; *BILD*, 28 August 1967; *Welt*, 5 December 1967.

37. *Der Spiegel* no. 24, 5 June 1967, p. 46 et seq., quotes p. 47 et seq.

38. Vogel, *Unruhe im Fernsehen*, pp. 226 et seq., 154 et seq., 201 et seq., 119 et seq. (quotes pp. 201, 120). See also p. 117.

39. Cf. Vogel, *Unruhe im Fernsehen*, pp. 203, 207 et seq.; Reichardt, *Authentizität*, p. 679 et seq.; Cornils, *Writing the Revolution*, p. 154 et seq.

40. *GA Bonn*, 1 June 1967. Cf. Bothien, *Protest und Provokation*, p. 68 et seq.; *akut* no. 32, May 1967, pp. 4–5, 12. As a result of an application from right-wing students, a hearing before the administrative court in Cologne denied the Bonn AStA its political mandate in April 1968.

41. Stadtmuseum Bonn (SMB) conversation with Rudolf Pörtner on 26 October 2005. Cf. *Aufruf des AStA*, undated, UAB 081/163. Quotes from Bracher and Penselin in Nevermann, ed., *Der 2. Juni*, pp. 44 et seq., 48 et seq.

42. Bothien, *Protest und Provokation*, p. 39 et seq.; *GA Bonn*, 5/6 June 1967.

43. SMB conversation with Rudolf Pörtner of 26 October 2005. On the protest demonstration of 6 June 1967 *GA Bonn*, 7 June 1967.

44. Letters to the editor of *GA Bonn*: Mrs A. W. on 13 June 1967; Th. Gansen on 7 June 1967; H. F. on 9 June 1967; Willy O. and Franz Merck on 7 June 1967; M. Schallus on 5 June 1967; H. Schl. on 16 June 1967; E. Vogel on 13 June 1967; W. E. on 16 June 1967; W. M. on 9 June 1967; W. B. and Dr E. on 16 June 1967; R. Kappis, K. Runge, and H. Ridder on 7 June 1967. Thirty-three correspondents and survey respondents in the editions dated 1 June to 28 June 1967 were evaluated.

45. Cf. *GA Bonn*, 2 June and 21 June 1967.

46. *GA Bonn*, 8 June and 15 June 1967. The *Bonner Rundschau* was even more student-friendly, cf. 16 June 1967 edition. Quote: *GA Bonn*, 6 June 1967.

47. According to a report by Maria Renner on an outing on 15 July 1965 (BO 2710, Dg. 1) relating to volunteers 2618, 2710, 2709, and 1715. On Schubert BO 2709, Dg.1, *Gesamtbeurteilung*. There is no surviving report from 1 June 1967.

48. Kieler Determinationsgerät invented by Mierke. Cf. Merker, *Generations-Gegensätze*, p. 310.

49. Erlemeier, *Die Bolsa-Freitagsgruppe*, pp. 1, 6.

50. She calls them 'gammlers and poffers', *Gammler* being a pejorative term from the 1960s for young drop-outs, and *Poffer* her misremembering of the term 'provo'.

51. TB 74 (2606) Dg. 3, GP; TB 59 (2604) Dg. 3, GP.

52. BO 1755, Dg. 2, GP; TB 67 (2605) Dg. 3, GP; BO 1709, Dg. 3, GP.

53. Helga Merker was 38 and somewhat older than the rest of the team. Like Maria Renner, she had previously worked as a social worker before her studies, and held a scholarship from the Victor Gollancz Foundation. Author interview with Helga Merker on 28 February 2017.

54. Cf. Merker, *Generations-Gegensätze*, p. 45 et seq.

55. *GA Bonn*, 9 June 1967. Author interview with Helga Merker on 28 February 2017.

ENDNOTES 185

56. On the SDS strategy see Brown, *West Germany and the Global Sixties*, p. 45 et seq.
57. *Der Spiegel* no. 9, 26 February 1968, p. 26; no. 24, 9 June 1969, p. 84; no. 27, 30 June 1969, p. 31.

Chapter 03

1. Heer, *'Mein 68'*, WDR television film 1988.
2. Quote *GA Bonn*, 27 October 2015. On Heer's biography cf. Bothien, *Protest und Provokation*, p. 111 et seq.; see also Rendel and Spitz, eds., *Das weite suchen*, p. 88.
3. Heer, *'Mein 68'*, WDR television film 1988.
4. Reconstruction of the preceding events according to UAB 081/163, SDS flyer of 12 February 1968 (*Diskutieren? Nein! Relegieren!*), chronology of events by Rudolf Pörtner. See also *Der Spiegel* no. 9, 26 February 1968, p. 26 et seq.; Fendrich, *Die Studentenproteste*, p. 70 et seq.
5. The GDR had had parts of the incriminating documents forged for its smear campaign against Lübke, but the accusation was based on facts. Fischer and Lorenz, eds., *Lexikon der 'Vergangenheitsbewältigung'*, p. 187 et seq. Contemporary press reports: *Der Spiegel* no. 45, 31 October 1966; no. 10, 4 March 1968; *Stern*, 26 February 1968, p. 64 et seq.
6. Cf. *Der Spiegel* no. 10, 4 March 1968, p. 21 et seq.; *Bonner Rundschau*, 2 March 1968 (wording of the speech).
7. Schneemelcher's speech to students on 13 February 1968, *Bonner Universitätsnachrichten* no. 4, 4 March 1968, p. 4.
8. Reconstruction of the preceding events according to UAB 081/163, SDS flyer of 12 February 1968, chronology. Cf. Pieper, *Die Studentenbewegung*, p. 45 et seq.
9. According to Peter Schon, in: UAB 081/163, SDS flyer of 12 February 1968.
10. UAB 081/167, *Stugew-Extra* no. 11 dated 8 February 1968.
11. AStA Bonn flyer, 8 February 1968, signed Pörtner, UAB 081/163. Similarly, leaflet from the Evangelische Studentengemeinde dated 8 February 1968, which criticized both the students' escalation methods and the policing, UAB 081/167.
12. UAB 081/167, SDS flyer of 2 February 1968. Cf. *Der Spiegel* no. 18, 27 April 1981; Rosskopf, *Friedrich Karl Kaul*, p. 325 et seq.
13. UAB 081/167, *Terror gegen Kaul*, SDS flyer of 7 February 1968.
14. von der Dollen, *'1968' an der Universität Bonn*, p. 212 et seq. UAB 081/167, 'Bürgerliche Hinterwäldler e. v. Ortsgruppe Bonn', anonymous flyer dated 4 February 1968, opposing 'extreme left-wing terrorization of opinion'.
15. UAB 081/167, *Terror gegen Kaul*, SDS flyer of 7 February 1968; *GA Bonn*, 7 February 1968.
16. UAB 081/163, leaflet of 12 February 1968 with contributions by left-wing students. *akut* no. 40, May/June 1968, p. 7.
17. SDS member Christoph Strawe, appearing belatedly to a disciplinary tribunal hearing, explained cheekily that 'he had just got back from Leipzig'. Von Weber 'retorted maliciously to ask why he hadn't just stayed in the GDR'. Cited by contemporary witness (and opponent of Strawe's) von der Dollen in *'1968' an der Universität Bonn*, p. 217.

186   ENDNOTES

18. Bothien, *Protest und Provokation*, p. 18 et seq. Pieper, *Die Studentenbewegung*, p. 46 et seq.

19. *akut* no. 39, April 1968, p. 16.

20. *akut* no. 39, April 1968, pp. 3 et seq., 8 et seq., 16. Cf. *Bonner Universitätsnachrichten* no. 6, 1 April 1968, p. 1 et seq.; no. 9, 30 April 1968, supplement. Cf. Bothien, *Protest und Provokation*, p. 28 et seq.

21. Hectographed declaration of 23 April 1968, in Folder Suhrbier, Handakte Bothien, Stadtmuseum Bonn (SMB). In the same folder: *Kölner Stadtanzeiger*, 24 April 1968. See also *Kölner Stadtanzeiger*, 15 June 1968 and 6 June 1968; *Frankfurter Rundschau*, 7 June 1968 and 18 June 1968.

22. The assistant professor was Alfred Jahn. Bothien, *Protest und Provokation*, pp. 17 et seq., 138.

23. SMB conversations with Bernd Ramm and Hartwig Suhrbier on 12 April 2006 and 31 August 2005. The controversy around the revocation of Thomas Mann's honorary doctorate by the University of Bonn in 1936 also played a role. Cf. von Schenck, *Autobiographie*, ch. 6, p. 1; Ulrich Wickert, 'Letzte Rettung', in: *Die Zeit*, 16 February 2006 (supplement '60 Jahre Zeit').

24. SMB conversations with Judith Olek, Rudolf Pörtner, Dieter Gutschick, and Christoph Strawe from 2005.

25. Anonymized SMB conversations.

26. SMB conversation with Eckehart Ehrenberg of 9 September 2005.

27. SMB conversation with Ulrich Rosenbaum of 11 April 2006.

28. von Schenck, *Autobiographie*, ch. 6, p. 6, cf. p. 10.

29. *akut* no. 39, April 1969, pp. 3, 10 et seq.

30. *Kölner Stadtanzeiger* no. 35, 10 February 1968, Siegkreis edition, author Hartwig Suhrbier.

31. *Kölner Stadtanzeiger* no. 35, 10 February 1968, Siegkreis edition, author Hartwig Suhrbier; in the AStA chronology of 9 February 1968 article quoted on p. 1 (UAB 081/167); *GA Bonn*, 20 May 1968.

32. Quote *GA Bonn*, 27 October 2015. Cf. 'Fanatische Söhne', *Netzeitung Voice of Germany*, 31 May 2005, http://www.netzeitung.de/voiceofgermany/331875.html (accessed 19 September 2005; printout in SMB Handakte Bothien).

33. Heer, '*Mein 68*', WDR television film 1988.

34. Author interview with Hannes Heer on 23 January 2017.

35. Heer, '*Mein 68*', WDR television film 1988.

36. Heer, *auch togo bleibt deutsch*, p. 82 (capitalization added).

37. *Neues Deutschland*, 26 January 2008.

38. Heer, *auch togo bleibt deutsch*, p. 84.

39. Bothien, *Protest und Provokation*, p. 112. On the Revolutionary Cells cf. UAB 081/173. On the VDS cf. *Der Spiegel no. 24*, 9 June 1969, p. 84 et seq.

40. 'Fanatische Söhne', *Netzeitung Voice of Germany*, 31 May 2005, http://www.netzeitung. de/voiceofgermany/331875.html (accessed 19 September 2005; printout in SMB Handakte Bothien).

41. Conze, *Die Suche nach Sicherheit*, p. 337; Judt, *Postwar*, p. 417. Cf. Kaelble, *Sozialgeschichte Europas*, p. 34.

ENDNOTES 187

42. Frei, *1968*, pp. 78 et seq., 87, 222. See also Wienhaus, *Bildungswege zu 1968*, p. 38 et seq.

43. Moses, *German Intellectuals*, p. 69.

44. Aly, *Unser Kampf 1968*, pp. 194 et seq., 189, 150 et seq.

45. Passerini, *Autobiography of a Generation*, p. 22 and ch. 2; Maslen, *Autobiographies of a Generation*, p. 30.

46. Here, they took up the literary trope of father–son conflict which has its roots in antiquity. Cf. Tölle, *Altern in Deutschland*, pp. 246 et seq., 276 et seq., 305 et seq.

47. Jureit, *Generationenforschung*, pp. 92, 119 et seq. Similarly, Lüscher and Liegle, *Generationenbeziehungen*, pp. 29 et seq., 251 et seq.

48. Calculation based on Bothien, *Protest und Provokation*, p. 94 et seq.

49. Wienhaus, *Bildungswege zu 1968*, p. 95.

50. Wienhaus, *Bildungswege zu 1968*, p. 40 et seq.

51. The Merker study interviewees were born between 1909 and 1934. See On Sources.

52. Cf. Herbert, *Drei politische Generationen*, p. 100; Wildt, *Generation des Unbedingten*. The regime's most senior leaders were by contrast rather older.

53. This assessment is based on contextual research in the participant files from the third round of the study and was not one of the variables encoded by the original research team.

54. Another of the activists mentioned a communist uncle. See On Sources for further details, and also Bothien, *Protest und Provokation*, p. 94 et seq.

55. Oseka, Voglis, and von der Goltz, *Families*, p. 51.

56. Calculation based on Passerini, *Autobiography of a Generation*.

57. SMB conversation with Christoph Strawe of 1 December 2005.

58. SMB conversation with Judith Olek of 8 December 2005. Cf. excerpts from the report in Bothien, *Protest und Provokation*, p. 107 et seq.

59. SMB conversation with Judith Olek of 8 December 2005. 'We' refers to her and her brother Bernd Ramm, who was also involved in student politics in Bonn.

60. This comes through particularly clearly in, for example, the SMB conversations with Dieter Gutschick, Rudolf Pörtner, Judith Olek, and Eckehart Ehrenberg.

61. SMB conversation with Rudolf Pörtner of 26 October 2005.

62. SMB conversation with Eckehart Ehrenberg of 9 September 2005.

63. SMB conversation with Ulrich Rosenbaum of 11 April 2006; email from Rosenbaum to the author on 24 August 2017. Things were similar for Guntram von Schenck, whose grandparents were committed Nazis and took their own lives in April 1945. His parents did not speak about it, but 'it would be dishonest to say that the circumstances of my grandparents' suicide ever particularly burdened me' (*Autobiographie*, ch. 1).

64. SMB conversation with Hans Günter Jürgensmeier of 28 February 2006.

65. SMB conversation with Jürgen Aretz of 10 November 2006; cf. emails from Jürgen Aretz to the author on 28 August 2017 and 11 September 2017.

66. The SMB conversations with Pörtner, Lotz, von Bredow, Ehrenberg, and Crueger show particularly clearly that this research was never done.

67. Cf. Frei, *Vergangenheitspolitik*, p. 403.

68. In eight of the sixteen reanalysed conversations, the speakers spontaneously compared their own parents, or their own roles, with those of Hannes Heer.

188   ENDNOTES

69. Heer, 'Mein 68', WDR television film 1988. See for example: *GA Bonn*, 27 October 2015 and 20 August 2008; *Hessisch-Niedersächsische Allgemeine*, 26 January 2009 and 14 January 2012; *Neues Deutschland*, 26 January 2008; *Spiegel online*, 15 August 2006 (http://www.spiegel.de/kultur/literatur/ss-bekenntnis-wie-hat-grass-damals-zum-holocaust-gestanden-a-431646.html, accessed 27 January 2017).

70. SMB conversation with Bernhelm Booß of 22 March 2006.

71. SMB conversations with Ulrich Rosenbaum on 11 April 2006; with Wolfgang Breyer on 29 November 2005; with Eberhard Crueger on 8 March 2006; with Wilfried von Bredow on 24 April 2006.

72. SMB conversations with Maria Zabel on 26 July 2006; with Hans Günter Jürgensmeier on 28 February 2006.

73. Welzer, Moller, and Tschuggnall, *Opa war kein Nazi*, esp. pp. 48 et seq., 51 et seq., quote p. 26.

74. SMB conversation with Hans Günter Jürgensmeier on 28 February 2006.

75. A further interviewee, Dieter Gutschick, saw his father as a 'dyed-in-the-wool Nazi' and met with the 'argument that he put forward ... that he personally was not to blame for anything and that he hadn't known anything. ... He had been classified as a fellow traveller by the Americans, and thus he also felt himself to have been only a fellow traveller and not a major perpetrator. Just like that. Easy.' In the 1960s, the son was prepared to tolerate his father's proximity to the Nazis as 'understandable', considering his experiences as a German from the Sudetenland, but he later changed his opinion: 'it was only later that I realized that he was fully aware of [the Nazi crimes]'. There is no indication of any such personal confrontation with his father at the time. SMB conversation with Gutschick on 28 September 2005.

76. Cf. UAB PF 138/194: Fakultätsprotokolle [faculty meeting minutes] 1968–1969.

77. SMB conversation with Heidrun Lotz on 4 May 2006.

78. Author interview with Hannes Heer on 23 January 2017.

79. See the letter quoted at the beginning of this chapter.

80. SMB conversation with Dieter Gutschick on 28 September 2005.

81. SMB conversation with Bernhelm Booß on 22 March 2006.

82. Oseka, Voglis, and von der Goltz, *Families*, p. 51.

83. Beate Klarsfeld, 'Ohrfeige für Pg. 2633930', in: *elan*, December 1968; Dutschke, *Die Tagebücher 1963–1979*, p. 27; Ensslin and Kunzelmann cited in: Koenen, *Das rote Jahrzehnt*, pp. 383, 160 et seq., cf. p. 384.

84. According to Lüscher and Liegle, *Generationenbeziehungen*, p. 256, see also p. 262. Higgs and Gilleard, *Generational Justice*, p. 252.

85. Siegfried, *Time Is on My Side*, p. 65 et seq.

86. Blücher, *Die Generation der Unbefangenen*, pp. 404, 102, 109 et seq., 393, 396, cf. 130, 399.

87. Siegfried, *Time Is on My Side*, p. 65 et seq.

88. *akut* no. 37, January 1968 (Rutger Booß, 'Der braungefleckte Dekan').

89. Cf. von Wiese, *Ich erzähle mein Leben*, p. 356 et seq.; *Internationales Germanistenlexikon*, entry on Benno von Wiese, p. 2025 et seq. (Klaus-Dieter Rossade).

90. Author interview with Georg Rudinger on 18 August 2016.

91. According to a student council leaflet of 26 April 1974, looking back at 1970: UAB 081/173.

ENDNOTES 189

92. *akut* no. 41, July 1968, p. 5 et seq.; no. 40, May/June 1968, p. 5 et seq. Cf. SMB conversation with Heidrun Lotz on 4 May 2006. Thomae cited in: Rudinger and Stöwer, *Innenansichten*, p. 91.

93. Cf. Rudinger and Stöwer, *Innenansichten*, pp. 79–80. Author interview with Georg Rudinger on 18 August 2016. SMB conversation with Heidrun Lotz on 4 May 2006.

94. UAB 081/173, leaflets 'Kommunistische Studentenpresse' 1/1974 and 'FSV Psychologie', 26 April 1974. Thomae was not involved in the Bund Freiheit der Wissenschaft (Federation for the Freedom of Scholarship), which had a strong presence in Bonn. Cf. Wehrs, *Protest der Professoren*.

95. Rudinger and Stöwer, 'Thomae, Hans', p. 441 et seq. Cf. Stöwer, *Erich Rothacker*, p. 13.

96. Thomae cited in: Rudinger und Stöwer, *Innenansichten*, p. 64, cf. pp. 55 et seq., 60.

97. Thomae, *Ruf des Lebens*, pp. 7, 9, 44 et seq., 57, 79, 158 et seq. See also pp. 74 et seq., 87 et seq., 104 et seq.

98. Thomae, *Immanuel Kant*, esp. p. 10 et seq. Thomae, *Das Wesen der menschlichen Antriebsstruktur*.

99. See also Oseka, Voglis, and von der Goltz, *Families*, p. 49 et seq.

100. Claus Leggewie, *A Laboratory of Postindustrial Society*, p. 281. On Wolff see *Frankfurter Allgemeine Zeitung*, 13 August 2010 (http://www.faz.net/aktuell/politik/staat-undrecht/rechtspersonen/kd-wolff-rebell-aus-der-waffenkammer-11024803.html, accessed 6 February 2017); *Forschung Frankfurt* 1/2014, p. 129.

101. Mitscherlich and Mitscherlich, *Die Unfähigkeit zu trauern*. Cf. Koenen, *Das rote Jahrzehnt*, p. 101 et seq.

102. E.g. Arno Plack, Dietrich Haensch, Dieter Duhm, and others. Cf. Herzog, *Sex after Fascism*, p. 156 et seq. On Theweleit see: Koenen, *Das rote Jahrzehnt*, pp. 31 et seq., 168 et seq. See also Cornils, *Writing the Revolution*, p. 41 et seq.

103. Reiche, *Sexuelle Revolution*, pp. 60, 64.

104. See for example, novels by Peter Schneider, Günter Kunert, Peter Härtling, and Niklas Frank. Cf. Seegers, 'Vati blieb im Krieg', p. 20 et seq.

105. On the second wave: Heer, *Literatur und Erinnerung*, p. 833. Cf. Cornils, *Writing the Revolution*, p. 146 et seq.

106. Bode, *Die vergessene Generation* (2004), 8th ed., pp. 158 et seq., 241 et seq., 290 et seq. Number of printings given as of 2016. Very similar interpretations can be found in Ennulat, *Kriegskinder* (2008); Lorenz, *Kriegskinder* (2003); Winterberg, *Kriegskinder*, the book to accompany the ARD television series of the same title; Radebold, Heuft, and Fooken, eds., *Kindheiten im Zweiten Weltkrieg* (2006); Stambolis, *Aufgewachsen in 'eiserner Zeit'* (2014, esp. p. 132 et seq.); Schulz, Radebold, and Reulecke, eds., *Söhne ohne Väter* (2004).

107. For critical analysis of the war children genre, see Heinlein, *Die Erfindung der Erinnerung*.

108. Kohut, *A German Generation*, pp. 3 et seq., 11, 218–219 and title. Cf. Kohut, *History, Loss and the Generation of 1914*, p. 254.

109. Wetterau, *68: Täterkinder und Rebellen*; Kundnani, *Utopia or Auschwitz*. Gabriele Rosenthal reaches the hasty conclusion that while the Sixty-Eighters tended to 'acquit' their own fathers of involvement with the Nazis, 'confrontation with their fathers and blockages to dialogue with them were [a very central issue] for this generation.' Rosenthal, *Historische und familiale Generationenabfolge*, p. 172.

190   ENDNOTES

110. Aly, *Unser Kampf 1968*, pp. 188 et seq., 196.
111. Deutscher Bundestag, 13. Wahlperiode, Stenographischer Bericht, 163. Sitzung, 13 March 1997, p. 14719 et seq.
112. *Der Spiegel* no. 16, 14 April 2014.
113. Habermas, *Interview mit Angelo Bolaffi*, p. 23; Habermas, *Studentenprotest in der Bundesrepublik*, p. 175.
114. On the process of creating a 'generational narrative', Möckel, *Erfahrungsbruch und Generationsbehauptung*, pp. 9, 16 et seq.
115. Lönnendonker, ed., *Linksintellektueller Aufbruch*, p. 2. He cites Robert Schindel, p. 223; Wolfgang Kraushaar, pp. 270, 276. See also: Gerd Weghorn (p. 198 et seq.), anonymous (p. 201), Hajo Funke and Thomas Mitscherlich (p. 224 et seq.), Klaus Schröder (pp. 303, 307).
116. Schildt, *Überbewertet?* p. 93.
117. SMB conversation with Bernhelm Booß on 22 March 2006. Christoph Strawe of the Bonn SDS also considered the Emergency Acts 'problematic' at the time, but qualified this by saying 'it wasn't as though we were on the brink of a new '33 or something'. SMB conversation with Strawe on 1 December 2005.
118. Cf. Mausbach, *Wende um 360 Grad*; Herzog, *Sex after Fascism*, p. 175 et seq.; Kiessling, *Die antiautoritäre Revolte*, p. 274 et seq.; Jureit, *Generationenforschung*, p. 119 et seq.; Herbert, *Geschichte Deutschlands*, p. 855.
119. For an example from Bonn see Dieter Gutschick and Eckehart Ehrenberg, who were cited in a 2008 article in the *Kölner Stadtanzeiger* as typical Sixty-Eighters, who argued for coming to terms with the Nazi past, and took a stand against their fathers. However, the SMB conversations with Gutschick and Ehrenberg on 28 September and 9 September 2005 show that there was no confrontation with their parents at the time.

Chapter 04

1. Quotations and details from *GA Bonn*, 4 May 1968, 13 May 1968. The 400 Protestant clergy took to the streets of Bonn on 8 May: *GA Bonn*, 9 May 1968. The German Trade Union Confederation (DGB) held its rally on 11 May in Dortmund, thus distancing itself from the Bonn APO march.
2. Meier cited in: '68er an Rhein, Ruhr und Weser', Documentary film for WDR television by Carsten Günther (2008), Part 2. Cf. Kozicki, *Aufbruch in NRW*, p. 47 et seq., esp. 52, 64; *Der Spiegel* no. 23, 3 June 1968, p. 21 et seq.
3. UAB 081/173: Declaration by lecturers and staff of the Psychology Department dated 29 May 1968, signed Thomae, Rudinger, Renner, Merker, Lehr, Erlemeier, von Langermann, Schaible, Schade, et al. Cf. Bothien, *Protest und Provokation*, p. 59 et seq.
4. On young people, see Siegfried, *Time Is on My Side*; Reichardt, *Authentizität*; on professors: Wehrs, *Protest der Professoren*; Moses, *German Intellectuals*. Enumerated according to Herbert, *Geschichte Deutschlands*, pp. 783 et seq., 835 et seq.: the section on the period from 1965 to the change of government in 1969 devotes twenty-seven of its sixty-nine pages (40 per cent) to youth culture and the 'Sixty-Eighter' movement. Older people are mentioned in passing on pp. 786, 814 et seq., and 819.

ENDNOTES   191

5. Herbert, *Geschichte Deutschlands*, p. 784.
6. *GA Bonn*, 14 May 1968, report on an Institute for Applied Social Sciences (infas) poll on the April unrest.
7. *Der Spiegel* no. 17, 22 April 1968, p. 28.
8. Among students it was 52 per cent. *GA Bonn*, 7 May 1968.
9. Allensbach poll from May/June 1968. The number of opponents of the acts aged between 30 and 44 (31 per cent), and 45 and 59 (26 per cent) lay between the values for the older and younger age groups. Noelle and Neumann, eds., *Jahrbuch der öffentlichen Meinung 1968-1973*, p. 229. On the survey of students of February 1968, cf. von der Goltz, *A Polarised Generation?*, p. 201.
10. *GA Bonn*, 8 June 1968.
11. BO 1724, Dg. 3, GP; BO 1605, Dg. 3, GP; BO 1756, Dg. 3, GP.
12. BO 1611, Dg. 3, Char., VB, GP, ZEW.
13. BO 1659, Dg. 3, ZEW, Citizenrolle, VB, GP. A steelworker who was bombed out in 1943 had a similar experience (BO 1750, Dg. 3, VB): 'It's a good thing to have pulled yourself together again in such a sorry state and got yourself back on your feet. Because there's twenty years in it, working in the moulding shop, in the sweat of your brow, and then in one night, it's all gone.'
14. Surveys from 1966 and 1965. On Russia: 45 vs. 30 per cent; respondents in the middle age group lay in between, with 41 and 37 per cent. Noelle and Neumann, eds., *Jahrbuch der öffentlichen Meinung 1965-1967*, pp. 456, 420.
15. Noelle and Neumann, eds., *Jahrbuch der öffentlichen Meinung 1965-1967*, pp. 478, 480. The men on the Bolsa study were particularly likely to express an opinion on the subject of the Vietnam War ranging from concern to criticism (BO 1738, 1746, 1750, 1753, 1758, 1659).
16. TB 14 (1629) Dg. 3.
17. BO 1618, Dg. 3, GP. Similarly, BO 1740, Dg. 3, GP.
18. BO 1744, Dg. 3, GP.
19. BO 1656, Dg. 3, GP; BO 1734, Dg. 3, GP; BO 1740, Dg. 3, VB. Similarly in BO 1758, Dg. 3, GP: 'We were exploited and deceived for political purposes.'
20. BO 1740, Dg. 3, GP.
21. E.g. BO 1644, Dg. 3, GP; cf. BO 1650, 1658, and 1659, Dg. 3.
22. 1721 cited in: Tismer, *Untersuchungen zur Lebensthematik*, p. 71.
23. TB 38 (1735) Dg. 3.
24. 1639 cited in: Renner, *Strukturen sozialer Teilhabe*, p. 201 et seq.
25. 2749 cited in: Renner, *Strukturen sozialer Teilhabe*, pp. 213, 215.
26. Transcript 1619 from 1967 in BO A7, p. 22; 1738 cited in: Tismer, *Untersuchungen zur Lebensthematik*, p. 34.
27. He also went fishing for carp and pike: 1729, cited in: Tismer, *Untersuchungen zur Lebensthematik*, p. 21.
28. Cf. Noelle and Neumann, eds., *Jahrbuch der öffentlichen Meinung 1965-1967*, p. 132.
29. Cf. Transcripts 1601 and 1705 in BO A7; transcript 1602 in BO A9.
30. Four per cent mentioned going to the cinema, putting it at the bottom of the rankings, far behind gardening, watching television, and walking. Evaluation 'Freizeit', signed Schmitz-Scherzer, Renner, Olbrich, in BO A3, p. 3 et seq.

192 ENDNOTES

31. Cf. TB 26 (1650) Dg. 5; Transcript 'Herr Br.' in BO A9, p. 13; Transcript 1705 in BO A7; 'Frau D.' in Renner, *Strukturen sozialer Teilhabe*, p. 213; 'Herr A.' in Tismer, *Untersuchungen zur Lebensthematik*, p. 33.

32. Cf. Tismer, *Untersuchungen zur Lebensthematik*, pp. 117 et seq., 105, 71; Renner, *Strukturen sozialer Teilhabe*, p. 211 et seq.

33. The standard pension was based on forty years of contributions. Hardach, *Der Generationenvertrag*, p. 89 et seq. Cf. Torp, *Gerechtigkeit im Wohlfahrtsstaat*, ch. 2; Grünendahl, *Generationenbeziehung im Wandel?*, p. 30; Künemund and Motel, *Verbreitung*, p. 126. See also Lüscher and Liegle, *Generationenbeziehungen*, p. 146.

34. Anna-Maria Hirsch, 'Interaktionsmuster', undated report in BO L9, pp. 4 et seq., 11.

35. Anna-Maria Hirsch, 'Interaktionsmuster', in BO L9, p. 11. E.g. TB 483 (2730) Dg. 1; TB 26 (1650) Dg. 5; Renner, *Strukturen sozialer Teilhabe*, pp. 213, 216, 225.

36. The term was coined by Rudolf Tartler in 1961, and subsequently popularized by Rosenmayr and Köckeis in 1965. Cf. Renner, *Strukturen sozialer Teilhabe*, p. 188 et seq.; Tismer et al., *Psychosoziale Aspekte der Situation älterer Menschen*, p. 71.

37. Anna-Maria Hirsch, 'Interaktionsmuster', in BO L9, p. 7 et seq.

38. Only one in ten lived in a three-generation family where there was a genuinely shared household. Ten per cent had children who lived over 100 kilometres away. Renner, *Strukturen sozialer Teilhabe*, pp. 59 et seq., 183 et seq.

39. Renner, *Strukturen sozialer Teilhabe*, pp. 142 et seq., 150, 190; similarly, Anna-Maria Hirsch, 'Interaktionsmuster', in BO L9, p. 7.

40. Renner, *Strukturen sozialer Teilhabe*, pp. 68, 73 et seq., 178, (quotation) 185 et seq.

41. Examples include study volunteers 1624, 1649, 1729, and 1734.

42. BO A3, draft interview guidelines for phase 1, probably 1965.

43. Author interview with Ingrid Tismer-Puschner on 4 August and 11 August 2015.

44. Author interviews with Ingrid Tismer-Puschner on 4 August and 11 August 2015; with Norbert Erlemeier on 27 April 2016; with Georg Rudinger on 18 August 2016.

45. Author interviews with Helga Merker on 28 February 2017 and 29 May 2017.

46. Author interview with Norbert Erlemeier on 27 April 2016.

47. Author interview with Georg Rudinger on 18 August 2016. Similarly, Helga Merker's primary experience of her parents was as victims of the war and the regime. Interview with Helga Merker on 28 February 2017.

48. 109 of 222 participants were born between 1898 and 1906.

49. Letter from Nurse Christa to Ursula Lehr, Kelsterbach, 8 February 1965, in BO A8.

50. BO 1728, Dg. 3; BO 1746, Dg. 3; cf. BO 1759, Dg. 3. The investigators were Georg Rudinger, Reinhard Schmitz-Scherzer, and Karl-Georg Tismer.

51. BO 1610, Dg. 3, AGD, Gesamteindruck (Investigator Tismer).

52. BO 1710, Dg. 3, VB (Investigator Tismer).

53. BO 1703, Dg. 1. The post-war FDP campaigned for drawing a line under the Nazi past.

54. Author's own statistical analysis of BO participant files and tape recordings 1601–1659, 1701–1759, Dg. 3 (n=96). This evaluation was limited to the male volunteers because in discussing their life histories they could scarcely evade the subjects of party membership, military service, and denazification.

55. BO 1606, Dg. 3, VB; interview script for phase three in BO L8.

56. BO 1645, Dg. 3, VB.

ENDNOTES 193

57. BO 1615, Dg. 3, VB.
58. The investigator was Heiser: TB 470 (2726) Dg. 1. My thanks to Carolin Schmidt, B. A., University of Halle, for this transcript.
59. TB 5 (1612) Dg. 5.
60. The only exception was an incriminated teacher from East Germany, who moved to the West after his retirement (BO 1704). On the 131ers, see: Frei, *Vergangenheitspolitik*, ch. 3; Garner, *Public Service Personnel*, p. 38 et seq.
61. On denazification cf. Niethammer, *Die Mitläuferfabrik*; Vollnhals, *Entnazifizierung*; Hayse, *Recasting West German Elites*.
62. BO 1653, Dg. 3, VB, investigator's notes.
63. 1706, cited in: Tismer, *Untersuchungen zur Lebensthematik*, p. 86 et seq.
64. BO 1654, Dg. 2–4, VB.
65. BO 1703, Dg. 1, Dg. 3.
66. This played out in East Germany. BO 1704, Dg. 1. Cf. BO 1703, Dg. 1, where another man put up with a housing problem because 'as a former Nazi Party member...he saw no option' to protest.
67. BO 1612, Dg. 3, VB. Similar cases: BO 1637, 1653, 1654 (all Dg. 3, VB); BO 1615, 1638, Dg. 1.
68. BO 2651, Dg. 3, VB.
69. BO 1703, Dg. 1.
70. BO 1610, Dg. 3.
71. BO 1746, Dg. 3, AGD.
72. Fifty-nine per cent of the 222 study participants had only primary education (*Volksschule*), and 25 per cent had further technical training with or without a leaving certificate (*Fachschule* or *Mittlere Reife*). Only 5 per cent had attended a *Gymnasium* (grammar school); 3 per cent had been to university. Schreiner, *Zur zukunftsbezogenen Zeitperspektive*, p. 275 et seq.
73. Variable 'Höchster Schulabschluß' (v35_t1) crossed with my own evaluation of every file relating to a male volunteer in Phase 3, 1967/68 (n = 95).
74. BO 1610, Dg. 3, Gesamteindruck.
75. 'nicht mitgelaufen, bin vorneweg gelaufen.' BO 1703, Dg. 2; Dg. 3, Char. Odermann mistrusted the study and, on several occasions, demanded that the tape be stopped before expressing his views against foreigners.
76. BO 1612, Dg. 3; TB 5 (1612) Dg. 5.
77. BO 1740, Dg. 3; BO 1746, Dg. 3; BO 1750, Dg. 3.
78. BO 1627, Dg. 3. Similarly: BO 1707, Dg. 3; BO 1610, Dg. 3.
79. BO 1618, Dg. 3; BO 1717, Dg. 3, Ex. 3. Similarly: BO 1733, Dg. 3; BO 1758, Dg. 3; BO 1601, Dg. 3; BO 1616, Dg. 3.
80. Renner, *Strukturen sozialer Teilhabe*, p. 176 et seq.
81. Fifteen instances vs. seventy-six, BO participant files, Dg. 3 (Citizenrolle: Aktivität).
82. Tismer, *Untersuchungen zur Lebensthematik*, p. 83 et seq. (quotation p. 85 et seq.) with reference to 1706.
83. BO 1712, Dg. 3, VB.
84. BO 1748, Dg. 3.
85. BO 1703, Dg. 1, esp. 'Ergänzungsbericht zur Bandaufnahme'. The row predated 1948.

194 ENDNOTES

86. Overall evaluation of BO participant files.
87. N = 144. Merker, *Generations-Gegensätze*, p. 186 et seq.
88. Poll from 1971 (30, 19, 14, and 8 per cent): Noelle and Neumann, eds., *Jahrbuch der öffentlichen Meinung 1968–1973*, p. 73.
89. BO A17: Herr Russ, p. 3; Frau Seifert, p. 3 et seq.; cf. Herr Seifert, p. 4.
90. BO A17, Herr Urban, p. 5 et seq.
91. Herr Senns, p. 4. Similar criticism of the elderly generation was expressed by Frau Faust, p. 2; Frau Kloppe, p. 3; Herr Scherz, p. 3; Herr Ebelt, p. 12.
92. On the Forty-Fivers, cf. Hodenberg, *Politische Generationen*; Moses, *German Intellectuals*. On the transcripts, see On Sources.
93. Of the sixteen men among the Forty-Fivers, six were aged between 45 and 56; the others were 36 to 42 years old. (Angermann, Groth, Russ, Kaym, Lochny, Reichelt, Senns, Sieber, Urban, Ebelt, Anschütz, Körber, Tetzlaff, Ullrich, Triene, Baumann). The female Forty-Fivers are Wagenknecht, Hahn, Stehr, Seifert, Rusp. The right-wing women are Weser, Strube, Kaiser, Hoffmann; right-wing men are Werder, Galen, Hahn, Schauer (all transcripts in BO A17).
94. Herr Russ, pp. 1 et seq., 8 et seq., 12.
95. Herr Kaym, p. 3. Cf. Herr Stehr, p. 5.
96. Frau Russ, p. 7 et seq.
97. E.g. in the media (cf. Hodenberg, *Konsens und Krise*) or politics.
98. See also Welzer, Moller, and Tschuggnall, *Opa war kein Nazi*, p. 246 et seq.
99. Siegfried, *Time Is on My Side*, p. 69.

Chapter 05

1. UAB Kl. Slg. 331, 'arbeitskreis emanzipation' documentation, p. 43 et seq.: AKE leaflet dated June 1971 ('Vorlesungskritik an der PH') and *Kölner Stadtanzeiger*, 13 July 1971. Hervé, *Studentinnen in der BRD*, p. 110 et seq. Author interview with Florence Hervé on 18 May 2017.
2. Author interview with Florence Hervé on 18 May 2017.
3. Interview with Florence Hervé in: *FrauenPerspektiven* no. 23, winter semester 2008/09, ed. Equal Opportunities Officer at the University of Bonn, p. 15. Quotation in: *Kölner Stadtanzeiger*, 13 July 1971. Letter from Hervé to Horst-Pierre Bothien of 11 September 2007, in SMB, Handakte Bothien.
4. Undated '*Flugblatt an Studentinnen*', October 1969, 'arbeitskreis emanzipation' documentation, p. 9 (UAB Kl. Slg. 331).
5. *akut* no. 56, 7 November 1969, pp. 6, 1. Sociology student Vetterlein, born in 1946, was the managing editor at *akut* in late 1969, under editor-in-chief Gerd Langguth.
6. The latter was the paper's specialist on sex-related matters. *akut no.* 58, 4 December 1969, pp. 1, 3. Author interview with Florence Hervé on 18 May 2017.
7. *GA Bonn*, 13 December 1967, 16 May 2014, and 11 June 2017; http://www.montag-club.de/pages/home.html (accessed 18 May 2017). The named speakers addressed the club in 1969/70, with the exceptions of Tismer-Puschner (1974) and Lehr (2008). When it was disbanded in 2017, the club still had 190 members. It was not possible to interview Hannelore Fuchs (1929–2017) for this book.

ENDNOTES 195

8. UAB Kl. Slg. 331, 'arbeitskreis emanzipation' documentation, p. 16 et seq.: Renger to Florence Murray-Hervé, 1 June 1970, and reply from the AKE.

9. Hervé to Horst-Pierre Bothien, 11 September 2007, in SMB, Handakte Bothien.

10. See esp. Kuhn et al., eds., *100 Jahre Frauenstudium*; *FrauenPerspektiven* no. 23, winter semester 2008/09, ed. Equal Opportunities Officer at the University of Bonn.

11. For instance: Frei, *1968*; Kraushaar, *Achtundsechzig*; Klimke, *The Other Alliance*; Cohn-Bendit and Dammann, eds., *1968: Die Revolte*; Gildea et al., eds., *Europe's 1968*; Fink, Gassert, et al., eds., *The World Transformed*.

12. Wehler, *Deutsche Gesellschaftsgeschichte 1949–1990*, pp. 172, 184. Herbert, *Geschichte Deutschlands*, pp. 861, 921 et seq.; cf. p. 844 for an almost word-for-word identical assessment of the American 'Women's Liberation Movement'. Conze, *Die Suche nach Sicherheit*, p. 403 et seq., cf. p. 355.

13. Westad, 'Preface', p. xxii. Maurer, *Gespaltenes Gedächtnis?* p. 119. Cf. Evans, *Sons, Daughters and Patriarchy*, p. 331 et seq.; Clifford, Gildea, and Warring, *Gender and Sexuality*, p. 239; special issue of the periodical *L'homme*, 2009.

14. Wienhaus, *Bildungswege zu 1968*, p. 102 (with reference to West Berlin).

15. Damm-Rüger died in 1995. Damm, *Meine Mutter, die 68erin*, p. 25.

16. The SDS broke up in 1970. Cf. Herbert, *Geschichte Deutschlands*, p. 859 et seq.; Koenen, *Das rote Jahrzehnt*.

17. Cited in: Bendkowski, ed., *Antiautoritärer Anspruch und Frauenemanzipation*.

18. Helke Sander on 13 September 1968 in: Lenz, ed., *Die neue Frauenbewegung*, pp. 63, 61 et seq. On the increasing numbers, see also Schulz, *Der lange Atem der Provokation*, p. 84.

19. Frei, *1968*, p. 228, cf. p. 134 et seq. On 'doing gender', see West and Zimmerman, *Doing Gender*, and periodical special issue *Gender and Society* 23 (1), 2009.

20. Gretchen Dutschke-Klotz in: Kätzel, ed., *Die 68erinnen*, pp. 284, 287, cf. pp. 282, 294 et seq.

21. Gretchen Dutschke-Klotz, *Nachwort*, pp. 374, 375 et seq., 385.

22. Gretchen Dutschke-Klotz, *Nachwort*, p. 376; Gretchen Dutschke-Klotz, *Wir hatten ein barbarisches, schönes Leben*, p. 160.

23. Gretchen Dutschke-Klotz, *Nachwort*, p. 393 et seq.

24. Pfeil, *Die 23jährigen*, pp. 36 et seq., 46 et seq., 55, 62 et seq.

25. Zellmer, *Töchter der Revolte*, p. 30 et seq.

26. Cf. von Oertzen, *Teilzeitarbeit und die Lust am Zuverdienen*.

27. Pfeil, *Die 23jährigen*, pp. 78 et seq., 87 et seq., 93.

28. Elke Regehr in Kätzel, ed., *Die 68erinnen*, pp. 82, 92, cf. p. 95 (similarly: Elsa Rassbach, p. 63; Hedda Kuschel, p. 122); Karin Adrian p. 254 et seq.; Helke Sander p. 177.

29. Cf. Pfeil, *Die 23jährigen*, p. 48 et seq. Sigrid Giersberg and Angelika Lehndorff-Felsko still spoke of the 1960s students as 'girls' in 2018 (in: KSM conversations on 8 August 2018 and 9 June 2018).

30. Elsa Rassbach in: Kätzel, ed., *Die 68erinnen*, p. 65 et seq., cf. pp. 69, 73; Sarah Haffner, p. 149; Dagmar Przytulla, née Seehuber, p. 205 (similarly, Elke Regehr and Helke Sander, pp. 85 et seq., 169; unnamed woman activist in Schulz, *Der lange Atem der Provokation*, p. 81). Gretchen Dutschke-Klotz in: Kätzel, ed., *Die 68erinnen*, p. 281, cf. p. 289 et seq.

31. Cited in: Günther, *'Meine Geschichte – die 68er-Generation'* (Broadcast on *Phönix*, 2008).

196   ENDNOTES

32. Christel Kalisch, née Bookhagen, in: Kätzel, ed., *Die 68erinnen*, p. 266; Elke Regehr, p. 85 et seq.

33. Cf. Reichardt, *Authentizität*, p. 612; Clifford, Gildea, and Warring, *Gender and Sexuality*, p. 252 et seq.

34. Buhmann, *Ich habe mir eine Geschichte geschrieben*, p. 162 (with reference to Frankfurt University); Steffen speaking on 24 November 1968 at an SDS conference in Hannover (cited in: Schulz, *Der lange Atem der Provokation*, p. 88); Sander speaking on 13 September 1968 at the 23rd SDS Conference of Delegates, in: Lenz, ed., *Die neue Frauenbewegung*, pp. 60, 63 (capitalization added).

35. See Ferree, *Varieties of Feminism*, p. 53; Brown, *West Germany and the Global Sixties*, p. 286; Thon, *Frauenbewegung*; Lenz, ed., *Die neue Frauenbewegung*; Schulz, *Der lange Atem der Provokation*; Bendkowski, ed., *Wie weit flog die Tomate?*; Wiggershaus, *Geschichte der Frauen*, p. 111 et seq.

36. Sander, *Der Seele ist das Gemeinsame eigen*, p. 52 et seq. Cf. Schulz, *Der lange Atem der Provokation*, p. 85.

37. 'Die Frauen im SDS oder In eigener Sache', *konkret* no. 12/1968.

38. Lenz, ed., *Die neue Frauenbewegung*, pp. 53 et seq., 55 et seq. Schulz, *Der lange Atem der Provokation*, p. 84. UAB Kl. Slg. 331, 'arbeitskreis emanzipation' documentation, pp. 9, 37.

39. Helke Sander in: Kätzel, ed., *Die 68erinnen*, p. 167, cf. p. 165 et seq.

40. Reichardt, *Authentizität*, p. 722 et seq.; cf. Zellmer, *Töchter der Revolte*, pp. 31, 70 et seq.

41. Figures from 1964, cited in Pfeil, *Die 23jährigen*, p. 84 et seq.

42. One in eight SDS members were married: Wienhaus, *Bildungswege zu 1968*, p. 100; Hervé, *Studentinnen in der BRD*, p. 74 (figure from 1971).

43. SMB conversation with Judith Olek, née Ramm, 8 December 2005.

44. Hervé, *Studentinnen in der BRD*, p. 110. On Bonn's *Kinderläden* see UAB 081/173, report by Morus Markand, *Psycho-Info* 7 of 25 January 1971.

45. KSM conversation with Anke Brunn on 14 July 2018. Author interview with Florence Hervé on 18 May 2017.

46. Author interview with Florence Hervé on 18 May 2017 and cited in: Günther, 'Meine Geschichte – die 68er-Generation' (Broadcast on *Phönix*, 2008). Helke Sander in: Kätzel, ed., *Die 68erinnen*, p. 163 et seq. Americans Gretchen Dutschke-Klotz and Elsa Rassbach brought their experience of women's colleges and knowledge of beatniks and communes to the movement: Kätzel, ed., *Die 68erinnen*, pp. 62 et seq., 282. Ute Canaris, Claudia Pinl, Anke Brunn, and Ursula Christiansen, who were active in politics in Cologne, had gained political experience at North American and French universities (KSM conversations on 16 June 2018, 16 June 2018, and 14 July 2018).

47. Helke Sander in: Kätzel, ed., *Die 68erinnen*, p. 163. Hanna B. cited in: Runge, *Emanzipationen*, p. 73 et seq.

48. Memorandum from the Board of Trustees to the *Studentenwerk*, 1967, cited in: Hervé, *Studentinnen in der BRD*, p. 84, see also p. 74 et seq.

49. Sarah Haffner, Karin Adrian, and Frigga Haug in: Kätzel, ed., *Die 68erinnen*, pp. 144, 243, 184 et seq., 191. See also Marlies Arndt in: Thon, *Frauenbewegung*, p. 190 et seq.

50. Zellmer, *Töchter der Revolte*, p. 49 et seq.

ENDNOTES   197

51. Figures from 1964: Pfeil, *Die 23jährigen*, p. 83 et seq.
52. Karin Adrian in: Kätzel, ed., *Die 68erinnen*, pp. 243, 246. Similar accounts come from Sigrid Fronius, p. 25, and Hedda Kuschel, p. 123. Beatrix Novy cited in: Günther, *'Meine Geschichte – die 68er-Generation'* (Broadcast on *Phönix*, 2008).
53. Hedda Kuschel in: Kätzel, ed., *Die 68erinnen*, p. 130; cf. an instance from the Munich SDS, 1967 in Zellmer, *Töchter der Revolte*, p. 64.
54. Sander, *Der Seele ist das Gemeinsame eigen*, p. 47. Sander cited in: *Der Spiegel*, no. 15, 11 April 2018, p. 47.
55. Susanne Schunter-Kleemann in: Kätzel, ed., *Die 68erinnen*, pp. 116, 112; Karin Adrian, p. 248; Christel Kalisch, née Bookhagen, p. 263.
56. For instance Dagmar Przytulla, née Seehuber, in: Kätzel, ed., *Die 68erinnen*, p. 207; Gretchen Dutschke-Klotz, p. 286; Gretchen Dutschke-Klotz, *Wir hatten ein barbarisches, schönes Leben*, p. 117.
57. Helke Sander in: Kätzel, ed., *Die 68erinnen*, p. 172. For more on this see Ingrid Schmidt Harzbach in a 1985 discussion between former SDS members, in: Lönnendonker, ed., *Linksintellektueller Aufbruch*, p. 228 et seq.
58. Lutz von Werder in: Lönnendonker, ed., *Linksintellektueller Aufbruch*, p. 209. See also Urs Müller-Plantenberg in: Lönnendonker, ed., *Linksintellektueller Aufbruch*, p. 231; Frigga Haug in: Kätzel, ed., *Die 68erinnen*, p. 192 et seq.
59. Cf. contributions to: Lönnendonker, ed., *Linksintellektueller Aufbruch*, pp. 207 et seq., 214 et seq., 226 et seq. Quotation from Annemarie Tröger, p. 214.
60. Cf. Annette Schwarzenau in: Kätzel, ed., *Die 68erinnen*, pp. 48 et seq., 56 et seq.; Helke Sander, p. 171 et seq. On the demonstration: *Der Spiegel* no. 24, 9 June 1969, p. 85.
61. On sexuality, see Chapter 6. Cf. here Dagmar Przytulla, née Seehuber, in: Kätzel, ed., *Die 68erinnen*, p. 208 et seq.
62. Cf. Helke Sander in: Kätzel, ed., *Die 68erinnen*, p. 167 et seq.; see also Hedda Kuschel, p. 128 et seq. More information on the nurseries in van Rahden, *Eine Welt ohne Familie*; Reichardt, *Authentizität*, p. 728 et seq., and (in Bavaria) Zellmer, *Töchter der Revolte*, p. 68 et seq.
63. Day-to-day operations required 'responsibility and discipline from the adults too, which they first had to learn'. UAB 081/173, report by Morus Markand in: *Psycho-Info* no. 7, 25 January 1971, p. 12 et seq.
64. Co-founder of the *Frankfurter Weiberrat*, Silvia Bovenschen in: 'Kinder sind die Falle', *Der Spiegel* no. 2, 10 January 2011, p. 108. See also Helke Sander in: Kätzel, ed., *Die 68erinnen*, p. 164, and Jutta Ditfurth in: *Protokoll Ringvorlesung Freie Universität Berlin vom 27. April 1988*, http://www.infopartisan.net/archive/1968/29703.html (accessed 27 April 2017).
65. Cited in: Bendkowski, ed., *Antiautoritärer Anspruch und Frauenemanzipation*.
66. Sarah Haffner in: Kätzel, ed., *Die 68erinnen*, p. 151, cf. p. 149 et seq. Cf. Elke Regehr and Gretchen Dutschke-Klotz, pp. 89, 282, 295; Claudia Pinl in: KSM conversation dated 16 June 2018.
67. Anonymized SMB conversation from 2005/2006. Silvia Bovenschen also remembered preparing 'fried potatoes' for the revolutionaries, cited in: Bendkowski, ed., *Antiautoritärer Anspruch und Frauenemanzipation*.

198   ENDNOTES

68. Gretchen Dutschke-Klotz, *Wir hatten ein barbarisches, schönes Leben*, p. 81; Annemarie Tröger in: Lönnendonker, ed., *Linksintellektueller Aufbruch*, p. 216; Susanne Schunter-Kleemann in: Kätzel, ed., *Die 68erinnen*, p. 111.

69. Cf. analysis of women's magazines from the 1960s to 1980s in Röser, *Frauenzeitschriften*; Langer-El Sayed, *Frau und Illustrierte*.

70. On the reaction to the series, see von Hodenberg, *Ekel Alfred und die Kulturrevolution*.

71. Cf. Obermaier, *High Times*; Cornils, *Writing the Revolution*, p. 141 et seq.

72. Quotations from: *Der Spiegel* no. 48, 25 November 1968, p. 60 et seq. See also *Der Spiegel* no. 39, 23 September 1968, p. 77 et seq.; Sarah Haffner and Gretchen Dutschke-Klotz in: Kätzel, ed., *Die 68erinnen*, pp. 151, 284.

73. Cf. Ashwin, *Women and the Transition from Communism*.

74. For example, Sigrid Fronius, then AStA chair at the Freie Universität Berlin: Kätzel, ed., *Die 68erinnen*, pp. 28, 36.

75. Cited in: Bendkowski, ed., *Antiautoritärer Anspruch und Frauenemanzipation*. Schrader-Klebert's essay *Die kulturelle Revolution der Frau* of June 1969, which saw woman as a household slave, kept in dependency, would become a key text.

76. On the forgotten tradition see Heinsohn, *Die eigene Geschichte erzählen*; Dischner, *Eine stumme Generation*; Gerhard, *Unerhört*; Hervé, ed., *Geschichte der deutschen Frauenbewegung*.

77. Cited in Bendkowski, ed., *Antiautoritärer Anspruch und Frauenemanzipation*. Similarly, author interview with Florence Hervé on 18 May 2017.

78. Cf. Annemarie Tröger in: Lönnendonker, ed., *Linksintellektueller Aufbruch*, p. 215; Gretchen Dutschke-Klotz in: Kätzel, ed., *Die 68erinnen*, p. 281; Dagmar Przytulla, née Seehuber, p. 218; Sander, p. 162 et seq.; Elsa Rassbach, p. 63.

79. Frigga Haug in: Kätzel, ed., *Die 68erinnen*, p. 192. Cf. Frigga Haug, *Wie Pelagea Wlassowa Feministin wurde*, p. 189 et seq. Similarly, Ingrid Schmidt-Harzbach on women's workplace groups in Berlin in: Lönnendonker, ed., *Linksintellektueller Aufbruch*, p. 227 et seq. On Frankfurt and Munich: Schulz, *Der lange Atem der Provokation*, p. 149 et seq.; on Bonn: Florence Hervé in: *FrauenPerspektiven* no. 23, winter semester 2008/09 ed. Equal Opportunities Officer at the University of Bonn, p. 15.

80. Bovenschen cited in: Bendkowski, ed., *Antiautoritärer Anspruch und Frauenemanzipation*; cf. Sander in: Kätzel, ed., *Die 68erinnen*, p. 174. See also Schulz, *Der lange Atem der Provokation*, p. 92 et seq.; Nave-Herz, *Die Geschichte der Frauenbewegung*, p. 56.

81. For more on this see Haug, *Wie Pelagea Wlassowa Feministin wurde*, p. 189 et seq.; Christel Kalisch, née Bookhagen, in: Kätzel, ed., *Die 68erinnen*, p. 264.

82. Kätzel, ed., *Die 68erinnen*, pp. 86, 130, 218, 253, cf. pp. 151, 253.

83. Nave-Herz, *Die Geschichte der Frauenbewegung*, p. 80.

84. For instance, Elsa Rassbach, in: Kätzel, ed., *Die 68erinnen*, p. 74 et seq., and Frau Schaal in: Dehnavi, *Das politisierte Geschlecht*, p. 272. On relationship-busting flat-shares, see Dehnavi, *Das politisierte Geschlecht*, pp. 270, 312 et seq.

85. Lehmann, *Matriarchat nicht Proletariat!*, p. 41 et seq.

86. Lehmann, *Matriarchat nicht Proletariat!*, p. 46.

87. Kommune 2, *Kindererziehung in der Kommune*, p. 174. For more on this, see Christel Kalisch, née Bookhagen, in: Kätzel, ed., *Die 68erinnen*, p. 267.

ENDNOTES 199

88. Karin Adrian in: Kätzel, ed., *Die 68erinnen*, p. 248 et seq., cf. p. 252 et seq. See also Gretchen Dutschke-Klotz, p. 286: 'Even loving someone was somehow wrong', i.e. 'patriarchal or bourgeois'.

89. Sven Reichardt, *Von 'Beziehungskisten'*, pp. 267 et seq., 280.

90. Lehmann, *Matriarchat nicht Proletariat!*, p. 45.

91. Reichardt, *Von 'Beziehungskisten'*, pp. 278, 280. See also Häberlen, *The Emotional Politics of the Alternative Left*, which follows the emotional experiments that West German leftists conducted on their private lives into the 1980s.

92. Viola Roggenkamp, 'Lysistrata geht um', *Die Zeit* no. 18, 22 April 1977.

93. Cf. Koenen, *Das rote Jahrzehnt*, p. 162 et seq., quotation p. 165.

94. Annette Schwarzenau in: Kätzel, ed., *Die 68erinnen*, pp. 50, 57; Kuschel, p. 125. See also two instances from Bavaria in the documentary film *'Die Kinder der sexuellen Revolution'*, WDR 2016.

95. Passerini, *Autobiography of a Generation*, esp. pp. 32 et seq., 84, 95 et seq.

96. Dagmar Przytulla, née Seehuber, in: Kätzel, ed., *Die 68erinnen*, pp. 169, 215 et seq. Others also reported on mutual rivalries, pp. 71, 151, 218, 255 et seq.

97. SMB conversation with Heidrun Lotz on 4 May 2006.

98. Elke Regehr in: Kätzel, ed., *Die 68erinnen*, p. 99, cf. Sigrid Fronius, pp. 27, 21. Sarah Haffner, p. 141 et seq.; Helke Sander, p. 161. See also Elsa Rassbach and Elke Regehr, pp. 62, 96. There are similar contemporary accounts from two women from Frankfurt in: Dehnavi, *Das politisierte Geschlecht*, pp. 165, 170.

99. Cited in: *'68er an Rhein, Ruhr und Weser'*, Documentary film for WDR television by Carsten Günther (2008), Part 2.

100. Frigga Haug in: Kätzel, ed., *Die 68erinnen*, p. 181 et seq. Further instances in pp. 76, 101 et seq., 203, 261. KSM conversation with Angelika Lehndorff-Felsko on 9 June 2018. See also author interview with Florence Hervé on 18 May 2017, with reference to one of her German host families.

101. Examples include Elke Regehr in: Kätzel, ed., *Die 68erinnen*, p. 98 et seq., and women interviewed by Thon, *Frauenbewegung*, pp. 428, 155.

102. Pfeil, *Die 23jährigen*, pp. 111 et seq., 136. Similar results from 1964 can be found in Blücher, *Die Generation der Unbefangenen*, p. 102.

103. Pfeil, *Die 23jährigen*, p. 136.

104. See Chapter 3. Cf. Stambolis, *Aufgewachsen in 'eiserner Zeit'*, p. 132 et seq.; Bode, *Die vergessene Generation*, p. 149 et seq.; Stambolis, *Töchter ohne Väter*, p. 87 et seq.

105. Author interview with Helga Merker on 28 February 2017. Merker, *Generations-Gegensätze*, pp. 45, 49 et seq. See also On Sources.

106. All transcripts from BO A17: Frau Hirsch, pp. 3 et seq., 6; Frau Angermann, p. 3; Frau Stehr, pp. 2, 5; Frau Faust, p. 2 et seq.; Frau Seifert, p. 3 et seq.

107. Frau Zorn, p. 1; Frau Banse, pp. 1, 4; Frau Eichhorn, pp. 2, 4.

108. For example, Frau Stamm, p. 2; Frau Borchert, p. 5; Frau Baumann, p. 3.

109. Merker, *Generations-Gegensätze*, p. 181, cf. pp. 183 et seq., 232 et seq. On the results of the PARI questionnaire (Parental Attitude Research Instrument) see p. 209 et seq., cf. pp. 313 et seq., 50.

110. Cf. table in Merker, *Generations-Gegensätze*, p. 180. On the young people's views, see also Blücher, *Die Generation der Unbefangenen*, p. 127 et seq.; Pfeil, *Die 23jährigen*, p. 142 et seq.

200 ENDNOTES

111. Cf. Merker, *Generations-Gegensätze*, pp. 88, 77, 94.
112. BO A17: Frau Borchert, p. 4 et seq.; Frau Fischer, p. 8; Frau Zabel, pp. 1 et seq., 9; Frau Rottorf, p. 1 et seq.; Frau Hahn, p. 3. See also Frau Russ, p. 1.
113. Frau Langer, p. 2; Frau Hirsch, pp. 5 et seq., 1; Frau Angermann, pp. 4, 6. Relatively strict: Frau Anz, p. 1 et seq.; Frau Ruhle.
114. Blücher, *Die Generation der Unbefangenen*, p. 109 et seq. See also Pfeil, *Die 23jährigen*, p. 106 et seq.; Siegfried, *Time Is on My Side*, p. 68 et seq.
115. Cf. BO A17: Frau Örtel, p. 2 et seq.; Frau Borchert, pp. 1, 3; Frau Sachse, p. 2; Frau Stehr, p. 1; Frau Hahn, p. 12.
116. Frau Strube, p. 1 et seq.; Frau Anz, pp. 2, 4. See also Frau Zorn, p. 1. The statistics bear out this tendency to assess their own children differently from other people's, cf. Merker, *Generations-Gegensätze*, p. 158.
117. Merker, *Generations-Gegensätze*, pp. 70, 141, 143 et seq., 300 et seq.
118. Seegers, '*Vati blieb im Krieg*', pp. 181, 196 et seq. Pfeil, *Die 23jährigen*, p. 82. Cf. Dehnavi, *Das politisierte Geschlecht*, pp. 167, 195.
119. BO A17: Frau Russ, p. 13 et seq. Similarly, Frau Wagenknecht, p. 9 et seq.; Frau Ruhle, p. 17 et seq.; Frau Esser, p. 10; Frau Hahn, p. 11 et seq.; Frau Linke, p. 6.
120. Frau Zabel, p. 14; Frau Märker, p. 4; Frau Gröpsch, p. 4. Similarly, Frau Schauer, p. 4.
121. *PARI-Skalen* nos. 3 and 13, analysis in Merker, *Generations-Gegensätze*, p. 209 et seq., cf. p. 313 et seq. and appendix table B (available in the Deutsche Nationalbibliothek Leipzig), p. 11.
122. BO A17: Frau Anz, p. 7; Frau Weser, p. 4 et seq.
123. Cf. Frau Kloppe, p. 4; Frau Baumann, p. 3 et seq.; Frau Damm, p. 4; Frau Gutsche, p. 6 et seq.; Frau Arnhold, p. 4; Frau Strube, p. 6.
124. In 1964, 13 per cent of girls (but only 4 per cent of boys) said that they had been forced into their current job against their expressed wishes: Pfeil, *Die 23jährigen*, p. 198 et seq. Cf. Merker, *Generations-Gegensätze*, p. 182. Lehr spoke in 1969 of a woman's 'constriction' by 'family considerations' (*Frau im Beruf*, p. 397).
125. Lehr, *Frau im Beruf*, pp. 136 et seq., 162 et seq.
126. Dagmar Przytulla, née Seehuber, in: Kätzel, ed., *Die 68erinnen*, p. 202. Dehnavi, *Das politisierte Geschlecht*, p. 195 et seq. See also similar accounts of father–daughter conflict from Frankfurt student Frau Schaal (in: Dehnavi, *Das politisierte Geschlecht*, p. 178 et seq.), Monika Cadenberg, and Marlies Arndt (Thon, *Frauenbewegung*, pp. 281, 186).
127. Cited in: Dehnavi, *Das politisierte Geschlecht*, p. 193 et seq. Hedda Kuschel's stepfather also thwarted her educational plans: Kätzel, ed., *Die 68erinnen*, p. 121 et seq.
128. Karin Adrian in: Kätzel, ed., *Die 68erinnen*, pp. 239, 254 et seq. Cf. Dehnavi, *Das politisierte Geschlecht*, p. 175 et seq.
129. Frau Esser, born 1945, cited in: Dehnavi, *Das politisierte Geschlecht*, pp. 173, 165.
130. BO A17: Frau Krause, p. 7; Frau Gröpsch, p. 1.
131. BO A17: Frau Weser, p. 4. Similarly, Frau Borchert, p. 6; Frau Rottorf, p. 3.
132. BO A17: Frau Esser, p. 2; Frau Gutsche, p. 3 et seq., cf. p. 6 et seq.
133. Lehr, *Frau im Beruf*, p. 132.
134. See for example Sarah Haffner in: Kätzel, ed., *Die 68erinnen*, p. 141; Helke Sander, p. 161. Cf. Zellmer, *Töchter der Revolte*, p. 32 et seq. on the expansion of education.

ENDNOTES 201

135. For more on the study design, see Chapter 2.
136. Author interview with Ingrid Tismer-Puschner on 4 August 2015.
137. Schmitz-Scherzer, *Freizeit und Alter*, pp. 65 et seq., 82 et seq.
138. Renner, *Strukturen sozialer Teilhabe*, pp. 211, 218, 228, cf. p. 177.
139. From 1966; agreement among 30- to 44-year-olds was at 29 per cent, and among 45- to 59-year-olds, it was at 31 per cent. Noelle and Neumann, eds., *Jahrbuch der öffentlichen Meinung 1965–1967*, p. 150.
140. Men and women combined: Noelle and Neumann, eds., *Jahrbuch der öffentlichen Meinung 1965–1967*, p. 65.
141. Cited in: Silies, *Liebe, Lust und Last*, p. 343.
142. Dagmar Przytulla, née Seehuber, in: Kätzel, ed., *Die 68erinnen*, p. 202.
143. Karin Adrian in: Kätzel, ed., *Die 68erinnen*, pp. 243, 255.
144. Cited in: Silies, *Liebe, Lust und Last*, p. 340 et seq.
145. Elisabeth Beck-Gernsheim cited in: Silies, *Liebe, Lust und Last*, p. 421; Thon, *Frauenbewegung*, p. 60.
146. Thon, *Frauenbewegung*, p. 268 et seq. Cf. Hausen, *Frauenerwerbstätigkeit*, p. 21 et seq.; Silies, *Liebe, Lust und Last*, p. 421.
147. She was ultimately unable to 'find a single case of this kind of emancipation' and instead gathered 'representative' tape recordings from women from various milieus. They included a Jew, several communists, and other political activists. Cited in: Frasl, *Studien zur Protokoll-Literatur*, p. 72. Runge, *Frauen: Versuche zur Emanzipation*, p. 271.
148. Thon, *Frauenbewegung*, pp. 186 and 255, cf. pp. 182 et seq., 260, 279, 413. Further examples in: Silies, *Liebe, Lust und Last*, p. 339 et seq.; Kätzel, ed., *Die 68erinnen*, p. 158.
149. Thon, *Frauenbewegung*, pp. 271 et seq., 288 et seq., 154 et seq.
150. Cf. Thon, *Frauenbewegung*, pp. 61, 155, 412, 430 et seq.
151. Annette Schwarzenau cited in: Kätzel, ed., *Die 68erinnen*, p. 58 et seq. See also Elke Regehr, Helke Sander, and Gretchen Dutschke-Klotz, pp. 96 et seq., 178 et seq., 294. KSM conversation with Anke Brunn on 14 July 2018.
152. Tröger wanted 'by no means' to claim that women in the SDS 'had been the main political teachers and not the men'. Cited in: Lönnendonker, ed., *Linksintellektueller Aufbruch*, pp. 218 et seq., 232, 234.
153. Cf. Helke Sander in: Kätzel, ed., *Die 68erinnen*, p. 177.
154. All quotations from Bendkowski, ed., *Antiautoritärer Anspruch und Frauenemanzipation*.
155. Susanne Schunter-Kleemann in: Kätzel, ed., *Die 68erinnen*, pp. 118 et seq., 115, 109. Cf. Elsa Rassbach, pp. 74, 77; Eke Regehr, p. 97; Gretchen Dutschke-Klotz, p. 296.
156. In the USA in particular, they are pigeonholed as white, middle-class groups, which excluded non-whites, lesbians, and women from lower social classes: Evans, *Women's Liberation*. On West Germany cf. Schulz, *The Women's Movement*, p. 290 et seq.; Zellmer, *Töchter der Revolte*, pp. 7 et seq., 266 et seq.; Stöhr, *Feminismen und politische Kultur*, p. 155 et seq.; Thon, *Frauenbewegung*, p. 51 et seq.
157. *Der Spiegel* no. 26, 21 June 1976, p. 144 et seq. Cf. *Der Spiegel* no. 37, 8 September 1975 ('Penetrieren unerwünscht [Penetration Unwanted]'), p. 130 et seq.; cover page no. 27, 30 June 1975; no. 36, 2 September 1974.
158. UAB Kl. Slg. 331, 'arbeitskreis emanzipation' documentation, p. 42.

202 ENDNOTES

159. *GA Bonn*, 16 May 2014; *Kölnische Rundschau*, 22 November 2005.
160. The band 'Bonner Blaustrümpfe' (Bonn Bluestockings) was actually founded in 1974. Cf. http://www.Lesbengeschichte.de/staedte_bonn_d.html (accessed 16 July 2017).
161. *Emma* no. 3/2018, pp. 4, 84 et seq.; cf. no. 4/2018, pp. 64–65.
162. Schulz, *Remembering 1968: Feminist Perspectives*, pp. 21 et seq., 29. For similar debates about other European cases, see Colvin and Karcher, eds., *Women*; Schulz, ed., *The Women's Liberation Movement*; Colvin and Karcher, eds., *Gender*.
163. Lucy Delap proposes a global history of mosaic feminisms to overcome the deceptively neat separation of numbered waves, and the Eurocentric narrative privileging white, educated Euro-American women: Delap, *Feminisms*, pp. 14–15.
164. Cf. von Hodenberg, *Writing Women's Agency*; Schmincke, *Von der Politisierung des Privatlebens*, p. 297 et seq. (quotation p. 297); cf. Paulus, Silies, and Wolff, *Die Bundesrepublik*, p. 15 et seq.
165. Cf. Benninghaus, *Das Geschlecht der Generation*; Möckel, *Erfahrungsbruch und Generationsbehauptung*.
166. Silies, *Liebe, Lust und Last*, p. 426 et seq.

Chapter 06

1. Anonymized contemporary conversation. I have reconstructed the *Konditorei* scene on the basis of the study participants' files. Quotations from investigator notes and tape recordings.
2. TB 168 (2624) Dg. 3; TB 88 (2610) Dg. 3; BO 2702, Dg. 3, GP; BO 1710, Dg. 3, Char., GP, Ex. 3; BO 1756, Dg. 3, TV, GP; BO 1628, Dg. 3, GP; TB 38 (1735) Dg. 3.
3. Frau Mutschmann would testify as a witness in the suit launched by her friend. BO 2702, Dg. 1 (1965), Char.
4. Schreiner noted: 'transcribed from tape as written transcript impossible'. BO 1628, Dg. 3, VB.
5. BO 1628, Dg. 3, AGD, Char.
6. The Bolsa team rejected Freud's notion of sexual drives as determiners of behaviour, cf. Thomae, *Das Individuum und seine Welt*, 1st ed., pp. 188–189.
7. Quotations: Steinbacher, *Wie der Sex nach Deutschland kam*, pp. 10–11.
8. Herzog, *Sexuality in Europe*, p. 133. See also: Herzog, *Sex after Fascism*, p. 141 et seq.; Steinbacher, *Wie der Sex nach Deutschland kam*; Heineman, *Sexuality in West Germany*; Balestracci, *La sessualità*; Eder, *Die lange Geschichte der 'sexuellen Revolution'*.
9. 'Stimmungsbericht über das Sommerfest vom 10. Juli 1968' (report on summer ball), UAB 081/13 (see also press reports, UAB 081/13).
10. Bonn students were lagging behind the West Berliners, 74 and 72 per cent of whom had experienced coitus. Giese and Schmidt, *Studenten-Sexualität*, pp. 23, 88 (quotation), 340–341.
11. Frigga Haug, who studied in Berlin, in: Kätzel, ed., *Die 68erinnen*, p. 196. *Bonner Rundschau*, 6 July 1968, UAB 081/13.

ENDNOTES 203

12. Cf. *Der Spiegel* no. 16, 15 April 1968, pp. 67–68; *Die Zeit*, 20 December 1996.

13. Krista Sager with reference to 1969, cited in: Silies, *Liebe, Lust und Last*, pp. 338–339. SMB conversation with Bernd Ramm on 12 April 2006.

14. Accounts from the time in: Heinzel, Fanelli, et al., *'Die 68er in Göttingen'* (DVD). See also Bonn student Ulrich Wickert on the subject in: *'68er an Rhein, Ruhr und Weser'*, Documentary film for WDR television by Carsten Günther (2008), Part 1. KSM conversation with Angelika Lehndorff-Felsko on 9 June 2018.

15. See KSM conversation with Angelika Lehndorff-Felsko on 9 June 2018 and Pardon-Dokumente, *Lieben und lieben lassen*, pp. 23 et seq., 27–28. See *Der Spiegel* no. 36, 2 September 1968, pp. 60–61.

16. Giese and Schmidt, *Studenten-Sexualität*, pp. 188, 392.

17. Four years earlier: Schmidt and Sigusch, *Arbeiter-Sexualität*, pp. 132–133, 84–85. Eder, *Die lange Geschichte der 'sexuellen Revolution'*, pp. 32, 43–44. Also, Herzog, *Sex after Fascism*, pp. 147, 151–152.

18. Herzog, *Sex after Fascism*, pp. 126–127.

19. Cited in: *Der Spiegel* no. 35, 26 August 1968, p. 50; see also Giese and Schmidt, *Studenten-Sexualität*, p. 192; Schmidt and Sigusch, *Arbeiter-Sexualität*, p. 56.

20. Eder, *Die lange Geschichte der 'sexuellen Revolution'*, p. 34 et seq.; Silies, *Liebe, Lust und Last*, p. 102 et seq.; Silies, *Wider die natürliche Ordnung*.

21. KSM conversation with Angelika Lehndorff-Felsko on 9 June 2018. The Bonn AStA had also frequently demanded places in halls of residence for married student couples. Cf. UAB 081/164; von der Goltz, *Von alten Kämpfern*, pp. 68–69.

22. von der Goltz, *Von alten Kämpfern*; SMB conversation with Rudolf Pörtner on 26 October 2005. Ehrenberg, *Ein Stück Erinnerung*. Similar campaigns took place in Hamburg (Silies, *Liebe, Lust und Last*, p. 309) and Göttingen, where the student newspaper published doctors' addresses (Heinzel, Fanelli, et al., *'Die 68er in Göttingen'*, DVD).

23. Cited in: *'68er an Rhein, Ruhr und Weser'*, Documentary film for WDR television by Carsten Günther (2008), Part 2.

24. Giese and Schmidt, *Studenten-Sexualität*, pp. 389–390. A similarly 'alarming negligence' was also found among young people in work (Schmidt and Sigusch, *Arbeiter-Sexualität*, pp. 54–55.). *Der Spiegel* no. 35, 26 August 1968, p. 48; Eder, *Die lange Geschichte der 'sexuellen Revolution'*, p. 44.

25. Schmidt and Sigusch, *Arbeiter-Sexualität*, p. 46, and interviewees' responses in Thon, *Frauenbewegung*, p. 188; Silies, *Liebe, Lust und Last*, pp. 303, 329–330, 333, 335.

26. UAB 081/37: AStA chair Booß to Rector, 24 April 1967; Rector to AStA chair Pörtner, 13 May 1967. Note about the Rector's conversation with the AStA on 18 May 67, dated 23 May 67 (signed Ne.). Pörtner in *akut* no. 35, October 1967, p. 17. See also *akut* no. 41, July 1968, p. 19. On Hackspiel, see Bothien, *Protest und Provokation*, p. 67.

27. See *akut* no. 42, 17 October 1968, pp. 1, 5; no. 43, 1 November 1968, pp. 4–5 (here on the reaction from the *Rheinische Merkur*); no. 44, 22 November 1968, p. 10. Jung was an SPD member and his self-description appeared in an SHB election leaflet, UAB 081/37. Two critical letters from male Catholic theology students appeared in *akut* no. 35, October 1967, p. 25. Quote: *Der Spiegel* no. 14, 27 March 1967, p. 66. *Express* (Bonn edition), 12 December 1966 and 11 March 1967. See also *akut* no. 29/30, Dec. 1966/Jan. 1967, pp. 4, 19.

204 ENDNOTES

28. Steinbacher, *Wie der Sex nach Deutschland kam*, pp. 304, 329, 356, 352 et seq. On mail order companies, cf. Heineman, *The Economic Miracle in the Bedroom*, esp. pp. 858–859.

29. Herzog, *Sex after Fascism*, pp. 129 et seq., 148.

30. Cf. surveys in Noelle and Neumann, eds., *Jahrbuch der öffentlichen Meinung 1956–1964*, pp. 589–590; Noelle and Neumann, eds., *Jahrbuch der öffentlichen Meinung 1968–1973*, p. 76 et seq. See also Eder, *Die lange Geschichte der 'sexuellen Revolution'*, pp. 26–27.

31. Here he is referring to the Sixty-Eighters' slogan: 'Wer zweimal mit derselben pennt, gehört schon zum Establishment [He who sleeps with the same girl twice is part of the establishment]'. Ehrenberg, *Ein Stück Erinnerung*. SMB conversation with Hans Günter Jürgensmeier of 28 February 2006.

32. Giese and Schmidt, *Studenten-Sexualität*, pp. 192–193, quotation 193. See also Noelle and Neumann, eds., *Jahrbuch der öffentlichen Meinung 1956–1964*, p. 589; Noelle and Neumann, eds., *Jahrbuch der öffentlichen Meinung 1968–1973*, p. 244; Noelle, ed., *Allensbacher Jahrbuch 1974–1976*, p. 25.

33. In June 1970, the AKE contributed to leaflets by the Bonn Medical Department, which decried the living conditions of '*Hausschwangeren*' (pregnant women in residence: heavily pregnant women on low incomes who received hospital accommodation and medical care in return for doing housekeeping work and allowing themselves to be examined by students), but focused more heavily on economic than bodily exploitation. UAB Kl. Slg. 331, 'arbeitkreis emanzipation' documentation, p. 18 et seq. Author interview with Florence Hervé on 18 May 2017.

34. Eitler, *Die 'sexuelle Revolution'*, pp. 238, 242; Balestracci, *The Influence of American Sexual Studies*.

35. Noelle and Neumann, eds., *Jahrbuch der öffentlichen Meinung 1968–1973*, p. 244; Noelle and Neumann, eds., *Jahrbuch der öffentlichen Meinung 1956–1964*, p. 591. Eder, *Die lange Geschichte der 'sexuellen Revolution'*, pp. 33, 36, 42, 44–45; Griffiths, *Gay Politics*, pp. 36–37.

36. Griffiths, *Gay Politics*, pp. 58–59, 79 et seq.

37. See Eitler, *Die 'sexuelle Revolution'*, p. 237 et seq.; Brown, *West Germany and the Global Sixties*, p. 309 et seq.

38. Herzog, *Sex after Fascism*, p. 152 et seq. Rainer Langhans cited in: Günther, '*Meine Geschichte – die 68er-Generation*' (Broadcast on *Phönix*, 2008).

39. On the Adorno incident on 22 April 1969 cf. Reimann, *Das 'Busen-Attentat'*; on the K1 photo: Herzog, *Sex after Fascism*, pp. 180–181; on the *Kinderläden*: Reichardt, *Authentizität*, p. 762 et seq.; Koenen, *Das rote Jahrzehnt*, p. 166.

40. See for example: Reichardt, *Authentizität*, p. 649 et seq.; Herzog, *Sex after Fascism*; Eitler, *Die 'sexuelle Revolution'*; Perinelli, *Longing, Lust, Violence*.

41. Herzog, *Sex after Fascism*, pp. 180–181.

42. Reichardt, *Authentizität*, pp. 679–680, 682; cf. Koenen, *Das rote Jahrzehnt*, p. 157 et seq. Przytulla, née Seehuber, in: Kätzel, ed., *Die 68erinnen*, p. 214, see also pp. 29–30 (Sigrid Fronius), 111–112 (Susanne Schunter-Kleemann).

43. Reichardt, *Authentizität*, pp. 719–720, 659 et seq. On the frustration resulting from polygamous experimentation see also Verlinden, *Sexualität und Beziehungen*, p. 382 et seq. On the militant porn wing of the seventies: Perinelli, *Longing, Lust, Violence*.

ENDNOTES   205

44. First-hand accounts from women in: Kätzel, ed., *Die 68erinnen*, pp. 152 (quotation), 197, 209 et seq., 241, 283. See also Clifford, Gildea, and Warring, *Gender and Sexuality*, p. 241 et seq.
45. KSM conversation with Angelika Lehndorff-Felsko on 9 June 2018. See also Evans, *Sons, Daughters and Patriarchy*, pp. 337, 342 et seq.
46. Cf. Brown, *West Germany and the Global Sixties*, pp. 294–295.
47. Steinbacher, *Wie der Sex nach Deutschland kam*, p. 356.
48. Reichardt, *Authentizität*, p. 675.
49. Report by Morus Markand on the 'AKV-Kinderladen' in *Psycho-Info* no. 7, 25 January 1971, pp. 12–13, UAB 081/173. See also van Rahden, *Eine Welt ohne Familie*.
50. This pseudonym is a concatenation of several Bonn psychology students whose work is documented in BO A17 and Helga Merker's dissertation (*Generations-Gegensätze*). I was unable to contact these women for this book and have therefore anonymized them in this way. The quotations are taken from conversation minutes in BO A17: Herr Stehr, pp. 2, 6; Herr Wittek, p. 4.
51. According to Merker, *Generations-Gegensätze*, p. 77 et seq.
52. The middle-aged men talked somewhat less often about sex, presumably as a result of the 'investigator effect': they held back because they were being interviewed by young, female psychology students. By contrast, most of the over-60s were talking to male interviewers. Merker, *Generations-Gegensätze*, p. 77 et seq. (quotation p. 82). On the sample Merker, *Generations-Gegensätze*, p. 47 et seq., and see On Sources.
53. According to Merker, *Generations-Gegensätze*, p. 88. Total values of 99 to 101 per cent are a result of rounding up.
54. Frau Borchert, pp. 1–2, 5. This and all subsequent quotations from conversations with the middle age group transcribed in BO A17.
55. Herr Russ, p. 6; Herr Anschütz, p. 5 et seq.; Frau Russ, p. 4; Herr Anz, p. 4; Frau Angermann, p. 6.
56. Frau Hahn, p. 10; Herr Hahn, pp. 8–9; Herr Lochny, p. 13.
57. Herr Senns and Frau Wagenknecht. See also Noelle and Neumann, eds., *Jahrbuch der öffentlichen Meinung 1958–1964*, p. 588.
58. Herr Arnhold, p. 5; Herr Tetzlaff, pp. 2–3; Herr Hagendorf, pp. 7–8.
59. Herr Körber, pp. 2–3; Herr Hanke, pp. 1–2.
60. Similar remarks were made by men: Knobl, Urban, Körber, Philipp, Tetzlaff, and Heldt; and women: Linke and Gutsche.
61. Frau Kloppe, pp. 6, 8. Frau Vormann had also 'bought a little book' (p. 3) for her six children.
62. Cf. Silies, *Liebe, Lust und Last*, p. 338.
63. Herr Anz, p. 7.
64. Silies, *Liebe, Lust und Last*, pp. 300 et seq., 334.
65. For examples see Silies, *Liebe, Lust und Last*, p. 333 et seq.
66. Herr Anschütz, pp. 17–18; Frau Hahn, pp. 11–12.
67. Herr Schauer, p. 5; see also Herr Berger, p. 8.
68. Frau Anz, pp. 7, 5; Herr Anz, p. 10.
69. He welcomed the fact that family 'life together…had become a touch more natural' because people let their children see them naked, whereas he had never seen his parents 'even half-undressed'. Herr Baumann, p. 2 et seq.

206 ENDNOTES

70. Examples: Herr Scherz, p. 9; Herr Hahn, pp. 2, 6; Herr Werder, p. 5; Herr Groth, pp. 6–7; Herr Kaym, p. 4; Herr Hagendorf, p. 5; Herr Lochny, p. 7; Herr Philipp, p. 1; Frau Sachse, p. 2.

71. Herr Tetzlaff, pp. 3–4; similarly, Herr Urban, p. 1. Herr Märker, p. 1. Herr Tetzlaff, p. 1, cf. Herr Örtel, pp. 3–4.

72. For example: Herr Hagendorf, p. 1 et seq.; Frau Wagenknecht, pp. 2–3.

73. Steinbacher, *Wie der Sex nach Deutschland kam*, pp. 15 et seq., 348 et seq. See also Höhn, *GIs and Fräuleins*.

74. On importation: Herr Knobl, Sieber, Galen; Frau Hirsch, Weser. On the media: Herr Werder, Groth, Stehr, Hagendorf, Schauer, Vormann; Frau Weser and Anz.

75. Conservatives: Herr Groth, Galen, Schauer, Vormann, Werder, and Frau Ruhle, Anz, Zorn, and Strube. Liberals: Herr Russ, Anz, Reichelt, Urban, Anschütz, Ebelt, Senns, Tetzlaff; Frau Wagenknecht, Hahn, Banse, Faust.

76. The interviews were conducted before the public debate sparked by Rosa von Praunheim's film, and before the '*Tuntenstreit*' (a row within the gay movement over effeminacy and drag, *Tunte* being a derogatory term for a gay man) in 1973.

77. Frau Ruhle, p. 1; Frau Anz, p. 5.

78. Herr Gröpsch, p. 3; Herr Ullrich, pp. 2, 4. See also Herr Anschütz, pp. 8–9; Frau Kloppe, p. 3; Frau Faust, p. 2.

79. Herr Wucherer, pp. 3, 7 (similarly, Herr Körber, p. 4). Frau Borchert, pp. 4–5.

80. Statistical evidence in Merker, *Generations-Gegensätze*, p. 78 et seq. The study volunteers were born between 1888 and 1908.

81. Participant 1711 cited in: Merker, *Generations-Gegensätze*, p. 93, where further evidence can also be found.

82. 2623 cited in: Merker, *Generations-Gegensätze*, p. 75. Similar remarks on TB 88 (2610) Dg. 3; BO 2616, Dg. 3, GP.

83. Quotations TB 168 (2624) Dg. 3; BO 1611, Dg. 3, GP. Comparable: BO 1603, 1709, 1728, 1739, 1756 (all Dg. 3, GP).

84. TB 168 (2624) Dg. 3. Transcript BO 1619, Dg. 3, pp. 74–75, in BO A7. See also TB 14 (1629) Dg. 3: 'Above all [it's] through the American influences, through the post-war influences, young people are following what they're told, aren't they?'.

85. BO 1617, Dg. 3, TV. Similarly: BO 1606, Dg. 3, GP; BO 1610, Dg. 3, TV; BO 1657, Dg. 3, GP; BO 1713, Dg. 3, GP.

86. BO 1646, Dg. 3, GP; BO 1654, Dg. 3, GP. See also BO 1709, Dg. 3, GP.

87. BO 1656, BO 1629, BO 1713. Cf. BO 1708, BO 1611 (all Dg. 3, GP).

88. Negative views on the 'pill' BO 1646, Dg. 3, GP; BO 1739, Dg. 3, GP; TB 152 (2621) Dg. 3.

89. Home: BO 2702, Dg. 1, Char. Club: BO 2711, Dg. 1, Ex. 3, transcript p. 6. Lady friend: BO 1757, Dg. 3, Ex. 1; BO 1755, Dg. 3, AGD. War: BO 1651, Dg. 3, VB. Woes: BO 1726, Dg. 3, VB; BO 1610, Dg. 3, Ex. 1; transcript 1619, Dg. 3 in BO A7, p. 43; transcript 1705, Dg. 1 in BO A7, pp. 56–57.

90. Cf. Herzog, *Sex after Fascism*, pp. 16, 24; Herzog, *Sexuality in Europe*, p. 19 et seq.

91. TB 88 (2610) Dg. 3; BO 2616, Dg. 3, GP; TB 368 (2709) Dg. 3; TB 56 (2603) Dg. 3.

92. Cited in: Lehr, *Frau im Beruf*, p. 151.

93. BO 2617, Dg. 3, GP. Cf. participant 2645, Dg. 3, in: Merker, *Generations-Gegensätze*, p. 75.

ENDNOTES   207

94. TB 113 (2614) Dg. 3. See also BO 2616, Dg. 3, GP.
95. TB 483 (1730) Dg. 1. Cf. BO 2612, Dg. 1, Ex. 1; BO 4604, Dg. 1.
96. BO 1644 and 1651, cf. 1655, 1707, 1757, 1758 (all Dg. 3, VB).
97. Participant 1721, Dg. 1, cited in: Tismer, *Untersuchungen zur Lebensthematik*, p. 71; BO 1721, Dg. 3, Ex. 1. On the stress of daughters or granddaughters being pregnant or sexually active 'too young': BO 1751, Dg. 3, Ex. 1; BO 1651, Dg. 3, AGD; BO 1638, Dg. 3, VB; TB 38 (1735) Dg. 3.
98. Cf. BO 1612, Dg. 3; BO 1656, Dg. 3, Ex. 1; on 1658 Renner, *Strukturen sozialer Teilhabe*, p. 200 et seq.
99. Participant 1729, Dg. 1, cited in: Tismer, *Untersuchungen zur Lebensthematik*, p. 118.
100. See for example transcript 1619, Dg. 3 in BO A7; BO 1732, Dg. 3, GP; BO 1743, Dg. 3, VB; TB 368 (2709) Dg. 3; BO 2616, Dg. 3, VB.
101. BO 1651, Dg. 3, Ex. 1, VB, GP, ZEW.
102. Transcripts 1619, Dg. 2, pp. 32–33, and Dg. 3, p. 73, in BO A7.
103. Scale 18 (Suppression of Sexuality) in the PARI tests, version IV. Cf. the (sometimes very) statistically significant differences in scale means. Merker, *Generations-Gegensätze*, pp. 208 et seq., 318; BO-Probandenakten, Dg. 3.
104. My own calculations using the Bolsa data from the third round, PARI-Items 18, 41, 64, 87 (n = 179, n = 181, n = 176, n = 180) show significant differences in the means by gender (v8_t1) for Item 41 (chi square 0.018) and Item 87 (chi square 0.031); by age group for Item 18 (chi square 0.043) and Item 64 (chi square 0.034).
105. Cf. Herzog, *Sexuality in Europe*, pp. 8, 15.
106. Examples of homophobia among the Bolsianers: transcripts 1619, Dg. 2, p. 105 et seq., and Dg. 3, pp. 92–93, in BO A7; BO 2730, Dg. 3, GP.
107. In 1966, almost 40 per cent of students considered homosexuality permissible while around 20 per cent thought it impermissible, making this group more tolerant than society as a whole. Giese and Schmidt, *Studenten-Sexualität*, pp. 195–196.
108. Steinbacher, *Wie der Sex nach Deutschland kam*; Heineman, *Sexuality in West Germany*.
109. Giese and Schmidt, *Studenten-Sexualität*, pp. 393–394, 396, cf. p. 386.
110. See Heinsohn, *Kommentar*, p. 98, and Silies, *Erfahrungen des Bruchs?*, pp. 206–207; Bänziger et al., *Sexuelle Revolution?*, p. 8.
111. Reichardt, *Authentizität*, p. 38 et seq.
112. *Der Spiegel* no. 27, 26 June 1967, p. 20; cf. no. 16, 10 April 1967, p. 34.

Chapter 07

1. Cf. *Frankfurter Allgemeine Zeitung*, 30 April 2018, p. 9 (Christian Geyer, 'Wie weiblich war 1968?'). Wolfgang Kraushaar, 'Umso schlimmer für die Tatsachen', *Süddeutsche Zeitung*, 25 April 2018, p. 9. Axel Schildt, review in *Sehepunkte* 18 (2018), http://www.sehepunkte.de/2018/05/31368.html (accessed 4 October 2022). Editorial 'über uns', *EMMA* 3 (2018), pp. 4, 84 et seq.
2. Cf. von der Goltz, *A Polarised Generation?*; von der Goltz, *The Other '68ers*; Schildt, *Die Kräfte der Gegenreform*; Schmidt, 'Die geistige Führung verloren'.

208 ENDNOTES

3. On France see Ross, *Establishing Consensus*; Zancarini-Fournel, *Le moment '68*. On the 'mediterranean pattern' of 68 in Italy, France, Portugal, and Spain: Horn, *The Spirit of '68*.
4. See 'Chapter 1', p. 8, notes 17–18.
5. See also Bracke, *One-Dimensional Conflict?*, p. 640 et seq.
6. Cf. the controversial discussion in Gilcher-Holtey, ed., *'1968' – eine Wahrnehmungs-revolution?*, esp. pp. 7, 101 et seq., 125–126; see also Evans, *Sons, Daughters and Patriarchy*, pp. 346–347.

Bibliography

Archives

Historisches Datenzentrum der Universität Halle-Wittenberg, BOLSA collection (Bonner Längsschnittstudie des Alterns), 1964–1985:
BO (files)
TB (tape recordings)
Database, 5,553 variables (evaluated with SPSS)
Stadtmuseum Bonn (SMB), files and collection on the exhibition 1967/68 (2007) by Horst-Pierre Bothien.
Rheinische Friedrich-Wilhelms-Universität Bonn, Universitätsarchiv (UAB):
Collection Allgemeiner Studenten-Ausschuss (AStA) 081
Collection of the Faculty of Philosophy (Philosophische Fakultät PF 138)
Collection of the Institute of Psychology (Psychologisches Institut PF 196)
Kleine Sammlungen Kl. Slg. 331
Bonner Universitätsnachrichten
Bonner Universitäts-Blätter

Author interviews

with Norbert Erlemeier on 27.4.2016
with Hannes Heer on 23.1.2017
with Florence Hervé on 18.5.2017
with Ursula Lehr and Georg Rudinger on 15.12.2014
with Helga Merker on 28.2.2017 and 29.5.2017
with Georg Rudinger on 18.8.2016
with Ingrid Tismer-Puschner, née Puschner, on 4.8.2015 and 11.8.2015

Interviews conducted by Horst-Pierre Bothien, Stadtmuseum Bonn (SMB)

with Jürgen Aretz on 10.11.2006
with Bernhelm Booß on 22.3.2006
with Wilfried von Bredow on 24.4.2006
with Wolfgang Breyer on 29.11.2005
with Eberhard Crueger on 8.3.2006
with Eckehart Ehrenberg on 9.9.2005
with Dieter Gutschick on 28.9.2005
with Hans Günter Jürgensmeier on 28.2.2006
with Heidrun Lotz on 4.5.2006

210 BIBLIOGRAPHY

with Judith Olek, née Ramm, on 8.12.2005
with Rudolf Pörtner on 26.10.2005
with Bernd Ramm on 12.4.2006
with Ulrich Rosenbaum on 11.4.2006
with Christoph Strawe on 1.12.2005
with Hartwig Suhrbier on 31.8.2005
with Maria Zabel on 26.7.2006

Interviews conducted by students at the Department of History at the University of Cologne, under the supervision of Michaela Keim and Stefan Lewejohann, Kölnisches Stadtmuseum, Cologne (KSM)

with Anke Brunn on 14.7.2018 at the Kölnisches Stadtmuseum, conducted by Judith Wonke
with Ute Canaris on 16.6.2018 at the Kölnisches Stadtmuseum, conducted by Katharina Wonnemann
with Sigrid Giersberg on 8.7.2018 at the Kölnisches Stadtmuseum, conducted by Daniel Sasse
with Angelika Lehndorff-Felsko on 9.6.2018 at the Kölnisches Stadtmuseum, conducted by Judith Wonke
with Claudia Pinl on 16.6.2018 at the Kölnisches Stadtmuseum, conducted by Jana Beinlich

Video Material

'Die Kinder der sexuellen Revolution: Freie Liebe und ihre Folgen', *Westdeutscher Rundfunk*: Menschen hautnah series, broadcast WDR 31.3.2016.
Günther, Carsten, '68er an Rhein, Ruhr und Weser', 2 parts, 45 minutes each, broadcast WDR 9.5.2008 and 16.5.2008.
'Meine Geschichte – die 68er-Generation', series 13, episodes 3–8: Hannes Heer, Florence Hervé, Beatrix Novy, Kurt Biedenkopf, Rainer Langhans, Johannes Stüttgen. Broadcast *Phönix* 7.9.2008, 14.9.2008, 21.9.2008, 28.9.2008, 5.10.2008, 12.10.2008, all 11.45–12.00.
Heer, Hannes, 'Mein 68: Ein verspäteter Brief an meinen Vater', broadcast Cologne (*West 3*) 1988, 45 minutes. Script: Hannes Heer, editor: Ludwig Metzger.
Heinzel, Matthias, Monika Fanelli, et al., 'Die 68er in Göttingen: Aufstand gegen die Nachkriegsgesellschaft'.
'Zeitzeugen berichten', *Göttinger Tageblatt* DVD (2008).

Newspapers

akut (Bonn student newspaper)
Der Spiegel
General-Anzeiger für Bonn und Umgegend (Bonn edition), cited as *GA Bonn*

BIBLIOGRAPHY   211

Literature

Abrams, Lynn, *Oral History Theory*, 2nd ed., London/New York 2016.

Aly, Götz, *Unser Kampf 1968: Ein irritierter Blick zurück*, Frankfurt am Main 2008.

Arbeitsgruppe Alternsforschung Bonn, *Altern psychologisch gesehen: Theorie und Praxis der Erwachsenenbildung*, Braunschweig 1971.

Ashwin, Sarah, 'Women and the Transition from Communism: Between a Rock and a Hard Place', in: *The Slavonic and East European Review* 71, no. 4 (1993), pp. 712–716.

Balestracci, Fiammetta, 'The Influence of American Sexual Studies on the "Sexual Revolution" of Italian Women', in: *Children by Choice? 20th Century Value Changes in Human Reproduction and Family Planning*, eds. Ann-Katrin Gembries, Isabel Heinemann, and Theresa Theuke, Munich 2018, pp. 145–162.

Balestracci, Fiammetta, *La sessualità degli italiani: Politiche, consumi e culture dal 1945 ad oggi*, Rome 2020.

Baltes, Paul B., and Margret M. Baltes, *Successful Aging: Perspectives from the Behavioral Sciences*, Cambridge 1993.

Bänziger, Peter-Paul, Magdalena Beljan, Franz Eder, and Pascal Eitler, 'Sexuelle Revolution? Zur Sexualitätsgeschichte seit den 1960er Jahren im deutschsprachigen Raum', in: *Sexuelle Revolution? Zur Geschichte der Sexualität im deutschsprachigen Raum seit den 1960er Jahren*, eds. Peter-Paul Bänziger, Magdalena Beljan, Franz Eder, and Pascal Eitler, Bielefeld 2015, pp. 7–24.

Bendkowski, Halina, ed., 'Antiautoritärer Anspruch und Frauenemanzipation: Die Revolte in der Revolte', Ringvorlesung vom 1.6.1988, http://www.infopartisan.net/archive/1968/29708.html#top (accessed 22.3.2017).

Bendkowski, Halina, ed., *Wie weit flog die Tomate? Eine 68erinnen-Gala der Reflexion*, Berlin 1999.

Benninghaus, Christina, 'Das Geschlecht der Generation: Zum Zusammenhang von Generationalität und Männlichkeit um 1930', in: *Generationen: Zur Relevanz eines wissenschaftlichen Grundbegriffs*, eds. Ulrike Jureit and Michael Wildt, Hamburg 2005, pp. 127–158.

Bernhard, Patrick, ' "Make love not war!" Die APO, der Zivildienst und die sozialliberale Koalition', in: *Reform und Revolte: Politischer und gesellschaftlicher Wandel in der Bundesrepublik vor und nach 1968*, ed. Udo Wengst, Munich 2011, pp. 11–30.

Blücher, Viggo Graf, *Die Generation der Unbefangenen: Zur Soziologie der jungen Menschen heute*, Düsseldorf 1966.

Bode, Sabine, *Die vergessene Generation: Die Kriegskinder brechen ihr Schweigen*, 8th ed., Stuttgart 2011.

Bothien, Horst-Pierre, *Auf zur Demo! Straßenprotest in der ehemaligen Bundeshauptstadt Bonn 1949–1999*, Essen 2009.

Bothien, Horst-Pierre, *Protest und Provokation: Bonner Studenten 1967/1968*, Essen 2007.

Bracke, Maud Anne, 'One-dimensional Conflict? Recent Scholarship on 1968 and the Limitations of the Generation Concept', in: *Journal of Contemporary History* 47, no. 3 (2012), pp. 638–646.

Bracke, Maud Anne, *Women and the Reinvention of the Political: Feminism in Italy, 1968–1983*, London/New York 2014.

Bracke, Maud Anne, ' "Women's 1968 Is Not Yet Over": The Capture of Speech and the Gendering of 1968 in Europe', in: *The American Historical Review* 123, no. 3 (1 June 2018), pp. 753–757.

Brown, Timothy S., *West Germany and the Global Sixties: The Anti-Authoritarian Revolt 1962–1978*, Cambridge 2013.

212 BIBLIOGRAPHY

Bude, Heinz, *Adorno für Ruinenkinder: Eine Geschichte von 1968*, Munich 2018.

Buhmann, Inga, *Ich habe mir eine Geschichte geschrieben*, Frankfurt am Main 1983.

Chappel, James, 'Old Volk: Aging in 1950s Germany, East and West', in: *Journal of Modern History* 90, no. 4 (December 2018), pp. 792–833.

Clifford, Rebecca, Robert Gildea, and Anette Warring, 'Gender and Sexuality', in: *Europe's 1968: Voices of Revolt*, eds. Robert Gildea, James Mark, and Anette Warring, Oxford 2013, pp. 239–257.

Cohn-Bendit, Daniel, and Rüdiger Dammann, eds., *1968: Die Revolte*, Frankfurt am Main 2007.

Colvin, Sarah, and Katharina Karcher, eds., *Gender, Emancipation, and Political Violence: Rethinking the Legacy of 1968*, London/New York 2020.

Colvin, Sarah, and Katharina Karcher, eds., *Women, Global Protest Movements, and Political Agency: Rethinking the Legacy of 1968*, London/New York 2019.

Conze, Eckart, *Die Suche nach Sicherheit: Eine Geschichte der Bundesrepublik Deutschland von 1949 bis in die Gegenwart*, Munich 2009.

Cornils, Ingo, *Writing the Revolution: The Construction of '1968' in Germany*, Rochester 2016.

Damm, Dorothee, 'Meine Mutter, die 68erin', in: *Wie weit flog die Tomate? Eine 68erinnen-Gala der Reflexion*, ed. Halina Bendkowski, Berlin 1999, pp. 25–29.

Dehnavi, Morvarid, *Das politisierte Geschlecht: Biographische Wege zum Studentinnenprotest von '1968' und zur Neuen Frauenbewegung*, Bielefeld 2013.

Delap, Lucy, *Feminisms: A Global History*, London 2020.

Denninger, Tina, Silke van Dyk, Stephan Lessenich, and Anna Richter, *Leben im Ruhestand: Zur Neuverhandlung des Alters in der Aktivgesellschaft*, Bielefeld 2014.

Derix, Simone, *Bebilderte Politik: Staatsbesuche in der Bundesrepublik Deutschland 1949–1990*, Göttingen 2009.

Dietz, Bernhard, Christopher Neumaier, and Andreas Rödder, eds., *Gab es den Wertewandel? Neue Forschungen zum gesellschaftlich-kulturellen Wandel seit den 1960er Jahren*, Munich 2014.

Dischner, Gisela, ed., *Eine stumme Generation berichtet: Frauen der dreißiger und vierziger Jahre*, Frankfurt am Main 1982.

Dollen, Busso von der, ' "1968" an der Universität Bonn – ein Zeitzeuge blickt zurück', in: *Bonner Geschichtsblätter* 60 (2010), pp. 197–229.

Dutschke, Rudi, *Jeder hat sein Leben ganz zu leben: Die Tagebücher 1963–1979*, Cologne 2003.

Dutschke-Klotz, Gretchen, 'Nachwort', in: Rudi Dutschke, *Jeder hat sein Leben ganz zu leben: Die Tagebücher 1963–1979*, Cologne 2003, pp. 373–407.

Dutschke-Klotz, Gretchen, *Wir hatten ein barbarisches, schönes Leben: Rudi Dutschke: Eine Biographie*, Cologne 1996.

Dutschke-Klotz, Gretchen, *1968: Worauf wir stolz sein dürfen*, Hamburg 2018.

Eder, Franz X., 'Die lange Geschichte der "Sexuellen Revolution" in Westdeutschland (1950er bis 1980er Jahre)', in: *Sexuelle Revolution? Zur Geschichte der Sexualität im deutschsprachigen Raum seit den 1960er Jahren*, eds. Peter-Paul Bänziger, Magdalena Beljan, Franz Eder, and Pascal Eitler, Bielefeld 2015, pp. 25–61.

Ehrenberg, Eckehart, 'Ein Stück Erinnerung: Aus meinen "1968er"-Jahren in Bonn (2007)', http://www.eckehartehrenberg.de/506n05.htm (accessed 29.9.2016).

Eitler, Pascal, 'Die "sexuelle Revolution" – Körperpolitik um 1968', in: *1968: Handbuch zur Kultur- und Mediengeschichte der Studentenbewegung*, eds. Martin Klimke and Joachim Scharloth, Heidelberg 2007, pp. 235–246.

Ennulat, Gertrud, *Kriegskinder: Wie die Wunden der Vergangenheit heilen*, 2nd ed., Stuttgart 2008.

BIBLIOGRAPHY 213

Erlemeier, Norbert, 'Die BOLSA-Freitagsgruppe – ein subjektiver Gesamteindruck', lecture at symposium celebrating Hans Thomae's 100th birthday, University of Bonn, 31 July 2015.

Evans, Sara M., 'Women's Liberation: Seeing the Revolution Clearly', in: *Feminist Studies* 41, no. 1 (2015), pp. 138–149.

Evans, Sara M., 'Sons, Daughters, and Patriarchy: Gender and the 1968 Generation', in: *The American Historical Review* 114, no. 2 (2009), pp. 331–347.

Fendrich, Stefanie, *Die Studentenproteste an der Rheinischen Friedrich-Wilhelms-Universität zu Bonn im Kontext der 68er-Bewegung in der Bundesrepublik Deutschland*, Master's Thesis, University of Bonn 2006.

Ferree, Myra Marx, *Varieties of Feminism: German Gender Politics in Global Perspective*, Stanford 2012.

Fink, Carole, Philipp Gassert, and Detlef Junker, eds., *1968: The World Transformed*, Cambridge/New York 2008.

Fischer, Torben, and Matthias N. Lorenz, eds., *Lexikon der 'Vergangenheitsbewältigung' in Deutschland: Debatten- und Diskursgeschichte des Nationalsozialismus nach 1945*, Bielefeld 2007.

Fooken, Insa, 'Die Bonner Gerontologische Studie des Alterns (BOLSA). Ausgangspunkt einer Differentiellen Gerontologie', in: *Sozial- und verhaltenswissenschaftliche Gerontologie: Alter und Altern als gesellschaftliches Problem und individuelles Thema*, ed. Fred Karl, Weinheim 2003, pp. 251–260.

Frasl, Monika, *Studien zur Protokoll-Literatur von Erika Runge*, Master's Thesis, University of Vienna 2009.

Frei, Norbert, *1968: Jugendrevolte und globaler Protest*, Munich 2008.

Frei, Norbert, *Vergangenheitspolitik: Die Anfänge der Bundesrepublik und die NS-Vergangenheit*, Munich 1996.

Garner, Curt, 'Public Service Personnel in West Germany in the 1950s', in: *Journal of Social History* 29, no. 1 (1995), pp. 25–80.

Gass-Bolm, Torsten, *Das Gymnasium 1945–1980: Bildungsreform und gesellschaftlicher Wandel in Westdeutschland*, Göttingen 2005.

Gerhard, Ute, *Unerhört: Die Geschichte der deutschen Frauenbewegung*, 20th ed., Reinbek 1995.

Giese, Hans, and Günter Schmidt, *Studenten-Sexualität*, Reinbek 1968.

Gilcher-Holtey, Ingrid, ed., *'1968' – eine Wahrnehmungsrevolution? Horizont-Verschiebungen des Politischen in den 1960er und 1970er Jahren*, Munich 2013.

Gilcher-Holtey, Ingrid, ed., *1968: Vom Ereignis zum Gegenstand der Geschichtswissenschaft*, Göttingen 1998.

Gildea, Robert, and James Mark, 'Introduction', in: *Europe's 1968: Voices of Revolt*, eds. Robert Gildea, James Mark, and Anette Warring, Oxford 2013, pp. 1–18.

Gitlin, Todd, *The Whole World Is Watching: Mass Media in the Making and Unmaking of the New Left*, Berkeley 2003.

Goltz, Anna von der, 'A Polarised Generation? Conservative Students and West Germany's "1968"', in: *'Talkin' 'Bout My Generation:' Conflicts of Generation Building and Europe's '1968'*, ed. Anna von der Goltz, Göttingen 2011, pp. 195–215.

Goltz, Anna von der, 'Making Sense of East Germany's 1968: Multiple Trajectories and Contrasting Memories', in: *Memory Studies* 6, no. 1 (2013), pp. 53–69.

Goltz, Anna von der, 'Other 68ers in West Berlin: Christian Democratic Students and the Cold War City', in: *Central European History* 50, no. 1 (2017), pp. 86–112.

Goltz, Anna von der, *The Other '68ers: Student Protest and Christian Democracy in West Germany*, Oxford 2021.

214 BIBLIOGRAPHY

Goltz, Anna von der, 'Von alten Kämpfern, sexy Wahlgirls und zornigen jungen Frauen. Überlegungen zur Beziehung von Generationalität, Geschlecht und Populärkultur im gemäßigtrechten Lager um 1968', in: *Hot Stuff: Gender, Popkultur und Generationalität in West- und Osteuropa nach 1945*, ed. Lu Seegers, Göttingen 2015, pp. 57–79.

Goltz, Anna von der, and Britta Waldschmidt-Nelson, eds., *Inventing the Silent Majority in Western Europe and the United States: Conservatism in the 1960s and 1970s*, Cambridge 2019.

Griffiths, Craig E., *The Ambivalence of Gay Liberation: Male Homosexual Politics in 1970s West Germany*, Oxford 2021.

Großbölting, Thomas, *1968 in Westfalen: Akteure, Formen und Nachwirkungen einer Protestbewegung*, Münster 2018.

Grünendahl, Martin, *Generationenbeziehung im Wandel? Untersuchungen zum Einfluss von Alter, Region und Kohorte auf familiäre Generationenbeziehungen im mittleren und höheren Erwachsenenalter*, Frankfurt am Main 2001.

Häberlen, Joachim C., *The Emotional Politics of the Alternative Left: West Germany, 1968–1984*, Cambridge 2018.

Habermas, Jürgen, 'Interview mit Angelo Bolaffi (1988)', in: Jürgen Habermas, *Die nachholende Revolution: Kleine politische Schriften VII*, Frankfurt am Main 1990.

Habermas, Jürgen, 'Studentenprotest in der Bundesrepublik', in: Jürgen Habermas, *Protestbewegung und Hochschulreform*, Berlin 2008, pp. 153–177.

Hacke, Jens, *Philosophie der Bürgerlichkeit: Die liberalkonservative Begründung der Bundesrepublik*, Göttingen 2006.

Hardach, Gerd, *Der Generationenvertrag: Lebenslauf und Lebenseinkommen in Deutschland in zwei Jahrhunderten*, Berlin 2006.

Haug, Frigga, 'Wie Pelagea Wlassowa Feministin wurde', in: *Wie weit flog die Tomate? Eine 68erinnen-Gala der Reflexion*, ed. Halina Bendkowski, Berlin 1999, pp. 189–198.

Hausen, Karin, 'Frauenerwerbstätigkeit und erwerbstätige Frauen: Anmerkungen zur historischen Forschung', in: *Frauen arbeiten: Weibliche Erwerbstätigkeit in Ost- und Westdeutschland nach 1945*, ed. Gunilla-Friederike Budde, Göttingen 1997, pp. 19–45.

Hayse, Michael R., *Recasting West German Elites: Higher Civil Servants, Business Leaders, and Physicians in Hesse between Nazism and Democracy, 1945–1955*, New York 2003.

Heer, Hannes, 'auch togo bleibt deutsch', in: *das weite suchen = expanding the gap*, eds. Martin Rendel and René Spitz, Stuttgart 2002, pp. 77–89.

Heer, Hannes, 'Literatur und Erinnerung: Die Nazizeit als Familiengeheimnis', in: *Zeitschrift für Geschichtswissenschaft* 53, no. 9 (2005), pp. 809–835.

Heineman, Elizabeth D., 'Sexuality in West Germany: Post-Fascist, Post-War, Post-Weimar or Post-Wilhelmine?', in: *Mit dem Wandel leben, Neuorientierung und Tradition in der Bundesrepublik der 1950er und 60er Jahre*, eds. Friedrich Kiessling and Bernhard Rieger, Cologne 2011, pp. 229–246.

Heineman, Elizabeth D., 'The Economic Miracle in the Bedroom: Big Business and Sexual Consumption in Reconstruction West Germany', in: *Journal of Modern History* 78, no. 4 (2006), pp. 846–877.

Heinlein, Michael, *Die Erfindung der Erinnerung: Deutsche Kriegskindheiten im Gedächtnis der Gegenwart*, Berlin 2010.

Heinsohn, Kirsten, 'Die eigene Geschichte erzählen: Erinnerungskulturen der deutschen Frauenbewegung (Düsseldorf 2020)', https://www.zeitgeschichte-hamburg.de/contao/files/fzh/pdf/p_ek_ap_16_2020.pdf (accessed 25.10.2022).

Heinsohn, Kirsten, 'Kommentar: Nachkriegszeit und Geschlechterordnung', in: *Zeitgeschichte als Geschlechtergeschichte. Neue Perspektiven auf die Bundesrepublik*, eds. Julia Paulus, Eva-Maria Silies, and Kerstin Wolff, Frankfurt am Main 2012, pp. 92–99.

BIBLIOGRAPHY 215

Herbert, Ulrich, 'Drei politische Generationen im 20. Jahrhundert', in: *Generationalität und Lebensgeschichte im 20. Jahrhundert*, ed. Jürgen Reulecke, Munich 2003, pp. 95–115.

Herbert, Ulrich, *Geschichte Deutschlands im 20. Jahrhundert*, Munich 2014.

Hervé, Florence, ed., *Geschichte der deutschen Frauenbewegung*, Cologne 1982.

Hervé, Florence, *Studentinnen in der BRD. Eine soziologische Untersuchung*, Cologne 1973.

Herzog, Dagmar, *Sex after Fascism: Memory and Morality in Twentieth-century Germany*, Princeton 2007.

Herzog, Dagmar, *Sexuality in Europe: A Twentieth-century History*, Cambridge 2011.

Higgs, Paul, and Chris Gilleard, 'Generational Justice, Generational Habitus and the "Problem" of the Baby Boomers', in: *Challenges of Aging: Pensions, Retirement and Generational Justice*, ed. Cornelius Torp, Basingstoke 2015, pp. 251–264.

Hillgruber, Christian, 'Die Studentenrevolte in Bonn: Vorgeschichte, Verlauf und Folgen', in: *Bonna Perl am grünen Rheine: Studieren in Bonn von 1818 bis zur Gegenwart*, ed. Thomas Becker, Göttingen 2013, pp. 189–215.

Hodenberg, Christina von, 'Ekel Alfred und die Kulturrevolution: Unterhaltungsfernsehen als Sprachrohr der 68er-Bewegung?', in: *Geschichte in Wissenschaft und Unterricht* 62 (2011), pp. 557–572.

Hodenberg, Christina von, *Konsens und Krise: Eine Geschichte der westdeutschen Medienöffentlichkeit, 1945–1973*, Göttingen 2006.

Hodenberg, Christina von, 'Politische Generationen und massenmediale Öffentlichkeit: Die "45er" in der Bundesrepublik', in: *Generationen: Zur Relevanz eines wissenschaftlichen Grundbegriffs*, eds. Ulrike Jureit and Michael Wildt, Hamburg 2005, pp. 266–294.

Hodenberg, Christina von, *Television's Moment: Sitcom Audiences and the Sixties Cultural Revolution*, New York 2015.

Hodenberg, Christina von, 'Writing Women's Agency into the History of the Federal Republic: "1968," Historians, and Gender', in: *Central European History* 52, no. 1 (March 2019), pp. 87–106.

Hodenberg, Christina von, and Katrin Moeller, 'Die Stimmen der Alten: Die BOLSA-Forschungsdaten als Quellen der deutschen Zeitgeschichte', in: *Zeithistorische Forschungen/Studies in Contemporary History* 17, no. 2 (2020), pp. 403–421.

Hodenberg, Christina von, and Detlef Siegfried, 'Reform und Revolte: 1968 und die langen sechziger Jahre in der Geschichte der Bundesrepublik', in: *Wo '1968' liegt: Reform und Revolte in der Geschichte der Bundesrepublik*, eds. Christina von Hodenberg and Detlef Siegfried, Göttingen 2006, pp. 7–14.

Höhn, Maria, *GIs and Fräuleins: The German–American Encounter in 1950s West Germany*, Chapel Hill 2002.

Horn, Gerd-Rainer, *The Spirit of '68: Rebellion in Western Europe and North America, 1956–1976*, Oxford 2007.

Howard, Ashley, *Prairie Fires: Urban Rebellions as Black Working-Class Politics in Three Midwestern Cities*, PhD Dissertation, University of Illinois at Urbana-Champaign 2012.

Inglehart, Ronald, *The Silent Revolution: Changing Values and Political Styles among Western Publics*, Princeton 1977.

Jackson, Julian, 'The Mystery of May 1968', in: *French Historical Studies* 33, no. 4 (1 October 2010), pp. 625–653.

Jian, Chen, Martin Klimke, Masha Kirasirova, Mary Nolan, Marilyn Young, and Joanna Waley-Cohen, eds., *The Routledge Handbook of the Global Sixties: Between Protest and Nation-Building*, London/New York 2018.

Judt, Tony, *Postwar: A History of Europe since 1945*, London 2005.

Jureit, Ulrike, *Generationenforschung*, Göttingen 2006.

Kaelble, Hartmut, *Sozialgeschichte Europas: 1945 bis zur Gegenwart*, Munich 2007.

216 BIBLIOGRAPHY

Kätzel, Ute, ed., *Die 68erinnen: Porträt einer rebellischen Frauengeneration*, Berlin 2002.

Keim, Michaela, and Stefan Lewejohann, eds., *Köln 68! Protest, Pop, Provokation: Begleitband zur Ausstellung des Kölnischen Stadtmuseums und der Universität zu Köln im Kölnischen Stadtmuseum vom 20. Oktober 2018 bis zum 24. Februar 2019*, Cologne 2018.

Kershaw, Ian, *Roller-Coaster: Europe, 1950–2017*, London 2018.

Kersting, Franz-Werner, Jürgen Reulecke, and Hans-Ulrich Thamer, eds., *Die zweite Gründung der Bundesrepublik: Generationswechsel und intellektuelle Wortergreifungen 1955–1975*, Stuttgart 2010.

Kiessling, Simon, *Die antiautoritäre Revolte der 68er: postindustrielle Konsumgesellschaft und säkulare Religionsgeschichte der Moderne*, Cologne 2006.

Klimke, Martin, *The Other Alliance: Student Protest in West Germany and the United States in the Global Sixties*, Princeton 2011.

Klimke, Martin, and Mary Nolan, 'Introduction: The Globalization of the Sixties', in: *The Routledge Handbook of the Global Sixties*, eds. Chen Jian, Martin Klimke, Mary Nolan, Masha Kirasirova, et al., London/New York 2018, pp. 1–9.

Klimke, Martin, and Joachim Scharloth, eds., *1968 in Europe: A History of Protest and Activism, 1956–1977*, New York 2008.

Koenen, Gerd, *Das rote Jahrzehnt: Unsere kleine deutsche Kulturrevolution 1967–1977*, Cologne 2001.

Kohut, Thomas August, *A German Generation: An Experiential History of the Twentieth Century*, New Haven 2012.

Kohut, Thomas August, 'History, Loss, and the Generation of 1914: The Case of the Freideutsche Kreis', in: *Generationalität und Lebensgeschichte im 20. Jahrhundert*, ed. Jürgen Reulecke, Munich 2003, pp. 253–277.

Kommune 2 (Christel Bookhagen, Eike Hemmer, Jan Raspe, and Eberhard Schultz), 'Kindererziehung in der Kommune', in: *Kursbuch* 17 (1969), pp. 147–178.

Kozicki, Norbert, *Aufbruch in NRW: 1968 und die Folgen*, Essen 2008.

Kraft, Sandra, *Vom Hörsaal auf die Anklagebank: Die 68er und das Establishment in Deutschland und den USA*, Frankfurt am Main 2010.

Kraushaar, Wolfgang, *1968: 100 Seiten*, Stuttgart 2018.

Kraushaar, Wolfgang, *Achtundsechzig: Eine Bilanz*, Berlin 2008.

Kraushaar, Wolfgang, *Die blinden Flecken der 68er Bewegung*, Stuttgart 2018.

Kruse, Andreas, 'Personale Geschehensordnung und Entwicklung des Individuums im Lebenslauf: Von der Philosophie zur Psychologie', in: *In Memoriam Hans Thomae: Reden, gehalten am 23. Mai 2003 anläßlich der Akademischen Gedenkfeier der Philosophischen Fakultät der Rheinischen Friedrich-Wilhelms-Universität Bonn*, eds. Georg Rudinger, Andreas Kruse, and Carl Friedrich Graumann, Bonn 2003, pp. 23–39.

Kruse, Andreas, Eric Schmitt, and Michael Wachter, 'Der Beitrag der Psychologie zur sozial- und verhaltenswissenschaftlichen Gerontologie', in: *Sozial- und verhaltenswissenschaftliche Gerontologie: Alter und Altern als gesellschaftliches Problem und individuelles Thema*, ed. Fred Karl, Weinheim 2003, pp. 59–86.

Kruse, Andreas, and Reinhard Schmitz-Scherzer, eds., *Psychologie der Lebensalter*, Darmstadt 1995.

Kuhn, Annette, Valentine Rothe, and Brigitte Mühlenbruch, eds., *100 Jahre Frauenstudium: Frauen der Rheinischen Friedrich-Wilhelms-Universität Bonn*, Dortmund 1996.

Kundnani, Hans, *Utopia or Auschwitz: Germany's 1968 Generation and the Holocaust*, London 2009.

Künemund, Harald, and Andreas Motel, 'Verbreitung, Motivation und Entwicklungsperspektiven privater intergenerationeller Hilfeleistungen und Transfers', in: *Generationen: Multidisziplinäre Perspektiven*, eds. Harald Künemund and Marc Szydlik, Wiesbaden 2009, pp. 122–137.

Langer-El Sayed, Ingrid, *Frau und Illustrierte im Kapitalismus: Die Inhaltsstruktur von illustrierten Frauenzeitschriften und ihr Bezug zur gesellschaftlichen Wirklichkeit*, Cologne 1971.

Leggewie, Claus, 'A Laboratory of Postindustrial Society: Reassessing the 1960s in Germany', in: *1968: The World Transformed*, eds. Carole Fink, Philipp Gassert, and Detlef Junker, Cambridge 1998, pp. 277–294.

Lehmann, Joachim, 'Matriarchat, nicht Proletariat! Ein Rückblick auf die feministische Revolte der siebziger Jahre', in: *Weiblichkeit als politisches Programm? Sexualität, Macht und Mythos*, eds. Udo Franke-Penski, Bettina Gruber, and Heinz-Peter Preußer, Würzburg 2005, pp. 40–50.

Lehr, Ursula, *Die Frau im Beruf: Eine psychologische Analyse der weiblichen Berufsrolle*, Frankfurt am Main 1969.

Lehr, Ursula, *Psychologie des Alterns*, Wiesbaden 1972.

Lehr, Ursula, 'Zur Geschichte der Entwicklungspsychologie der Lebensspanne', in: *Psychologie der Lebensalter*, eds. Andreas Kruse and Reinhard Schmitz-Scherzer, Darmstadt 1995, pp. 3–14.

Lehr, Ursula, and Hans Thomae, eds., *Formen seelischen Alterns: Ergebnisse der Bonner gerontologischen Längsschnittstudie (BOLSA)*, Stuttgart 1987.

Lehr, Ursula, and Hans Thomae, 'Stichprobe und Ablauf der Untersuchung in der Bonner Gerontologischen Längsschnittstudie (BOLSA)', in: *Formen seelischen Alterns*, eds. Ursula Lehr and Hans Thomae, Stuttgart 1987, pp. 7–17.

Lenz, Ilse, ed., *Die neue Frauenbewegung in Deutschland: Abschied vom kleinen Unterschied*, Wiesbaden 2008.

Levsen, Sonja, *Autorität und Demokratie: Eine Kulturgeschichte des Erziehungswandels in Westdeutschland und Frankreich, 1945–1975*, Göttingen 2020.

Lönnendonker, Siegward, ed., *Linksintellektueller Aufbruch zwischen 'Kulturrevolution' und 'kultureller Zerstörung': Der Sozialistische Deutsche Studentenbund (SDS) in der Nachkriegsgeschichte 1946–1969*, Wiesbaden 1998.

Lorenz, Hilke, *Kriegskinder: Das Schicksal einer Generation*, Munich 2003.

Lüscher, Kurt, and Ludwig Liegle, *Generationenbeziehungen in Familie und Gesellschaft*, Constance 2003.

Marwick, Arthur, *The Sixties: Cultural Revolution in Britain, France, Italy, and the United States, 1958–1974*, Oxford/New York 1998.

Maslen, Joseph, 'Autobiographies of a Generation? Carolyn Steedman, Luisa Passerini and the Memory of 1968', in: *Memory Studies* 6, no. 1 (2013), pp. 23–36.

Maurer, Susanne, 'Gespaltenes Gedächtnis? "1968 und die Frauen" in Deutschland', in: *L'homme* 20, no. 2 (2009), pp. 118–128.

Mausbach, Wilfried, 'Wende um 360 Grad? Nationalsozialismus und Judenvernichtung in der "zweiten Gründungsphase" der Bundesrepublik', in: *Wo '1968' liegt: Reform und Revolte in der Geschichte der Bundesrepublik*, eds. Christina von Hodenberg and Detlef Siegfried, Göttingen 2006, pp. 15–47.

Mercer, Ben, *Student Revolt in 1968: France, Italy and West Germany*, Cambridge 2019.

Merian: Das Monatsheft der Städte und Landschaften 9, no. 29 (1976): 'Bonn'.

Merker, Helga Margarete, *Generations-Gegensätze: Eine empirische Erkundungsstudie über die Einstellung Erwachsener zur Jugend*, Darmstadt 1973.

218 BIBLIOGRAPHY

Michels, Eckard, *Schahbesuch 1967: Fanal für die Studentenbewegung*, Berlin 2017.

Mitscherlich, Alexander, and Margarete Mitscherlich, *Die Unfähigkeit zu trauern: Grundlagen kollektiven Verhaltens*, Munich 1967.

Möckel, Benjamin, *Erfahrungsbruch und Generationsbehauptung: Die 'Kriegsjugendgeneration' in den beiden deutschen Nachkriegsgesellschaften*, Göttingen 2014.

Möhring, Maren, *Fremdes Essen: Die Geschichte der ausländischen Gastronomie in der Bundesrepublik Deutschland*, Munich 2012.

Moses, A. Dirk, *German Intellectuals and the Nazi Past*, Cambridge 2007.

Müller-List, Gabriele, 'Bonn als Bundeshauptstadt (1949–1989)', in: *Geschichte der Stadt Bonn, Bd. 4: Bonn: Von einer französischen Bezirksstadt zur Bundeshauptstadt 1794–1989*, eds. Dietrich Höroldt and Manfred van Rey, Bonn 1989, pp. 639–744.

Nagel, Katja, *Die Provinz in Bewegung: Studentenunruhen in Heidelberg 1967–1973*, Heidelberg 2009.

Nave-Herz, Rosemarie, *Die Geschichte der Frauenbewegung in Deutschland*, 1st ed., Opladen 1982.

Nevermann, Knut, ed., *Der 2. Juni 1967: Studenten zwischen Notstand und Demokratie*, Cologne 1967.

Niethammer, Lutz, *Die Mitläuferfabrik: Die Entnazifizierung am Beispiel Bayerns*, Berlin 1982.

Noelle, Elisabeth, ed., *Allensbacher Jahrbuch der Demoskopie 1974–1976*, Vienna 1976.

Noelle, Elisabeth, and Erich Peter Neumann, eds., *Jahrbuch der öffentlichen Meinung 1956–1964*, Allensbach 1965.

Noelle, Elisabeth, and Erich Peter Neumann, eds., *Jahrbuch der öffentlichen Meinung 1965–1967*, Allensbach 1967.

Noelle, Elisabeth, and Erich Peter Neumann, eds., *Jahrbuch der öffentlichen Meinung 1968–1973*, Allensbach 1974.

Obermaier, Uschi, *High Times. Mein wildes Leben*, Munich 2008.

Oertzen, Christine von, *Teilzeitarbeit und die Lust am Zuverdienen: Geschlechterpolitik und gesellschaftlicher Wandel in Westdeutschland 1948–1969*, Göttingen 1999.

Olbrich, Erhard, *Der ältere Mensch in der Interaktion mit seiner sozialen Umwelt*, PhD Dissertation, University of Bonn 1976.

Olbrich, Erhard, and K. Pöhlmann, 'Prozeß und Interaktion in der Persönlichkeits- und Entwicklungspsychologie', in: *Psychologie der Lebensalter*, eds. Andreas Kruse and Reinhard Schmitz-Scherzer, Darmstadt 1995, pp. 81–92.

Oseka, Piotr, Polymeris Voglis, and Anna von der Goltz, 'Families', in: *Europe's 1968: Voices of Revolt*, eds. Robert Gildea, James Mark, and Anette Warring, Oxford 2013, pp. 46–71.

Pardon-Dokumente, *Lieben und lieben lassen: Sexualfreud und -neid an deutschen Universitäten*, Frankfurt am Main 1966.

Passerini, Luisa, *Autobiography of a Generation: Italy 1968*, Middletown, 1996.

Paulus, Julia, Eva-Maria Silies, and Kerstin Wolff, 'Die Bundesrepublik aus geschlechterhistorischer Perspektive', in: *Zeitgeschichte als Geschlechtergeschichte: Neue Perspektiven auf die Bundesrepublik*, eds. Julia Paulus, Eva-Maria Silies, and Kerstin Wolff, Frankfurt am Main 2012, pp. 11–29.

Perinelli, Massimo, 'Longing, Lust, Violence, Liberation: Discourses on Sexuality on the Radical Left in West Germany, 1969–1972', in: *After the History of Sexuality: German Genealogies with and beyond Foucault*, eds. Dagmar Herzog, Helmut Puff, and Scott Spector, New York 2012, pp. 248–281.

Pfeil, Elisabeth, *Die 23jährigen: Eine Generationenuntersuchung am Geburtenjahrgang 1941*, Tübingen 1968.

BIBLIOGRAPHY 219

Pieper, Kirsten Julia, *Die Studentenbewegung an der Universität Bonn in den Jahren 1965 bis 1970*, Master's Thesis, University of Bonn, undated.

Radebold, Hartmut, Gereon Heuft, and Insa Fooken, eds., *Kindheiten im Zweiten Weltkrieg: Kriegserfahrungen und deren Folgen aus psychohistorischer Perspektive*, Weinheim 2006.

Rahden, Till van, 'Eine Welt ohne Familie: Der Kinderladen als ein demokratisches Heilsversprechen', in: *Autorität: Krise, Konstruktion und Konjunktur*, eds. Till van Rahden, Oliver Kohns, and Martin Roussel, Paderborn 2016, pp. 255–282.

Reichardt, Sven, *Authentizität und Gemeinschaft: Linksalternatives Leben in den siebziger und frühen achtziger Jahren*, Berlin 2014.

Reichardt, Sven, 'Von "Beziehungskisten" und "offener Sexualität"', in: *Das alternative Milieu: Antibürgerlicher Lebensstil und linke Politik in der Bundesrepublik Deutschland und Europa 1968-1983*, eds. Sven Reichardt and Detlef Siegfried, Göttingen 2010, pp. 267–289.

Reiche, Reimut, 'Sexuelle Revolution: Erinnerung an einen Mythos', in: *Die Früchte der Revolte. Über die Veränderung der politischen Kultur durch die Studentenbewegung*, eds. Lothar Baier et al., Berlin 1988, pp. 45–72.

Reimann, Bruno W., 'Das "Busen-Attentat" auf Adorno, oder: Agonie und Ende der studentischen Protestbewegung', http://www.bruno-w-reimann.de/das-busenattentat-auf-adorno-arbeitsmanuskript/ (accessed 20.9.2016).

Rendel, Martin, and René Spitz, eds., *das weite suchen = expanding the gap*, Stuttgart 2002.

Renner, Maria Theresia, *Strukturen sozialer Teilhabe im höheren Lebensalter mit besonderer Berücksichtigung der sozialen Beziehungen zwischen den Mitgliedern der erweiterten Kernfamilie*, PhD Dissertation, University of Bonn 1969.

Roggenkamp, Viola, 'Mainstreaming: Feminismus zwischen EMMA und ZEIT', in: *Wie weit flog die Tomate? Eine 68erinnen-Gala der Reflexion*, ed. Halina Bendkowski, Berlin 1999, pp. 208–216.

Rohstock, Anne, *Von der 'Ordinarienuniversität' zur 'Revolutionszentrale'? Hochschulreform und Hochschulrevolte in Bayern und Hessen 1957-1976*, Munich 2010.

Rosenthal, Gabriele, 'Historische und familiale Generationenabfolge', in: *Generationen in Familie und Gesellschaft*, eds. Martin Kohli and Marc Szydlik, Opladen 2000, pp. 162–178.

Röser, Jutta, *Frauenzeitschriften und weiblicher Lebenszusammenhang: Themen, Konzepte und Leitbilder im sozialen Wandel*, Opladen 1992.

Ross, Kristin, 'Establishing Consensus: May '68 in France as Seen from the 1980s', in: *Critical Inquiry* 28, no. 3 (2002), pp. 650–676.

Ross, Kristin, *May '68 and its Afterlives*, Chicago 2008.

Rosskopf, Annette, *Friedrich Karl Kaul: Anwalt im geteilten Deutschland (1906-1981)*, Berlin 2002.

Rudinger, Georg, 'Hans Thomae als Wegbereiter einer Psychologie für den Menschen', in: *In Memoriam Hans Thomae: Reden, gehalten am 23. Mai 2003*, eds. Georg Rudinger, Andreas Kruse, and Carl Friedrich Graumann, Bonn 2003, pp. 10–21.

Rudinger, Georg, and Ralph Stöwer, 'Innenansichten eines akademischen Lebens: Prof. Dr. Dr. h. c. Hans Thomae: Abschrift der Tonbandaufzeichnung eines biographischen Interviews vom 22. und 29. August 1994', in: *In Memoriam Hans Thomae: Reden, gehalten am 23. Mai 2003*, eds. Georg Rudinger, Andreas Kruse, and Carl Friedrich Graumann, Bonn 2003, pp. 45–94.

Rudinger, Georg, and Ralph Stöwer, 'Thomae, Hans', in: *Deutschsprachige Psychologinnen und Psychologen, 1933-1945: Ein Personenlexikon*, eds. Uwe Wolfradt, Elfriede Billmann-Mahecha, and Armin Stock, Wiesbaden 2015, pp. 441–442.

220 BIBLIOGRAPHY

Runge, Erika, 'Emanzipationen: Auszüge aus vier Lebensläufen', in: *Kursbuch* 17 (1969), pp. 69–89.

Runge, Erika, *Frauen: Versuche zur Emanzipation*, 7th ed., Frankfurt am Main 1978.

Sander, Helke, 'Der Seele ist das Gemeinsame eigen, das sich mehrt', in: *Wie weit flog die Tomate? Eine 68erinnen-Gala der Reflexion*, ed. Halina Bendkowski, Berlin 1999, pp. 43–56.

Schildt, Axel, '"Die Kräfte der Gegenreform sind auf breiter Front angetreten": Zur konservativen Tendenzwende in den Siebzigerjahren', in: *Archiv für Sozialgeschichte* 44 (2004), pp. 449–478.

Schildt, Axel, 'Überbewertet? Zur Macht objektiver Entwicklungen und zur Wirkungslosigkeit der "68er"', in: *Reform und Revolte: Politischer und gesellschaftlicher Wandel in der Bundesrepublik vor und nach 1968*, ed. Udo Wengst, Munich 2011, pp. 89–102.

Schildt, Axel, Detlef Siegfried, and Karl Christian Lammers, eds., *Dynamische Zeiten: Die 60er Jahre in den beiden deutschen Gesellschaften*, Hamburg 2000.

Schmidt, Daniel, '"Die geistige Führung verloren": Antworten der CDU auf die Herausforderung "1968"', in: *Die zweite Gründung der Bundesrepublik: Generationswechsel und intellektuelle Wortergreifungen 1955–1975*, eds. Franz-Werner Kersting, Jürgen Reulecke, and Hans-Ulrich Thamer, Stuttgart 2010, pp. 85–107.

Schmidt, Günter, and Volkmar Sigusch, *Arbeiter-Sexualität: Eine empirische Untersuchung an jungen Industriearbeitern*, Neuwied 1971.

Schmincke, Imke, 'Von der Politisierung des Privatlebens zum neuen Frauenbewusstsein: Körperpolitik und Subjektivierung von Weiblichkeit in der Neuen Frauenbewegung Westdeutschlands', in: *Zeitgeschichte als Geschlechtergeschichte: Neue Perspektiven auf die Bundesrepublik*, eds. Julia Paulus, Eva-Maria Silies, and Kerstin Wolff, Frankfurt am Main 2012, pp. 297–317.

Schmitz-Scherzer, Reinhard, *Freizeit und Alter*, PhD Dissertation, University of Bonn 1969.

Schrader-Klebert, Karin, 'Die kulturelle Revolution der Frau', in: *Kursbuch* 17 (1969), pp. 1–46.

Schreiner, Manfred, *Zur zukunftsbezogenen Zeitperspektive älterer Menschen*, PhD Dissertation, University of Bonn 1969.

Schulz, Hermann, Hartmut Radebold, and Jürgen Reulecke, eds., *Söhne ohne Väter: Erfahrungen der Kriegsgeneration*, Berlin 2004.

Schulz, Kristina, *Der lange Atem der Provokation: Die Frauenbewegung in der Bundesrepublik und in Frankreich 1968–1976*, Frankfurt am Main 2002.

Schulz, Kristina, 'Remembering 1968: Feminist Perspectives', in: *Women, Global Protest Movements, and Political Agency: Rethinking the Legacy of 1968*, eds. Sarah Colvin and Katharina Karcher, London/New York 2019, pp. 19–32.

Schulz, Kristina, ed., *The Women's Liberation Movement: Impacts and Outcomes*, Oxford/New York 2017.

Schulz, Kristina, 'The Women's Movement', in: *1968 in Europe: A History of Protest and Activism 1956–1977*, eds. Martin Klimke and Joachim Scharloth, Basingstoke 2008, pp. 281–293.

Sedlmaier, Alexander, *Konsum und Gewalt: Radikaler Protest in der Bundesrepublik*, Berlin 2018.

Seegers, Lu, ed., *Hot Stuff: Gender, Popkultur und Generationalität in West- und Osteuropa nach 1945*, Göttingen 2015.

Seegers, Lu, *'Vati blieb im Krieg': Vaterlosigkeit als generationelle Erfahrung im 20. Jahrhundert*, Göttingen 2013.

Siegfried, Detlef, *1968 in der Bundesrepublik: Protest, Revolte, Gegenkultur*, Stuttgart 2018.

Siegfried, Detlef, *Time is on My Side: Konsum und Politik in der westdeutschen Jugendkultur der 60er Jahre*, Göttingen 2006.

Silies, Eva-Maria, 'Erfahrungen des Bruchs? Die generationelle Nutzung der Pille in den sechziger und siebziger Jahren', in: *Zeitgeschichte als Geschlechtergeschichte: Neue Perspektiven auf die Bundesrepublik*, eds. Julia Paulus, Eva-Maria Silies, and Kerstin Wolff, Frankfurt am Main 2012, pp. 205–224.

Silies, Eva-Maria, *Liebe, Lust und Last: Die Pille als weibliche Generationserfahrung in der Bundesrepublik 1960–1980*, Göttingen 2010.

Silies, Eva-Maria, 'Wider die natürliche Ordnung: Die katholische Kirche und die Debatte um Empfängnisverhütung seit den 1960er Jahren', in: *Sexuelle Revolution? Zur Geschichte der Sexualität im deutschsprachigen Raum seit den 1960er Jahren*, eds. Peter-Paul Bänziger, Magdalena Beljan, Franz Eder, and Pascal Eitler, Bielefeld 2015, pp. 153–180.

Stambolis, Barbara, *Aufgewachsen in 'eiserner Zeit': Kriegskinder zwischen Erstem Weltkrieg und Weltwirtschaftskrise*, Gießen 2014.

Stambolis, Barbara, *Töchter ohne Väter: Frauen der Kriegsgeneration und ihre lebenslange Sehnsucht*, Stuttgart 2012.

Steinbacher, Sybille, *Wie der Sex nach Deutschland kam: Der Kampf um Sittlichkeit und Anstand in der frühen Bundesrepublik*, Munich 2011.

Stöhr, Irene, 'Feminismen und politische Kultur', in: *Wie weit flog die Tomate? Eine 68erinnen-Gala der Reflexion*, ed. Halina Bendkowski, Berlin 1999, pp. 154–165.

Stöwer, Ralph, *Erich Rothacker: Sein Leben und seine Wissenschaft vom Menschen*, Göttingen 2012.

Thomae, Hans, 'Alltagsbelastungen im Alter und Versuche ihrer Bewältigung', in: *Formen seelischen Alterns: Ergebnisse der Bonner gerontologischen Längsschnittstudie (BOLSA)*, eds. Ursula Lehr and Hans Thomae, Stuttgart 1987, pp. 92–114.

Thomae, Hans, *Das Individuum und seine Welt: Eine Persönlichkeitstheorie*, 1st ed., Göttingen 1968.

Thomae, Hans, *Das Individuum und seine Welt: Eine Persönlichkeitstheorie*, 2nd completely revised ed., Göttingen 1988.

Thomae, Hans, *Das Wesen der menschlichen Antriebsstruktur*, Leipzig 1944.

Thomae, Hans, 'Gerontologische Längsschnittstudien: Ziele, Möglichkeiten, Grenzen', in: *Formen seelischen Alterns: Ergebnisse der Bonner gerontologischen Längsschnittstudie (BOLSA)*, eds. Ursula Lehr and Hans Thomae, Stuttgart 1987, pp. 1–6.

Thomae, Hans, *Immanuel Kant: Von der Würde des Menschen*, Leipzig 1941.

Thomae, Hans, *Ruf des Lebens: Gedanken großer Deutscher der Vergangenheit*, Potsdam 1939.

Thome, Helmut, 'Value Change in Europe from the Perspective of Empirical Social Research', in: *The Cultural Values of Europe*, eds. Hans Joas and Klaus Wiegandt, Liverpool 2008, pp. 277–319.

Thon, Christine, *Frauenbewegung im Wandel der Generationen*, Bielefeld 2015.

Tismer, Karl-Georg, *Untersuchungen zur Lebensthematik älterer Menschen*, PhD Dissertation, University of Bonn 1969.

Tismer, Karl-Georg, Ulrich Lange, Norbert Erlemeier, and Ingrid Tismer-Puschner, *Psychosoziale Aspekte der Situation älterer Menschen*, Stuttgart 1975.

Tölle, Domenica, *Altern in Deutschland 1815–1933: Eine Kulturgeschichte*, Grafschaft 1996.

Torp, Cornelius, *Gerechtigkeit im Wohlfahrtsstaat: Alter und Alterssicherung in Deutschland und Großbritannien von 1945 bis heute*, Göttingen 2015.

Verhey, Jeffrey, *The Spirit of 1914: Militarism, Myth, and Mobilization in Germany*, Cambridge 2000.

222 BIBLIOGRAPHY

Verheyen, Nina, *Diskussionslust: Eine Kulturgeschichte des 'besseren Arguments' in Westdeutschland*, Göttingen 2008.

Verlinden, Karla, *Sexualität und Beziehungen bei den '68ern': Erinnerungen ehemaliger Protagonisten und Protagonistinnen*, Bielefeld 2015.

Vinen, Richard, *1968: Radical Protest and Its Enemies*, London 2018.

Vogel, Meike, *Unruhe im Fernsehen: Protestbewegung und öffentlich-rechtliche Berichterstattung in den 1960er Jahren*, Göttingen 2010.

Vollnhals, Clemens, ed., *Entnazifizierung: Politische Säuberung und Rehabilitierung in den vier Besatzungzonen 1945–1949*, Munich 1991.

Wehler, Hans Ulrich, *Deutsche Gesellschaftsgeschichte, vol. 5: 1949–1990*, Munich 2008.

Wehrs, Nikolai, *Protest der Professoren: Der 'Bund Freiheit der Wissenschaft' in den 1970er Jahren*, Göttingen 2014.

Weisbrod, Bernd, 'Generation und Generationalität in der Neueren Geschichte', in: *Aus Politik und Zeitgeschichte* 8 (2005), pp. 3–9.

Welzer, Harald, Sabine Moller, and Karoline Tschuggnall, *Opa war kein Nazi: Nationalsozialismus und Holocaust im Familiengedächtnis*, 8th ed., Frankfurt am Main 2012.

Wengst, Udo, ed., *Reform und Revolte: Politischer und gesellschaftlicher Wandel in der Bundesrepublik vor und nach 1968*, Munich 2011.

West, Candace, and Don H. Zimmerman, 'Doing Gender', in: *Gender and Society* 1, no. 2 (1987), pp. 125–151.

Westad, Odd Arne, 'Preface: Was There a "Global 1968"?', in: *The Routledge Handbook of the Global Sixties*, eds. Chen Jian, Odd Arne Westad, Masha Kirasirova, et al., London/ New York 2018, pp. xx–xxiii.

Wetterau, Karin, *68. Täterkinder und Rebellen: Familienroman einer Revolte*, Bielefeld 2017.

Wienhaus, Andrea, *Bildungswege zu '1968': Eine Kollektivbiografie des Sozialistischen Deutschen Studentenbundes*, Bielefeld 2014.

Wiese, Benno von, *Ich erzähle mein Leben: Erinnerungen*, Frankfurt am Main 1982.

Wiggershaus, Renate, *Geschichte der Frauen und der Frauenbewegung in der Bundesrepublik Deutschland und in der Deutschen Demokratischen Republik nach 1945*, Wuppertal 1979.

Wildt, Michael, *Generation des Unbedingten: Das Führungskorps des Reichssicherheitshauptamtes*, Hamburg 2002.

Winterberg, Yury, and Sonya Winterberg, *Kriegskinder: Erinnerungen einer Generation*, Berlin 2009.

Zancarini-Fournel, Michelle, *Le moment 68: Une histoire contestée*, Paris 2008.

Zellmer, Elisabeth, *Töchter der Revolte? Frauenbewegung und Feminismus der 1970er Jahre in München*, Munich 2011.

Ziemann, Benjamin, *Front und Heimat: Ländliche Kriegserfahrungen im südlichen Bayern 1914–1923*, Essen 1997.

Glossary and Abbreviations

Abitur: school-leaving exams taken at the end of year 12 or 13, primarily at a *Gymnasium*, qualifying students for university entry.

Arbeitskreis Emanzipation (AKE): Emancipation Working Group, a Bonn-based feminist collective.

Allgemeiner Studentenausschuss (AStA): General Students' Committee, the student government at German universities.

Außerparlamentarische Opposition (APO): Extra-Parliamentary Opposition, a political protest movement in the late sixties and early seventies disillusioned with the Grand Coalition government of the CDU/CSU and SPD.

Beziehungskiste (literally 'relationship crate'): a colloquial term for a non-traditional romantic or intimate coupledom outside of marriage.

Bildungsbürgertum (Bildungsbürger/bildungsbürgerlich, adjective): the university-educated middle classes. Considered a cultural elite, they traditionally dominated certain professions.

Bolsa: Bonn Longitudinal Study of Ageing, or *Bonner Längsschnittstudie des Alterns*.

Blockwart: block warden, low-ranking Nazi party functionary who collected party fees and informed on neighbours.

Blut und Boden (blood and soil): while the term predates the Nazis, it became a slogan summarizing their ideology of 'blood' as a racially-defined *Volk* (people or nation), united with the 'soil' of the land.

Bund Deutscher Mädel (BDM): League of German Girls, the girls' section of the Hitler Youth.

Christlich-Demokratische Union Deutschlands (CDU): Christian Democratic Union of Germany, centre-right, conservative political party, linked to its sister party, the Christian Social Union (CSU) in Bavaria.

Freie Demokratische Partei (FDP): Free Democratic Party, liberal political party.

FRG: Federal Republic of Germany (*Bundesrepublik Deutschland*).

German Democratic Republic (GDR): East German state, ruled by the SED from 1949 to 1989.

Gymnasium: a type of secondary school intended to offer an academic education and *Abitur*, leading to university study.

224 GLOSSARY AND ABBREVIATIONS

Humanistische Studentenunion (HSU): Humanist Students' Union, a left-liberal, anti-clerical student group.

Liberaler Studentenbund Deutschlands (LSD): Liberal Student Association of Germany, the official student group of the FDP from 1950–1969.

Mittelschule (literally 'middle school'): A term used for various types of secondary school of an intermediate academic level, depending on the state and the era.

Provo: Dutch counter-culture of the mid-1960s that aimed to provoke violent responses from the authorities to non-violent actions.

Nationalsozialistische Partei Deutschlands (NSDAP, Nazi): National Socialist Party of Germany.

Parteigenosse (PG): member of the National Socialist Party of Germany.

Radikalenerlass: Anti-Radical Decree, passed on 28 January 1972. It banned anyone considered a member of or aligned to an extremist organization from civil service or other public sector positions, including teaching. Applicants could be checked for their loyalty to the constitution and the liberal-democratic order.

Realschule: a type of secondary school intended to offer a practical education and lead to vocational training.

Ring Christlich-Demokratischer Studenten (RCDS): Association of Christian Democratic Students, student group affiliated with the CDU and CSU conservative parties.

Sozialdemokratische Partei Deutschlands (SPD): Social Democratic Party of Germany, centre-left, social democratic political party.

Sozialdemokratischer Hochschulbund (SHB): Social Democratic Higher Education League, affiliated with the SPD.

Sozialistische Einheitspartei Deutschlands (SED): Socialist Unity Party of Germany, the ruling party in the GDR.

Sozialistischer Deutscher Studentenbund (SDS): Socialist German Students' Union, founded in 1946 as the student branch of the SPD. Tensions rose between the SDS and the SPD leading to all SDS members being expelled from the party in 1961.

Studentenwerk: student welfare office, student services: a state-run, non-profit student affairs organization, covering one or more local universities. They run university cafeterias and halls of residence, and issue student grants and loans.

Verband Deutscher Studentenschaften (VDS): Association of German Student Unions, umbrella group for student associations in Germany.

List of Credits

2.1, 4.2, 6.3. extracted from Bothien, *Protest und Provokation*

2.2, 2.3, 2.5, 2.6, 2.7. © Ursula Lehr/photo: Werner Verhey

2.4, 6.1. © Schafgans Archiv, Bonn/photo: Hans Schafgans

3.1. © Bonner Stadtarchiv, Collection Georg Munker

3.2. © Bonner Stadtarchiv

3.3. © Verlag *Der Spiegel*

4.1. © Bonner Stadtarchiv/photo: Engels

5.1. extracted from *akut* no. 56, 7 November 1969

5.2. extracted from Kätzel, ed., *Die 68erinnen*

5.3. © Ulrich Wienke

6.2. © Bonner Stadtarchiv, Collection Camillo Fischer

6.4. © Hans Günter Jürgensmeier

Index

131ers 80–5

Abortion 96–7, 112, 132, 140, 147, 161, 169
Adenauer, Konrad 40, 53, 77
Adolescents 7, 48–9, 56, 59–60, 88, 118–9, 122–3, 126, 154–5, 159–60
Adorno, Theodor W. 150, 167
Adrian, Karin 101, 104, 107–9, 115, 126, 128
Ageing 11, 17, 24–5, 60, 127, 173, 177
Ahr valley 19, 27, 33–4
Albertz, Heinrich 29
Aly, Götz 47, 59, 65, 179 n.4
Anniversaries of '68 5, 12–3, 95–6, 133, 168
Anti-nuclear movement 49
Anti-Semitism 57, 61–2, 65, 68, 78–80, 117, 164
APO 6, 22, 31, 49, 58, 67, 71–2, 89, 96–7
Aretz, Jürgen 51
Augstein, Rudolf 7
Auschwitz 39–40, 45–7, 52, 58, 62, 64, 80
Austria 19, 81
Authoritarianism 31, 43, 51, 60, 63–4, 67–8, 72, 74, 76, 88–91, 99, 118, 121, 130, 134, 150, 164, 166, 169–72, 174–5

Bacia, Hubert 150
Beat, beatniks 1, 12, 35, 122–3, 141, 142*f*, 160, 163, 180 n.32, 196 n.46
Beauvoir, Simone de 93, 112
Bebel, August 93, 112
Bendkowski, Halina 131
Berlin 1, 3–6, 9, 14–5, 17, 26, 28–30, 32–3, 35, 38, 40–2, 47, 58, 72–4, 76, 86, 95, 98, 101, 103–4, 106–16, 128, 131, 134, 148–52, 154, 163, 166, 169
Bildungsbürgertum 5–7, 64
Bode, Sabine 64, 118
Böll, Heinrich 69

Bonn 3, 6, 11–33, 36–51, 53, 57–8, 60–2, 68–71, 73, 76, 78, 80–1, 85, 88, 92–5, 99, 104–6, 110–11, 116–9, 121–4, 126–7, 132–4, 141–9, 152, 163–4, 167, 170, 177–8, 181 n.39
Bookhagen, Christel *see* Kalisch, Christel
Booß, Bernhelm 52–3, 68, 145
Bothien, Horst-Pierre 12, 47–8, 50, 178, 181 n.37
Böttiger, Helmut 16
Bovenschen, Silvia 97–8, 112, 131
Bracher, Karl Dietrich 31
Bredow, Ferdinand von 53
Bredow, Wilfried von 53
Breyer, Wolfgang 53
Brühl 15
Brunn, Anke 106, 131, 196 n.46
Bude, Heinz 48
Buhmann, Inga 102
Busenattentat 150, 167

Canaris, Ute 196 n.46
Capitalism 53, 68, 97–8, 109–10, 113, 134, 150, 152, 166, 173
Chamberlain, Houston Stewart 62
Christiansen, Ursula 196 n.46
Christlich-Demokratische Union Deutschlands (CDU) 39, 74–5, 160, 171
Centre party 51
Childcare 93, 104–6, 108–9, 112–4, 129, 132
Churches 46, 62, 74, 127, 139–40, 144, 148
    Catholics 49, 51, 74, 138–9, 144
    Protestants 69, 144
Cohn-Bendit, Daniel 3, 9, 96, 99, 131, 168
Cold War 30, 38, 171, 173
Cologne 12–3, 33, 38, 88, 102, 106–8, 117–9, 121–2, 131, 134, 143–4, 149, 151, 178
Communes 3–5, 30, 38, 58, 99, 102, 108–10, 113–6, 148, 150–1, 157, 167

228 INDEX

Communists 39–43, 46, 48–9, 57, 61, 68,
  73, 81–2, 91, 95, 97, 116, 149, 171
Concentration camps 40–1, 43–4,
  50, 52, 69
Conservatives 9, 31, 41–2, 46, 48–9, 51, 53,
  68, 93, 127, 141, 144–5, 147, 155,
  158–9, 165, 167–8, 171, 175
Consumerism 59–60, 76–7, 91, 98, 123,
  141, 147, 165, 172
Contraception 111, 135, 140, 143–5,
  147–8, 154, 156–7, 160–1, 165,
  167, 173
Conze, Eckart 96
Courrèges, André 146f
Crueger, Eberhard 53
Cultural revolution 5, 10, 174
Czechoslovakia 74

Dahrendorf, Ralf 7
Damm, Dorothee 97
Damm-Rüger, Sigrid 96–7, 99, 103,
  109–10, 131
Darmstadt 16
Daughters 8, 28, 55–6, 64, 76–7, 87, 97–8,
  100–1, 108, 111, 114, 118–26,
  128–30, 152, 155–8, 161–3, 167, 173,
  200 n.126
Demonstrations 1–2, 4–6, 15, 17, 27–9,
  31–3, 44–5, 49, 55f, 69–70, 72–3, 75,
  97, 109–10
Denazification 56, 61, 80–6, 90, 172
Divorce 78, 84, 104, 113–5, 140, 147
Dollen, Busso von der 42
Drop-outs (Gammler) 35–6, 136, 154,
  157–8, 167, 172, 184 n.50
drugs 157, 160
Duisburg 26
Düsing, Mechtild 117
Dutschke, Rudi 3–5, 29–30, 38–9, 58, 70,
  89, 96, 99–100, 131, 140, 150, 171
Dutschke-Klotz, Gretchen 99–100, 102,
  168, 196 n.46

Education 4–6, 72, 85, 90–2, 100–1, 104,
  119, 123, 125–7, 128–30, 134, 156,
  173–4, 178, 193 n.72
Egypt 26–7, 32
Ehrenberg, Eckehart 44, 50, 144, 148,
  190 n.119

Emergency Acts 40–1, 68–73, 90–1, 97,
  170, 173
Engels, Friedrich 112
Ensslin, Gudrun 58, 115
Erlemeier, Norbert 18, 23f, 24–5, 34f,
  36, 79
Essen 18
Expellees 28, 40, 45

Farah Diba, Empress of Persia 15, 17
Father–son conflict 8, 47, 63, 68, 135,
  170, 173
Feminist groups
  Aktionsrat zur Befreiung der Frauen
    104, 110, 112, 128
  Emancipation Working Group
    (AKE) 92–5, 105, 116, 132, 149,
    204 n.33
  Monday Club 94–5, 132–3, 194 n.7
  reading groups 93, 112
  Weiberrat 97, 112, 126, 151, 167
Fest, Joachim 7
Fichte, Johann Gottlieb 62
Flakhelfer (anti-aircraft
  auxiliaries) 7, 12, 88
Florence 19
France 4, 9–10, 69, 104, 133, 143, 173–4
Francis of Assisi 127, 131
Frankfurt 4–6, 11, 15–6, 30, 38, 95–7,
  103, 112, 126, 134, 144, 149–51,
  166–7, 169
Frei, Norbert 48, 98–9
Freie Demokratische Partei (FDP) 31, 69,
  81, 192 n.53
Freud, Sigmund 62
Fried, Erich 69
Friedan, Betty 112
Fronius, Sigrid 111, 131
Fuchs, Hannelore 94–5, 133

Gaulle, Charles de 70
Gay and lesbian rights *see* homosexuality
Generations
  familial generations 3–4, 8–9, 12, 14,
    45–7, 51–2, 54, 58–9, 63–5, 67–8,
    77–9, 86–8, 90, 98, 118, 125–30, 134,
    141, 156, 170–5
  female generations 7, 13, 95–6, 98, 130,
    133–5, 169–70

Forty-Fivers 7–8, 88–9, 134, 194 n.93
political generations 6–8, 64, 67, 98,
  134–5, 170–1, 173, 175
German Democratic Republic (GDR) 10,
  26, 29, 31–2, 39–43, 45–6, 57, 78, 171
Gerontology 11, 24–5, 28
Giese, Hans 142–3
Globke, Hans 40, 55
Goltz, Anna von der 9, 49
Göring, Hermann 80, 84
Grandparents 8, 14, 47–8, 66, 72, 77,
  88–91, 121, 127–8, 141, 153, 159–60,
  164, 166, 172–3
Grass, Günter 32
Greece 141
Gutschick, Dieter 57, 186 n.24, 187 n.60,
  188 n.75, 190 n.119

Habermas, Jürgen 7, 29, 67
Hackspiel, Madeleine 145
Haffner, David 107f
Haffner, Sarah 102, 104, 106, 107f, 110
Hairstyles 1–3, 5, 35, 98, 121, 138, 140,
  153, 157, 180 n.32
Hamburg 6, 94, 101, 107, 118, 146, 203 n.22
Haug, Frigga 107, 117
Häußermann, Hartmut 30
Heer, Hannes 38–46, 48, 50–3, 55–8, 60–1,
  63, 99, 141
Heer, Paul 39, 44–6, 48, 50–3, 56–8, 63
Heidelberg 16, 25, 177
Heine, Heinrich 62
Hemmer, Eike 109
Hemmer, Nessim 115
Herbert, Ulrich 48, 72, 96
Herrmann, René 16
Hervé, Florence 93–5, 99, 104–6, 149
Herzog, Marianne 104
Hitler, Adolf 7–8, 12, 41, 48, 63, 79–81, 89,
  118, 158
Höfer, Werner 95
Homosexuality 109, 132–3, 139–40, 147–9,
  159, 164, 166, 174, 206 n.76, 207 n.107
Horkheimer, Max 150
Housewives 2, 6–7, 11, 35, 76, 84–5, 93, 95,
  101, 107, 111–2, 117, 123–4, 126,
  128–30, 156
Housework 93, 100, 107–8, 112,
  123, 127

Inflation 74–5, 91
Inglehart, Ronald 180 n.31
Intimacy at a distance 77–8, 172
Intimacy through silence 77–8, 90, 172
Israel 26–7, 32, 36, 68, 81
Italy 9–10, 19, 49, 104, 116, 173–4, 180 n.26

Jahn, Alfred 43–4, 186 n.22
Jahn, Friedrich Ludwig 62
Jahn, Gerhard 95
Jaide, Walter 95
Jews 33, 40–1, 52, 54, 62, 68, 79, 85,
  138, 164
Judges 49, 60, 83, 170
Jung, Mathias 146
Jureit, Ulrike 47
Jürgensmeier, Hans Günter 51,
  54–5, 148

Kalisch (née Bookhagen),
  Christel 102, 109
Kant, Immanuel 62
Kätzel, Ute 181 n.38
Kaul, Friedrich Karl 41–3
Keim, Michaela 178, 181 n.40
Kelsterbach 11, 16
Kierkegaard, Søren 102
Kiesinger, Kurt Georg 26, 40, 57–8, 60
Kinderläden 104–6, 109–10, 114–5, 134,
  150, 152, 169
Kinsey, Alfred C. 147, 158
Klarsfeld, Beate 58
Knitting 92
Köckeis, Eva 192 n.36
Kohl, Helmut 7
Kohut, Thomas 8, 64
Kölbel, Prof. Dr Dr 92
Kolle, Oswalt 146–7, 160
Krahl, Hans-Jürgen 103, 131
Kruse, Andreas 181 n.34
Kundnani, Hans 64
Kunzelmann, Dieter 58, 99, 167
Kurras, Karl-Heinz 29
Kuschel, Hedda 108, 113, 116

Langguth, Gerd 93
Langhans, Rainer 39, 58, 96, 111,
  150, 179 n.4
Lehmann, Joachim 113–4

230 INDEX

Lehr, Ursula 11, 17, 22–6, 34*f*, 36, 95, 126, 181 n.34
Leisure 24, 59, 76, 130, 147
Lessing, Doris 112
Lessing, Gotthold Ephraim 62
Lewejohann, Stefan 178, 181 n.40
Lindner, H. 141
Lotz, Georg 56, 58
Lotz, Heidrun 48, 55–6, 58, 61, 116–7
Lübke, Heinrich 6, 15, 28, 40–2, 44, 60, 185 n.5
Lucke, Albrecht von 48
Lüneburg, Max 73
Lützeler, Heinrich 31, 60

Mahler, Horst 30, 38
Mann, Thomas 186 n.23
Mannheim, Karl 7
Mannheim 11, 22
Marcuse, Herbert 150
Marriage 90, 92, 97, 99–101, 114–5, 117, 124–5, 130, 134, 138–40, 143–4, 147, 154, 156–7, 161–3, 165–6, 168, 173–4, 196 n.42
Marx, Karl 62, 92, 112
Marxism 30, 39–40, 49, 53, 58, 166
Mehnert, Klaus 95
Meier, Friedhelm 70–1
Meinhof, Ulrike 58, 103–4, 115
Memorials 15–6, 31
Menschik, Jutta 132
Merker, Helga 12, 35–6, 48, 79, 88, 118, 120, 152–3, 178, 181 n.36, 184 n.53, 192 n.47
Mexico 96
Milan 3, 9
Military 2, 7, 30, 38, 46, 52, 141
Mini-skirts 12, 35–6, 121–3, 128, 146*f*, 160
Mitscherlich, Alexander 63
Mitscherlich, Margarete 63
Moser, Hans 33
Moser, Hugo 43–4
Mothers, motherhood 8, 27, 39, 44, 49–52, 54, 56–8, 64–5, 92, 95, 97–8, 101–2, 104–8, 110–11, 113–30, 132, 142, 154–6, 161, 167, 173
Mozart, Wolfgang Amadeus 29
Munich 26, 28, 33
Museums 12–3, 44, 48, 50, 95, 178

Nägler, Helga 148*f*
Nasser, Gamal Abdel 85
National community 32
Nationalism 73, 76, 172
Nave-Herz, Rosemarie 113
Nazi (National Socialist)
   crimes 54, 56
   fellow travellers 45, 47–8, 52, 56, 58, 61, 85, 150, 188 n.75
   Führer 45, 62, 81
   mass organisations 7, 12, 51, 61, 82, 89, 158
   party membership 39, 45, 53–4, 57, 60–2, 79–82, 84, 87, 193 n.66
   past 3, 8, 10, 25, 40, 42–3, 46–7, 50, 54–6, 60, 68, 72, 80, 86–7, 90, 118, 150, 170, 172–4
   perpetrators 42, 45, 47–8, 52, 54, 56–8, 64–5, 68, 173
   Schutzstaffel (SS) 51, 65, 84
   Sturmabteilung (SA) 29, 56, 84
Nevermann, Knut 30
New Left 4, 7, 65, 68, 95, 109, 112–3, 132, 140, 149–50, 166–9, 171, 175
Nickels, Christa 65
Nietzsche, Friedrich 62
Novy, Beatrix 102, 108
Nudity 140, 146–7, 150, 157, 165–7, 205 n.69

Oberhausen 11, 76
Oberländer, Theodor 40
Obermaier, Uschi 111, 150
Ohnesorg, Benno 4, 6, 15, 17, 29–33, 38, 58, 171
Olek (née Ramm), Judith 49, 105
Oral History 9, 12–3, 64, 177

Paedophilia 150
Parents, parenting styles 3, 8, 12, 14, 39–68, 72, 77, 79–80, 87–8, 90–1, 97, 100, 108–9, 114–6, 118–23, 125–8, 136, 141, 143, 148, 152–7, 164–6, 172–4
Paris 3, 9, 69, 73
Parliament (*Bundestag*) 42, 65, 69–70, 86, 95, 147, 170
Part-time employment 101, 125
Passau 19

Passerini, Luisa 116, 180 n.26
Pate, Glen 40–1, 43–4
Peace movement 32, 56, 70, 72–3, 140, 171
Penselin, Siegfried 31
Pensions 77, 83–4, 90, 172
Persia 2, 15–6, 28–9, 33, 75
Petting 141–2
Pinl, Claudia 196 n.46
Plack, Arno 150
Plogstedt, Sibylle 112, 131
Police 1, 4–6, 15–7, 26–9, 31–3, 38, 41, 42*f*,
    44–6, 49, 58, 60, 68–70, 72–3, 75, 83,
    89, 109, 141, 147, 160, 170
Pornography 140, 146–7, 150–1, 157,
    160, 165–6
Pörtner, Rudolf 31–2, 41, 50, 144–5
Portz, Valentin 28
Post-materialism 10
Prague Spring 74
Praunheim, Rosa von 149, 206 n.76
Pregnancy 103–4, 106, 113, 140, 145,
    156–7, 161–3, 167, 204 n.33, 207 n.97
Pre-marital sex 140, 143, 145, 147, 154,
    156–7, 160–3, 165–7, 172–3
Press
    akut 3, 16, 50–1, 93–4, 96, 145–6, 148
    BILD 5, 29, 136
    Der Spiegel 5, 23–30, 65, 66*f*, 103, 111,
        132, 146, 150, 167–8
    General-Anzeiger (Bonn) 6, 15,
        32–3, 70, 94
    Stern 5, 40, 96, 109–11
Professors 4, 7, 28, 30, 33, 35, 43–4, 46, 58,
    60–2, 69, 71–2, 74, 93, 102, 105, 170
Promiscuity 148, 150–1, 157, 165
Prostitution 93, 154
Przytulla (née Seehuber), Dagmar
    102, 113, 116, 125, 128, 151
Psychology
    explorations 20, 23, 81, 127
    personality theories 11, 24, 34
    tests 16, 18, 20–2, 24–5, 27–8, 34, 136

Race, Racism 62, 74, 78, 87, 89, 117, 143,
    160, 164
Radicals Decree (*Radikalenerlass*) 46
Radio 26, 73, 168
Ramm, Bernd 143
Ramm, Judith *see* Olek, Judith

Rape 96, 121, 148, 166
Rassbach, Elsa 102, 196 n.46
Reemtsma, Jan Philipp 46
Regehr, Elke 101–2, 113
Renger, Annemarie 94
Renner, Maria Theresia 18*f*, 19–20, 24,
    33–6, 127
Reich, Wilhelm 63, 150, 152
Reiche, Reimut 30, 63, 150
Resistance 48–9, 51, 53, 57, 62, 67, 80, 97, 157
Retirement 7, 28, 33, 76–7, 80, 83–4, 127–8
Reza Pahlavi, Shah of Persia 15, 17, 26, 29
Ridder, Helmut 33
Ring Christlich-Demokratischer Studenten
    (RCDS) 41–2, 53, 144–5
Rosenbaum, Ulrich 2–3, 44, 50–1, 53
Rosenberg, Alfred 60
Rosenmayr, Leopold 192 n.36
Rosenthal, Gabriele 189 n.109
Rosorius, Jürgen 41, 144–5
Rothacker, Erich 61
Rothenburg 26
Rudinger, Georg 23–5, 60, 79–80
Ruff, Siegfried 43–4
Runge, Erika 129
Russians 39, 74, 121

Sander, Friedrich 61
Sander, Helke 96–9, 101, 103–4, 106, 108,
    112, 116, 128, 168
Schelsky, Helmut 7
Schenck, Guntram von 44, 187 n.63
Schiller, Friedrich 63, 170
Schmidt, Günter 142–3
Schmidt, Helmut 95
Schmitz-Scherzer, Reinhard 18*f*,
    19, 22, 24
Schneemelcher, Wilhelm 40–1, 60
Schneider, Peter 179 n.4, 189 n.104
Schnibben, Cordt 65, 66*f*
Schrader-Klebert, Karin 198 n.75
Schreiner, Manfred 24, 138–9
Schunter-Kleemann, Susanne 108,
    111, 131
Schwarzenau, Annette 110, 115, 131
Schwarzer, Alice 96–7, 132–3, 169
Seehuber, Dagmar *see* Przytulla, Dagmar
Sex education 140, 145–7, 154, 157, 159,
    163, 165, 173

232 INDEX

Sexual revolution 110, 140–1, 147–52, 158,
    164–7, 173–4
Silies, Eva-Maria 135
Simons, Heribert 18*f*
Stergar, Grischa 115
Strawe, Christoph 49, 185 n.17, 190 n.117
Struck, Karin 117
Six Days' War 27, 32, 68
Social science data 13, 177–8
Soviet Union 74, 112
Sozialdemokratische Partei Deutschlands
    (SPD) 3, 44, 75, 87, 94–5, 144, 171
Sozialistische Einheitspartei Deutschlands
    (SED) 41–2
Sozialistischer Deutscher Studentenbund
    (SDS) 1, 4–5, 28–31, 38–44, 46–7,
    49, 55, 58, 63, 67, 73, 92–3, 96–9,
    101–5, 107–12, 116, 131, 134, 141,
    149, 151, 168–9, 171, 175, 196 n.42,
    201 n.152
Spain 9, 98
Strikes 9, 70–1, 110
Student
    Allgemeiner Studentenausschuss
        (AStA) 16, 30–3, 41, 44, 46, 50, 52,
        68, 93, 105, 144–5, 148, 184 n.40,
        203 n.21
    associations 6, 29, 31, 38, 41–2, 46, 53,
        141–2, 144–5
    halls of residence 142–3, 203 n.21
    parliament 6, 31, 39, 41, 44, 105,
        144–5, 149
    press 146
    welfare office (*Studentenwerk*) 106
    See also *Ring Christlich-Demokratischer*
        Studenten, Sozialistischer Deutscher
        Studentenbund, Verband Deutscher
        Studentenschaften

Tartler, Rudolf 192 n.36
Teachers 46, 51, 57, 80, 82, 83–4, 86, 89,
    104–6, 110, 115, 123, 125–6, 150,
    154, 157
Teenagers *see* adolescents
Teiner, Ursula-Regine 93–4
Television 4–5, 19, 26–30, 38, 40, 45, 59,
    67, 73, 96, 122, 136–7, 144, 157, 160,
    167, 172, 177, 191 n.30
Terrorists 103, 115

Teufel, Fritz 30, 58, 96, 109
Theweleit, Klaus 63, 150
Thomae, Hans 11–2, 17, 19–20, 22–6,
    34–6, 37*f*, 60–2, 79, 118, 127
Thon, Christine 129
Tismer, Karl-Georg 18*f*, 19, 22, 24, 26, 86
Tismer-Puschner, Ingrid 18*f*, 79, 95,
    127, 137–8
Tomato throw 96–7, 103–4, 109, 131,
    133, 169
Tornow, Georgia 131
Tourism 19, 33, 59, 98, 143
Trauma 47, 56, 63–4, 67, 162
Treitschke, Heinrich von 62
Tröger, Annemarie 131, 201 n.152
Trümmerfrauen 54, 117

Uhse, Beate 136, 146–7
Unemployment 56, 163
United States, America 5, 10, 23, 25, 30, 36,
    40, 74–5, 80, 85, 99–100, 106, 141, 158,
    160, 164
University reform 7, 60, 62, 171, 174
Utopia 64, 75, 89–90, 133, 151,
    170–2, 174–5

Value change 10, 59, 88–9, 130, 140, 150,
    155, 173
Väterliteratur 47, 63–4
Verband Deutscher Studentenschaften
    (VDS) 29, 46
Vesper, Bernward 63
Vesper, Will 63
Vetterlein, Thomas G. 93
Vietnam War 28, 31, 40, 74–5, 90–1, 98,
    167, 170–1, 191 n.15
Violence 2, 12, 17, 28–9, 38, 41,
    63, 70, 72–3, 75, 78, 89–91, 150,
    166, 171
    sexual violence 148–9, 158, 166, 174
Vocational choice 88, 90, 125, 162, 173
Volkswagen Foundation 11, 17, 25,
    177, 182 n.9

Walter-Lehmann, Regine 113–4
War children (*Kriegskinder*) 63–5,
    189 n.106
Weber, Hellmuth von 43–4, 60, 185 n.17
Wehler, Hans-Ulrich 7, 96

INDEX   233

Wehrmacht Exhibition 38, 46, 52
Weiden 11
Welfare 77, 106, 163
Werder, Lutz von 109
Westernization 7, 173
Wetterau, Karin 64
Wickert, Ulrich 203 n.14
Widows 18, 77, 118–9, 159, 162
Wiese, Benno von 60
Wolff, KD 63
Women's movements *see* feminist groups

Workers 6–7, 9, 11, 18, 35, 70–1, 76–7,
    80–2, 85–6, 100, 125, 136, 143, 161–2,
    171, 173, 191 n.13
World War One 5, 48, 74, 163
World War Two 28, 38, 40, 45, 64–5, 74,
    78, 80, 86, 155, 160
Wuppertal 11

Zabel, Maria 53
Zetkin, Clara 93, 112
Zundel, Rolf 95